Continental Films

WISCONSIN FILM STUDIES

Patrick McGilligan, *series editor*

Continental Films

French Cinema under German Control

Christine Leteux

THE UNIVERSITY OF WISCONSIN PRESS

Publication of this book has been made possible, in part, through support from the Programmes d'aide à la publication de l'Institut français and from the Anonymous Fund of the College of Letters and Science at the University of Wisconsin–Madison.

The University of Wisconsin Press
728 State Street, Suite 443
Madison, Wisconsin 53706
uwpress.wisc.edu

Gray's Inn House, 127 Clerkenwell Road
London ECIR 5DB, United Kingdom
eurospanbookstore.com

Originally published under the title *Continental Films: Cinéma français sous contrôle allemand*. Published by arrangement with La Tour Verte. © 2017 by La Tour Verte. All rights reserved.
Translation copyright © 2022 by the Board of Regents of the University of Wisconsin System

Printed in the United States of America
This book may be available in a digital edition.

Library of Congress Cataloging-in-Publication Data

Names: Leteux, Christine, author.
Title: Continental Films : French cinema under German control / Christine Leteux.
Other titles: Continental films. English | Wisconsin film studies.
Description: Madison, Wisconsin : The University of Wisconsin Press, [2022] | Series: Wisconsin film studies | Foreword by Bertrand Tavernier. | Includes bibliographical references and index.
Identifiers: LCCN 2021060226 | ISBN 9780299339807 (hardcover)
Subjects: LCSH: Continental films—History. | Motion picture industry—France—History—20th century. | Fascism and motion pictures—France—History—20th century. | France—History—German occupation, 1940-1945.
Classification: LCC PN1993.5.F7 L47513 2022 | DDC 384/.8094409044—dc23/eng/20220705
LC record available at https://lccn.loc.gov/2021060226

This book is dedicated to the memory of my mother,

GENEVIÈVE,

and to

BERTRAND TAVERNIER,

who proved to be this book's fairy godfather

Contents

Illustrations

Foreword

I have been waiting for such a book for years, a book that shakes beliefs and prejudices, scrubs certain tall stories, and shows what lies below the tip of the iceberg, a whole part of history of whose contours I thought I knew. During the research, the preparation, and the shooting of *Laissez-passer*, the only fiction picture that tackles what happened at Continental, I asked myself dozens of questions. I had questioned many witnesses who had lived this story—Jean Aurenche, Jean-Paul Le Chanois, Jean Devaivre, and Rosine Delamare. And I came up against gray areas. I had difficulties understanding Greven's personality, even his artistic sensitivity, why he was so determined to hire Jean Aurenche to offer him a project as demoralizing as Fernandel's *Adrien*, adapted from Jean de Letraz, whom Aurenche couldn't stand, a film I never managed to watch to the end. It was common knowledge that Fernandel, especially if he was supposed to direct, was going to insist that his brother-in-law, Jean Manse, rewrite the dialogue. Christine Leteux describes, for example, the treatment inflicted on the *Simplet* script, written by Carlo Rim, by a band of knuckleheads, Robert Beunke, Fernandel's agent, a character we can call highly unpleasant—that's an understatement!—and a pathological liar, the notorious Manse, and Greven. Rim was not even allowed to direct the picture.

It's just one of the thousands of discoveries brought to light in the pages of *Continental Films*. All these documents, these testimonies, often unpublished, these very probing insights that show without bias Greven's mysterious personality. He appears as a studio man, clever, cyclothymic, irascible, with a real sense of organization, knowledge that allows him to spot successful directors, very good technicians, cinematographers, set designers, and editors and real commercial flair. We must give him credit for noticing very quickly Henri-Georges Clouzot's talent. But it's hard to detect any conception of filmmaking in its diversity, any artistic sense of the kind that spots good subjects, that intuits the right director for a project. And the films he made in Germany in the 1950s do not change my mind.

In any case, it's the way I described him in *Laissez-passer*, where he spoke mostly about work schedules and shooting timetables, and it is how Christian Berkel played him. We are a long way from Alexander Korda championing the editing of *The Third Man*, from Harry Cohn supporting Robert Rossen, ignoring twenty-two very negative previews of *All the King's Men*, and from Darryl Zanuck ignoring the early very negative reactions to *The Grapes of Wrath* and refusing to tamper with the editing. Admittedly, those tycoons had to face mostly their shareholders and board of directors, a formidable breed but less so than Goebbels or the Nazi dignitaries. And Greven had to manage, in addition, those dignitaries concerned about the progress of the war while managing productions in an occupied country.

Nevertheless, it becomes apparent in reading this book that the main artistic choices were those imposed by filmmakers and screenwriters from the first two pictures. It is to Christian-Jaque, Charles Spaak, and Pierre Véry that we owe the merits of *L'Assassinat du Père Noël*, which is in the same artistic tradition as *Les Disparus de Saint-Agil*, to Henri Decoin, the charm and enthusiasm of *Premier Rendez-vous*, and to Jean-Paul Le Chanois, Clouzot, and to Maurice Tourneur, the strength and originality of *La Main du diable*. Jean Devaivre repeatedly told me, for example, that the choice of Palau to play the devil was a masterstroke from Tourneur, not the management. *Le Corbeau* was a Clouzot project, *La Vie de Plaisir*, a Charles Spaak project. I learned from *Continental Films* that Greven was even opposed to Albert Valentin. It was Decoin and Clouzot who dictated the critical content and the style of *Les Inconnus dans la maison*, and I am glad that Leteux underlines the director's personal input, which draws on his sports background, in Raimu's final plea. Decoin had in fact been saved from destitution by sports. But I'm also glad she made me see how he had to fight to lessen, even to try to suppress, the Jewishness of the character played by Mouloudji, which makes him even more likeable. By the way, this plea, which has often been considered pro-Pétain, takes up numerous arguments in favor of sports developed during the Popular Front by Minister Léo Lagrange.

And Leteux also makes convincing arguments regarding Greven's double speech and double dealing: on the one hand, he protected Jean-Paul Le Chanois, something confirmed by the latter and by Max Douy, and asked Aurenche at Fouquet's restaurant to give him the names of Jewish screenwriters "because they are the most talented"—"One of the most frightening moments of my life," Aurenche repeatedly told me—and on the other hand, he fired composer Roland-Manuel, preventing him from making the music for *La Main du diable* because he was Jewish. According to Henri Dutilleux, Roland-Manuel was the author of one of the most beautiful scores in French film, that of *Remorques*, and would have been certainly inspired by Tourneur's picture. Leteux shows how Greven's margin of freedom could be limited by quarrels with other Nazi dignitaries or by denunciations that sparked official suppression, which was what happened in the case of Roland-Manuel. It didn't prevent Greven's double dealing in the case of *Caprices* and in Harry Baur's tragic destiny.

Of course, some books, some studies, from those by Jean-Pierre Bertin-Maghit, the great pioneer, up through those by Jacques Siclier, René Chateau, and Philippe d'Hughes, had already partly raised the curtain, explained some decisions, revealed a fact, a text, a vivid statement such as Henri Jeanson's pamphlet "Cocos contre Corbeau" or his letter to Armand Salacrou, then president of the writers from the Resistance ("But, my dear Armand, you know very well that Clouzot has never been anymore a collaborator than you have been a Resistance member"). But, besides those, there have been many texts in which the same old tales, the same rumors, even the same lies or errors are peddled. For example, it had been said that Harry Baur spoke German, which is not true, as Leteux demonstrates brilliantly in pointing out that the production dates in Germany for *Symphonie eines Lebens* were postponed to allow him time to learn the language.

During numerous debates after *Laissez-passer*, I often came up against spectators stating that *Le Corbeau* had been released in Germany, that technicians and authors who signed on at Continental did so to join the collaboration, even to support Germany. Some clichés die hard. In the United States, it was even worse; the majority of journalists and critics didn't have any idea that French filmmaking continued during the Occupation. And some didn't see the necessity: "Why make films when your country is occupied?" You had to try to explain that film people had the right to earn a living, to feed themselves, like journalists during the McCarthy era. They weren't all able to move to another job, to move to another country (very few screenwriters spoke English). In addition, from 1942 onward, if they couldn't produce a contract, they had to go to Germany. And the head electrician at the Neuilly studios told me that he had hired many young people so that they could avoid compulsory work service.

Indeed, there was still an amount of dross surrounding Continental history, a comfortable mixture of ignorance, prejudice, and an attachment to rumors reported in the press ("The journalist's main enemy is information," Bob Woodward reiterated), a refusal to confront the facts, the "burning stones of reality," as Virginia Woolf used to say, and the absence of new documents. Marc Bloch saw a reason for the 1940 defeat in the lack of curiosity.

And this lack of curiosity, this dross, Leteux shatters it. She dynamites it and makes us feel we are reliving history day by day. We feel her surprise, her astonishment with these discoveries that shatter received ideas. And she makes us share in her astonishment, which garners our admiration.

I had felt the same feeling of happiness and jubilation while reading her remarkable book about Maurice Tourneur, a biography that set the record straight. She brought back to us this so unjustly forgotten filmmaker, sharing with us his creative commitment, his moments of doubt, and his artistic successes. It was one of those milestone French biographies like the one about Nicholas Ray by Bernard Eisenschitz and the one about Jean Renoir by Pascal Merigeau.

And, here too, through all these pages, I had the feeling of finally understanding certain facts, certain choices, what linked them to the historical context, which sheds new light on this or that position (Decoin's accepting the job at Continental) or this or that decision. To my great astonishment, I realize that, contrary to the legend, in the end, few Continental pictures were released in Germany. Not only was *Le Corbeau* never distributed because it was considered too dark (it was one of the lies invented by the Communist Party and the Popular Republican Movement, which had the longest life), nor was an export visa ever signed for it but numerous other works were never screened.

The *Caprices* story was like a bullet in the heart, as I discovered all its force and horror. Léo Joannon's scandalous and despicable behavior when he stole a script using blackmail, Companeez's suffering, Raymond Bernard's stoicism and also his incredible courage when he dared to sue the Majestic Film company despite his being a Jew—all this was completely new to me. And through these terrible pages, I felt a great empathy toward victims such as Bernard and Companeez, rushes of anger toward Joannon ("The Hun's fly," as Jeanson used to call him), an increased respect for Cayatte, an escaped prisoner who had been abused and asked for his name to be removed from the film credits after the liberation. Yes, there was a closeness, a friendship among these filmmakers, these screenwriters, as in American books—Victor Navasky's *Naming Names*, Patrick McGilligan's *Tender Comrades*, and Eric Bentley's *30 Years of Treason*—about the blacklist and the witch hunt.

Leteux went through masses of archives and read tons of documents, mostly unpublished and never quoted, including those in German archives, never-before-translated excerpts from Goebbels diary, and above all, professional purge files that have hardly ever been consulted and that provide a wealth of precious information, which use often very well written, precise, and warm French. I felt my first shock in the first pages, when reading the first excerpt of Pierre Blanchar's statement about his encounter with Greven at Maxim's. The clarity of the sentences, the precision of certain details (the piles of military caps in the cloakroom, the swastika lapel badge, which was Greven's only distinctive sign), the desire to use a precise present tense, all that offers such a different perspective on Blanchar, so different from the grotesque caricature repeated ad nauseam. And I found this quality in all his comments the clear-headedness and judgment of which reminded me of the intelligence with which he played the abortionist doctor in *Un Carnet de bal* (1937), the dreamy hero in *L'Homme de nulle part* (1936), and the fanatical and delirious student in *Crime et châtiment* (1935). As Leteux points out, we are very far from Jean Cocteau's famous and obviously very unfair description of him as having "an eagle eye in the head of a birdbrain." He probably wanted people to forget some of his own enthusiasm for certain Pétain supporters.

After this first discovery, I went from one surprise to the next. All of Henri Decoin's statements are so fascinating, so intelligently argued, that we regret he never wrote any memoirs or the fact that no magazine ever interviewed him, if only to ask him about his often talented use of music. The kinship I felt with this filmmaker became even greater when I discovered his often very critical outspokenness, his acute judgment, the way he managed to work twice on the sly with a Jewish screenwriter for a German company, in particular on the delightful *Premier Rendez-vous*. He later helped the screenwriter flee to Switzerland. I also felt a kinship with Carlo Rim, so acute, so clear sighted. Leteux had already mentioned his creative input on the marvelous Maurice Tourneur picture, *Avec le sourire*.

Yes, Leteux made me understand the choices, the hesitations of those authors, filmmakers, actors, and actresses. Pierre Fresnay, for example, was certainly pro-Pétain, a defender of the order, which didn't prevent him from protecting Claude Bourdet, Édouard Bourdet's son, but he never was pro-German or a mainstay of Continental. And what about the stupefying revelations about Mireille Balin? Each page reveals facts and stances that surprise us and touch us and make us revise our judgments, thanks to telling details about many different people. Because she is not only interested in famous people, filmmakers, and film stars. She understands intuitively and intimately, as her previous books on Capellani (where she rectified dozens of errors) and on Maurice Tourneur show, how a film crew works together, and she knows that it is not just the big names who make history.

Leteux conveys with precision all of Bauermeister's efforts to spy on film sets. I had shown in *Laissez-passer* that he always tried to come first into the sound control room to listen to conversations. But I also showed how, the French crews being often united and resourceful, his departure from his office on the Champs-Élysées was signaled by a phone call to the studio watchman, who ran to the set and shouted: "He is on his way!" People stopped smoking; cigarette butts were hidden. They put their ties back on (you had to wear one) and most important, the sound engineer hid the usual boom and replaced it with another kind, as the Germans preferred this tool to record dialogue. And Bauermeister was often unsuccessful.

In this book, she reveals astonishing characters, pays a moving tribute to Armand Thirard, a mainstay of Continental, a great cinematographer, a master of chiaroscuro who could light a scene without a photoelectric cell and measured the intensity of the light by blinking. From rummaging through the archives, Leteux discovered extraordinary characters, all those Russians, often Armenians, often patriots, like the great art director André Andrejew, who gathered his team to warn them there was an informer among them, the chief makeup man Chakhatouny, whom Jean Devaivre mentioned so often and whom I learned mixed with the Armenian arm of the Resistance movement led by Missak Manouchian and was very much anti-German, and also that complex, strange figure, stage manager Grégoire Metchikian. His obsession for his work generated feelings of animosity. He was suspected, perhaps unfairly, of siding with the management, and some people were wary of him. And suddenly, as if by accident, we learn his son Georges's story, fired from Continental because he was too frank in his judgment regarding a script (Devaivre reiterated to me that to survive in this firm, you had to keep your mouth shut). And after being forced to enter the compulsory work service, he went underground. And Greven and Bauermeister never again spoke to his father. This is the very example of a small poignant drama I had never heard about that Leteux uncovers, a drama that confirms the complexity of human relationships and the difficulties of imposing rigid judgment.

It will be impossible after this book to talk about "the trip to Berlin" as we did for decades. Leteux has unearthed fascinating testimony, that of André Legrand, the screenwriter of *La Symphonie fantastique*, which gives this story a more complex color. She reveals the hesitations, in particular Danielle Darrieux's, and also the courageous and honorable attitudes of those who refused to go on the trip and who are never mentioned, from Decoin to Pierre Blanchar. They had to threaten Junie Astor with the closure of her movie theaters to make her consent to go on the trip. In this group, there was no spirit and no enthusiasm, Leteux underlines, unlike the writers' trip from Chardonne to Brasillach, except from a journalist, Heuzé, who was a caricature of the fanatic collaborator.

It will also be impossible to keep trotting out the same story about Harry Baur's tragic end. What Leteux has found is terrifying and flies in the face of all the hearsay. Far from wanting to cash in on a juicy contract as some still insist these days, Baur absolutely refused to shoot Hans Bertram's picture *Symphonie eines Lebens* in Germany. He used every pretext—failing health, lack of knowledge of the language, all these excuses to avoid having to do it. But he was denounced by a childhood friend, Édouard Bouchez, who had become a crazed antisemite, a Nazi supporter. The text of his denunciation is beyond depressing. It put Goebbels in an awkward position, as he wasn't in favor of arresting Baur and it gave a great power to Captain Dannecker, who Leteux describes as a sadist, even though Goebbels, who had proof that Baur was not a Jew, appointed another officer to control him. It resulted in a long imprisonment, beatings "with a stool," and an appalling death. This murder of one of the greatest French actors, whose genius is not celebrated properly, was tarnished by groundless rumors. It is terrible to think that the two leads of Duvivier's *Poil de carotte* (1932), Harry Baur and Robert Lynen, were both murdered by the Germans.

Yes, I must confess, I had an amazing time perusing this book that I couldn't stop reading, which destroys so many clichés, makes certain behaviors more human, certain motivations more complex. We are at times surprised by the naivete, even the lack of thought of some, the dirty tricks of Joannon and Bouchez. And I felt again a genuine admiration, as I did during the shooting of *Laissez-passer*, for those directors, screenwriters, technicians, and grips who on the whole behaved more than honorably. Romain Rolland said, "A hero, I don't really know what it is, but, I imagine a hero is somebody who does what he can. The others don't."

Bertrand Tavernier, September 2017

Continental Films

Prologue

Movies shot in France during World War II still hold a special fascination for the general public. Their subjects and treatments are commented on endlessly in an attempt to ferret out a propaganda or resistance message hidden under a veneer of entertainment. The attitudes of members of the film industry are also discussed in order to separate the patriots from the collaborators. Yet the facts behind the rumors that were spread for decades have often gone unchecked. The dark years of the occupation have become mythical now that very few eyewitnesses are still alive. Trying to understand the attitude of everybody seems like a difficult exercise. However, during my research for my biography of Maurice Tourneur, I discovered thousands of pages of transcripts from the purge committees of the film industry that record what these eyewitnesses remembered of their occupation years when it was still vivid in their memories. It consists of statements that film directors and technicians made to committees in explaining their activities inside Continental Films. There were some villains, some Resistance fighters, but mostly men and women like us who tried to survive and keep working during a difficult period when each decision could lead them down a dangerous path. Those who worked for the German-owned company Continental Films were no different from other film people. I seek to understand their motives, fears, lives, and careers.

As I was born well after the period, I can only refer to the memories of those who lived it. I remember two telling anecdotes my maternal grandparents told me regarding the state of France in 1939. My grandmother worked as a stenographer for Gnome et Rhône until June 1940. Although rumors of war were on the rise, this company went on regularly exporting airplane engines to Germany right until the declaration of war. As my grandmother used to say, "We sent them engines to equip the planes that were going to bomb us!" This prewar economic collaboration also took place in the film industry. Numerous

French films were produced in Germany by the Alliance Cinématographique Européenne, a subsidiary of the powerful UFA company.[1] The Nazis' accession to power did not result in this special relationship changing. The France of 1939 was very antiwar, and it felt an economic collaboration with Germany would prevent war. This reasoning sounds simplistic and ridiculous nowadays, but, then, nobody wanted to acknowledge the brewing disaster. The lack of preparation seemed total. When my grandfather was called up, he was given a gun and ammunition. Only the ammunition he was given did not match the caliber of his weapon . . .

Although most remained unaware of the coming perils, a few enlightened commentators managed to accurately recognize the flaws of a sick society. One of those witnesses was the journalist and screenwriter Carlo Rim—who would become screenwriter for Continental Films. He wrote down his impressions in his diary with a rare clear headedness. In April 1938, the actress Charlotte Lysès, Sacha Guitry's first wife, who had been invited to lunch by Carlo Rim and his wife, did not hesitate to say in front of the appalled guests, "Personally, I only know two living geniuses: Sacha and Hitler!"[2]

Without a shadow of a doubt, antisemitism was present in the society of that time, even if it didn't express itself as directly. On September 3, 1939, Carlo Rim was seated in a café with actor Raimu and painter Moïse Kisling in Bandol, in the south of France. Raimu suddenly cried: "There you are! We're going to get killed for Polish Jews! I do not know if you have an opinion on Polish Jews, my dear Kisling, but, as for me, to hell with them!" Kisling turned pale and replied: "I am a Polish Jew." Raimu suddenly switched topics and began talking about giving the Krauts a thrashing together with his Polish Jewish friends. Carlo Rim quite rightly remarked on his naive and monumental impudence.

On June 17, 1940, Carlo Rim and his comrades-in-arm listened to an elderly man's quavering voice on the radio announcing the armistice with Germany. In Maréchal Pétain's speech, he immediately noticed an attack against a republic already moribund: "The spirit of pleasure prevailed. . . . We wanted to avoid effort, today we are meeting misfortune." Around Rim, some men were in tears. He perceptively asked, "Tears of anger, despair or sadness? Of humiliation, rather. A great country collapses in shame with slaps and kicks in the ass, like in a circus."[3]

A man predicted to Carlo Rim in 1938 that "the war that's looming will be more atrocious than the others because it will be a civil war which doesn't dare mention its name."[4] Antoine de Saint-Exupéry was right.

CHAPTER 1

Paris, Fall 1940

Germans began occupying the City of Lights on June 14, 1940. Hitler came to contemplate his spoils as soon as July 28. Paris was his finest war trophy, the capital of the richest country among those he conquered. He glanced admiringly at the Eiffel Tower. His henchman, Propaganda Minister Joseph Goebbels, arrived four days later, on July 2, and took a rapid tour of the coveted capital. Jubilant, he contemplated the magnificent view of Paris from Montmartre with some German soldiers. "I'd love to live here for a few weeks," he wrote in his diary.

From the very start of the occupation, Paris served a particular function for the German authorities. It was the city of pleasures, the place where soldiers came on furlough to have a rest before going back to the front. As soon as July 15, 1940, the occupying military command began publishing a new semimonthly magazine in German called *Der deutsche Wegleiter für Paris* (The German guide to Paris) designed for soldiers who wanted to take advantage of all the French capital had to offer.[1] Paris was now their city; they came to enjoy restaurants, museums, and shows and to shop in luxury outlets. It was therefore important that the economic life of the capital resumed as quickly as possible. Filmmaking was among those entertainment industries that needed to quickly resume.

During the spring offensive of the German army, three-quarters of the Parisians had fled the city. Most of the movie people had gone to the French Riviera. The film industry had been at a standstill since May 1940. Some movies that had been started in summer 1939 had been finished between March and May 1940, like Jean Grémillon's *Remorques* (1941) and Maurice Tourneur's *Volpone* (1941). Other works remained unfinished, such as Henri Decoin's *Coup de foudre* with Danielle Darrieux. During the fall, in September and October, actors and directors began slowly coming back to the capital, hoping that the film industry would start up again in the occupied zone. Not a single movie had been shot since May 1940, and the film industry could only resume its activity if the German authorities gave the go ahead. Nobody knew how long this occupation would last. Therefore, one had to find work where one could.

All those who arrived in Paris during that fall were in a state of shock. For them, until then, occupation had been a vague notion, hard to define after spending time in the free zone, in the south. A young singer and actor, who was then Edith Piaf's boyfriend, captured this first impression. Just having arrived back in Paris, Paul Meurisse sat outside Fouquet's on the Champs-Elysées. This smart café-restaurant was the favorite place of movie people and where Raimu ate almost every day. Meurisse had barely sat down at a table when he saw a group of German soldiers accompanied by a brass band parading in the middle of the Champs-Elysées toward place de la Concorde. Suddenly, "occupation" became a tangible word, and he made an effort not to burst into tears because some German officers were sitting at a nearby table. He remarked, "We were defeated, but at that precise moment, we understood that humiliation escorted defeat."

Actor Pierre Blanchar came back to Paris after a long exodus across France. He remembered,

> In 1940, the Armistice found me in Royan, where I had been with my family since May 15. And I stayed in Royan until the end of July. I therefore saw the Jerries, and I understood that it was impossible to stay there. We were nervous wrecks, which could have dire consequences from one day to the next. Besides I escaped from incidents with Germans. . . . I decided to leave with my family for the south of France, the free zone. So, from August until the end of September, I was successively in Marseille, Théoule, and in the Cannes region. . . . In September, we were cut off from news, we didn't know exactly what was happening in Paris, but still, we knew, thanks to rumors and gossip, that theaters were reopening in Paris. . . . At that time, the safe-conduct system was very unstable. Finally, I managed to get a pass from the Cannes police station, which was perfectly irregular, but I was benefiting from that kind of uncertainty, mess.[2]

One day after his return to Paris, Blanchar had an appointment with Roger Capgras, a theater producer at Maxim's.

> I arrived for the appointment at around half past twelve or one, and just when I entered the restaurant, I saw there . . . It was the moment when I realized that

we were truly occupied, because I arrived on Place de la Concorde just when the music was descending from the Arc de Triomphe, and there was a rather pretty bloom of flags with swastikas. I entered Maxim's, and I saw in the cloakroom a pile of caps, and it turned out, there were only two civilians at Maxim's, Capgras and me. And just when I was removing my coat, I was held up. I felt I was being pulled. I turned around and as I was moving, I saw an enormous lap badge, a swastika, what's happening to me? . . . I found myself in the presence of Greven, who was in civvies, and asked me for news: "How did it go for you?" and all that. . . . I knew Greven from Berlin, and I had met him three times. . . . It was late 1937 or early 1938. It was during the shooting of *L'Étrange Monsieur Victor* directed by [Jean] Grémillon. . . . And Greven was there making a film at UFA and on the verge of becoming head of the production. So, I saw him there and later at the studios where he was getting ready to direct a production. I saw him casually as one sees people in studios. At the time, I recognized him immediately, but I couldn't remember his name. . . . And he tells me, "You know, I am in Paris for a while. I'd like to see you because I'm preparing some things. At the moment, cinema is in a state of extraordinary disorder." And he gives me his address and tells me, "Do come one morning." We make an appointment.[3]

At the time of this unexpected meeting with Alfred Greven, Pierre Blanchar was unaware that the German producer was in the process of creating a new film production company, Continental Films.

CHAPTER 2

Alfred Greven

Those who had been in close contact with Alfred Greven in France had very diverse and clear-cut opinions about him. Screenwriter André Cayatte spoke of "an extravagant human animal," screenwriter H. André Legrand spoke of a man of "dangerous joviality," and actress Edwige Feuillère of "a kind of upper-class bourgeois dummy," while Henri-Georges Clouzot and Jean-Paul Le Chanois celebrated the man who loved cinema.[1] In any case, his personality left few people indifferent. He arrived in France during the summer of 1940, sent by propaganda minister Joseph Goebbels to control and manage the French film industry.

Who was Alfred Greven really?[2] We know he was born on October 9, 1897, in Eberfeld (northern Westphalia) to a lower middle-class family.[3] His father, Franz Joseph Greven, was a shopkeeper; he had a brother and two sisters. Greven trained as a typographer. World War I changed his life forever. He volunteered for the infantry in 1914 and was severely wounded twice, once in 1914 and then again in 1915 before he ended up joining the air force in July 1917 as a lieutenant. Greven was part of Jagdstaffel 12 (Flying Squadron 12) stationed in the north of France, then occupied by the Germans. We can therefore assume he learned French during this stay. His squadron was later merged with others to form Jagdgeschwader 2 (Fighter Wing 2).[4] He was decorated with the Iron Cross twice and credited with four air combat victories.

He formed new friendships that proved useful later for his career. "Air force men are thick as thieves—is that not what they say? This comradeship got me into the movies in 1920, when I met an old air force buddy who had invested a lot of money in a film and asked me to supervise the production."[5] He ended up working in film distribution and production companies such as Maak, Mars, Landlicht, Stern, Sphinx, Deulig-Scala, and Tonfilm AG. By the end of the 1920s, he was in charge of a prestigious Berlin film theater, the UFA-Palast am Zoo.

Greven was injured in a car accident in 1930 and spent two years in the hospital.[6] On December 24, 1931, he joined the National Socialist German Workers' Party after getting to know the doctors in the hospital, who were already members of the Nazi Party. This early membership in the party, even before Adolf Hitler's rise to power, shows that Greven agreed fully with the ultranationalist and antisemitic ideology of the party. He later explained his membership to his nephew in the following way: "We must change things. Germany needs changes."[7] His membership would, of course, help him climb the social ladder inside the film industry after 1933.

Indeed, Greven's career took a new turn thanks to the production of *Der alte und der junge König* (1935), a Hans Steinhoff biopic of King Frederick William I of Prussia with Emil Jannings in the title role, for the Deka film production company. The film was celebrated by the Nazi Party and the Third Reich for its authoritarian vision of the main character that was in perfect phase with the new regime. To thank him for this film, Greven was given his own production unit inside UFA. He produced Franco-German versions of three pictures, one of which was *Le Domino vert* (1935), codirected by Henri Decoin and Herbert Selpin and featuring a young Danielle Darrieux. In parallel, a German version titled *Der grüne Domino* (1935) was directed by Selpin and starring Brigitte Horney.

In June 1937, Greven became the head of a new film production company called Terra-Filmkunst. In less than two years, the company profit increased by 45 percent. Greven produced essentially commercial films that only had entertainment value. In February 1939, he left Terra when propaganda minister Joseph Goebbels appointed him head of production at UFA. He kept this coveted job only for three months owing to a violent conflict with Goebbels. Greven would antagonize the powerful propaganda minister time and again in the years to come. He liked to make decisions without seeking approval from his superior.

The story behind the conflict is like a Georges Feydeau farce in which the main characters are the pillars of the Nazi regime. Joseph Goebbels had had an affair with Czech actress Lída Baarová from 1936 until 1938. They had been blissfully happy, to the great displeasure of Magda Goebbels. The deceived wife had taken her revenge by taking a lover, Karl Hanke, her husband's secretary. When the Goebbelses began contemplating divorce, Adolf Hitler decided to intervene. He couldn't allow his most famous minister to destroy the illusion of the perfect Nazi family he had created with Magda and their six children. Leading Nazi dignitaries had to set an example. Goebbels had to separate from

Lída and fall into line, while the actress was sent back to Prague. However, one of her movies produced by UFA was still awaiting distribution.

Greven decided to authorize the distribution of *Prüssische Liebesgeschichte*, in which Lída Baarová played the part of Princess Elisa Radziwill, the mistress of Kaiser Wilhelm I. This decision was motivated by economic considerations, but Greven made things worse by entering into negotiations with the actress for a new exclusive contract. One wonders why Greven made a move like this that was so at odds with his interests. He either wasn't aware of Goebbels's affair or else he had been misinformed about it.

Magda Goebbels immediately took action, sending her lover Karl Hanke to Babelsberg studios. Hanke, escorted by two SS, asked to see Greven and once admitted, he slapped his face. Rumors of the scandal made the rounds in the film industry, arousing Goebbels's anger. On May 27, 1939, Goebbels sacked Greven from UFA. The film *Prüssische Liebesgeschichte* was banned and wasn't released until 1950.

Greven's career came to an abrupt halt, but the film world had not heard the last of him. His days of glory came in summer 1940. He was sent to Paris to reorganize the French film industry. In spite of their differences, Goebbels acknowledged his business skills even as he considered him a "vulgar upstart."[8] Goebbels wrote, "It is a shame that there is often a discrepancy between personality and ability. Most of the time the questionable characters are the most able."[9] The comment is particularly ironic coming from a Nazi dignitary.

The fact that Greven could speak French and knew already a number of big names in French cinema was certainly an argument in his favor. He had, for example, authorized the production of *L'Héritier des Mondésir* (1939) in Berlin, a comedy directed by Albert Valentin featuring Fernandel shortly before he left UFA. In addition, he had a solid experience in film production and distribution, which made him the ideal candidate. And he was—of course—a distinguished member of the Nazi party.

In the rare pictures remaining of Greven, we see a man wearing a hat to hide his bald head. He had piercing eyes and a bold chin. We surmise that he was a tough character. Assistant director Jean Devaivre described him as a towering giant at six foot, seven inches. He certainly impressed his interlocutors with his powerful build. Guy de Carmoy spoke of a quick-tempered man wearing old clothes and a straw hat who could suddenly lose his temper and call his collaborators "pederasts."[10]

The films he produced in Germany—propaganda pictures, musicals, costume dramas, thrillers, and adaptations of novels by H. G. Wells, Arthur Conan

Doyle, and Theodor Fontane—would leave very little trace in the history of cinema. But that would not be the case with films he made at Continental Films. Greven was going to have full control over the French film industry and would be able to choose the cream of the crop among French filmmakers and the best available technicians. With such collaborators, he could only succeed in producing quality pictures that would leave a lasting mark on French film history.

CHAPTER 3

The Beginnings
of a Company

To establish a new company in Paris, it had to be registered with the commercial court. Continental Films was created on October 1, 1940, as a private company for ninety-nine years with a capital investment of 1 million francs. It was officially registered on October 25 under the number 282 789B. Apparently, Greven followed French laws and regulations to create the company. However, the first letterhead for Continental Films lists a different number, 282 739B, which suggests shoddy secretarial work, even if the error was later corrected, unless it was intentional to prevent the commercial court register from being consulted.

However, Greven was not all powerful at the helm of Continental Films. He received his orders from the top executive of the German film industry, Max Winkler, who founded the company Cautio Treuhand in 1929 in Berlin. Greven had signed a contract on June 1, 1940, that specified that his work would be "the representation of the interests of the German Reich film industry, as curated by our chairman Dr. (honoris causa) Winkler, in the Netherlands, Belgium, and France."[1] Winkler was working directly under the propaganda minister.

The creation of the company was mentioned in the trade press as soon as November 1, 1940. The company's 1 million francs were divided up as follows: Alfred Greven got the most, with 98 percent of the shares, while Fritz R. Langenscheidt and Richard Ehrt received 1 percent each. Film professionals therefore had to be aware of the fact that the company's capital came from Germany and of the fact that Alfred Greven was its manager with extensive power.

Greven didn't come alone from Germany to manage Continental Films. His righthand man, while the company existed, was Rudolf Hans Bauermeister. In the commercial court register Bauermeister was described as a sales manager, but in reality, he was the production manager, in direct contact with filmmakers and technicians on the set. Like Greven, Bauermeister was born in northern Westphalia in Barmen, a small town close to Wuppertal, on February 1, 1902. He spoke French and had previously worked for UFA. The rest of the company staff was German: the two authorized representatives, Robert Henking (who stayed in Berlin) and Hans Jurgen von Eike und Polwitz (who lived in Paris). The head of the secretarial pool was a Miss Gertrud Aschbrenner, born on April 18, 1894, in Berlin, in the Charlottenburg district. She supervised the work of a pool of German secretaries who never completely mastered the French language. Greven's mail was always peppered with grammatical errors. The company's accountant, Henri Contour, was the only Frenchman on the staff. Greven was certainly unable to employ a German for a job requiring in-depth knowledge of French laws and regulations.

Beyond administratively creating the company, it was also necessary to recruit artists, technicians, and film directors and also to search for scripts. Greven tackled these issues as soon as he arrived in Paris. He quickly realized he was going to need help from the French. Trying to recruit French artists for a German company in an occupied and humiliated country was not going to be easy. Even if some people wanted to get back to work, there was no doubt that most of them were ill at ease with the idea of collaborating with the occupying power. Greven therefore enlisted the services of two men, agent Robert Beunke and production manager Aimé Chemel, to help him.

Aimé Chemel remembered, "I was the first technician hired by Continental. I was fully aware of what it was. . . . I joined Continental with the agreement and at the injunction of Mr. de Carmoy who was then the government commissioner [for cinema]. This was for the sole purpose of enabling the French film industry to resume, to ensure that French film producers could get authorizations, because it's certain that if Continental had not started, French producers would never have been authorized to produced films."[2] In October 1940, Chemel began working with Greven on the first productions of the company. At that time, Continental was lodged in the offices of the German distribution company Tobis at 2 rue de La Baume in the very chic eighth arrondissement of Paris.

At the same time Greven was maneuvering, the new Vichy government was fighting to reorganize French cinema in the free zone, while also trying to control French film personnel in the occupied zone. For that purpose, the new French state headed by Maréchal Pétain promulgated a law on October 3, 1940, that banned Jews from all professions in filmmaking, whether as producers, directors, actors, or even usherettes. On August 16, 1940, the Vichy government created the Organizing Committee of the Cinema Industry. Although during the 1930s, film people had dreamed of regulation, the government was now offering them an administrative straitjacket for controlling staff through compulsory professional cards and censorship of the film contents in line with "national renewal" propaganda. To receive a trade card, film technicians had to fill out a two-page form noting their full civil status and that of their spouse and their four grandparents as well as their nationality and status as Jew or non-Jew. This systematic filing system allowed the government to eliminate those considered undesirable by the new regime from the film industry.

In December 1940, following the publication of the law's implementing decrees, the government appointed a tax inspector, Guy de Carmoy, as government commissioner of the Organizing Committee of the Cinema Industry, while producer Raoul Ploquin took over as the head of it. This brilliant producer was the ideal candidate: he had worked for UFA in Berlin from 1927 until 1939 and spoke German fluently. As head of French production inside UFA, he had produced *Un Mauvais garçon* (1936), directed by Jean Boyer with Danielle Darrieux, several Jean Grémillon masterpieces such as *Gueule d'amour* (1937) and *L'Étrange Monsieur Victor* (1938), and two films directed by Albert Valentin, *L'Entraîneuse* (1938) with Michèle Morgan and *L'Héritier des Mondésir* (1939) with Fernandel. Ironically, it was actor Pierre Blanchar—later a pillar of the Resistance within the film industry—who supported Ploquin's appointment during a meeting with Greven. "At that time, we needed to find a man who could act as go-between between Vichy regulations and the French film industry. So [Greven] had his own ideas, and Ploquin had already been mentioned. During this conversation, I emphasized Ploquin's qualities. I said, 'Ploquin looks to me to be the right man for you, as he worked in Germany for a long time. His past collaborations will make his future ones with you easier, and besides, he is a Frenchman who certainly knows French cinema. He is capable to seeing to the French film industry's interests.'"[3]

As early as October 1940, Greven hoped to hire five famous French directors: Maurice Tourneur, Marcel Carné, Christian-Jaque, Léo Joannon, and Georges Lacombe. He did not choose them at random; he knew they had directed successful pictures before the war and his main aim was to produce entertaining films that would please a wide audience. These directors were obviously uncomfortable with the idea of joining Continental Films. They did not wish to become propaganda tools.

Those five men's testimonies tally regarding the steps they took following Greven's injunctions. Marcel Carné remembered:

I came back from the summer of 1940 exodus. Greven asked for me. He asked me if I wanted to sign a contract with him. We discussed the terms. We readily agreed on the terms of the contract, except with respect to two clauses. First of all, I demanded that my films be shot in France, because I didn't want to make films in Germany, and secondly, that the subject be chosen by mutual agreement so that there wouldn't be any propaganda pictures. Greven refused these conditions. I said, "In this case, I'm not signing." I thought the affair was dead and buried, but then, I was summoned to the rue de Varenne by the head of the government, where I met Mr. Mary, Mr. de Carmoy's secretary. Mr. Mary told me, "We have a complaint from Mr. Greven; you do not want to sign a contract. . . . You have been discharged. . . . They are offering you a very good contract." I explained to him the two clauses I had asked for and the reasons why I asked for them. De Carmoy told me, "Things need to be sorted out, because, frankly, Continental's position is the following: if you and your colleagues do not agree, French cinema won't restart. It's sine qua non. Continental demands its directors and its stars. Once it has the people it wants under contract, then it will grant an authorization to French producers." . . . After that, Mr. Mary told me, "Listen, first, I'll try to settle the matter of the two clauses you are asking for, and second, if there are any disagreement with Continental people, the French government will support you, you can be sure of that."[4]

Director Christian-Jaque also met with Greven and then de Carmoy. "We were summoned with Carné. Mr. Greven told us, 'A two-year contract.' I said, 'I have never signed such a contract. I'm not going to start now. I asked for some time to consider the case.' Immediately, we made an appointment with de Carmoy. We told him, 'Here is the situation, what should we do?' De Carmoy, 'Actually, if he cannot get what he wants, he will axe French production. There is no doubt.'"[5] Georges Lacombe, Maurice Tourneur, and Léo Joannon later met Carné and Christian-Jaque, who briefed them regarding their conversation with Guy de Carmoy.

Tourneur was in a delicate situation in relation to the French and German authorities.[6] After becoming an American citizen in 1921, he had come back to France in 1926, hoping to resume his career as filmmaker. But his past caught up with him. He had been a draft dodger during World War I, and France expelled him in 1928. He managed to have his expulsion suspended in 1929 and was finally able to come back to France. His status remained precarious until 1940. He had to ask the police prefect in writing for authorization to remain legally in France every year. Tourneur related how he and his colleagues made up their minds. "Several of my comrades and myself to whom this contract was offered reflected that, on the one hand, a significant mass of capital was going to flow to France, allowing thousands of people belonging to our industry, including staff dedicated to distribution and exhibition, to earn a living at a critical time and that on the other hand, if we refused, the Germans were going to import their own authors, directors, etc., into France, who were not likely to have the same scruples as us. And so we thought we should accept."[7]

At the same time the film directors were being recruited, the agent Robert Beunke had been busy in the unoccupied zone meeting the famous actors Greven wished to hire. Born in Paris in 1887, Beunke had worked first as a secretary and later as journalist before becoming secretary of the Paris Theaters Academy in 1926. In 1940, he was Fernandel's agent and knew theater and film people inside out. As he needed a letter of transit to travel to Paris in December 1940, Beunke agreed to work for Greven for a salary of 8,000 francs a month. His job was to hire a number of actors for Continental. He acted as go-between for three years and signed up actors Raimu, Fernandel, Michel Simon, Jules Berry, Louis Jourdan, and Tino Rossi. Beunke showed real enthusiasm doing the job. It looked as if he had no qualms in working for a German company. Famous still photographer Roger Forster remembered how he offered him a job working on *Simplet* in April 1941: "He proposed that I shoot at Continental. He said that France would be occupied for thirty years, and if I didn't sign a contract with Continental, I'd never be able to work, and in any case, I'll never get a letter of transit to go to Paris."[8] Screenwriter Carlo Rim, as we will see, would have a similar experience with Beunke.

The company had been established. Continental now had to start producing its first films.

CHAPTER 4

First Productions

On February 15, 1941, the corporate press announced that Continental Films had just put two feature films into production: *L'Assassinat du Père Noël* (1941), directed by Christian-Jaque, and *Le Dernier des six* (1941), directed by Georges Lacombe. Production resumed at last at the Billancourt studios on February 28 with the Lacombe picture while Christian-Jaque went on locations to Chamonix in the French Alps on February 17.

Christian-Jaque had signed his contract in October 1940, his conditions having been accepted. Between the two Continental Films he had been requested for, he choose to direct *Premier Bal* (1941) for French producer André Paulvé. Greven agreed to his conditions; there was no doubt he was anxious to secure the cooperation of this famous filmmaker. Christian-Jaque also managed to get permission to film *L'Assassinat du Père Noël* (1941), which he had already been working on before the war with author Pierre Véry, and a fictionalized account of the life of composer Hector Berlioz (*La Symphonie fantastique* [1942]). He also specified various clauses to make sure his works wouldn't be tampered with:

1) You hire me to collaborate on the shooting script and to supervise the preparation, the staging, the production, and the editing of two films in French, which will be shot in France.

2) The choice of subjects for these two films will be settled by mutual agreement.

3) The final shooting script and dialogue as well as model sets must be agreed on beforehand in writing by your company.

4) In shooting the film, I promise to do my best to not exceed the estimated budget provided by you and to keep to the schedule we mutually agreed on. . . .

11) In the case that cuts are made to the films produced by me and if those cuts are likely to alter the artistic value of my work as well as in the case where

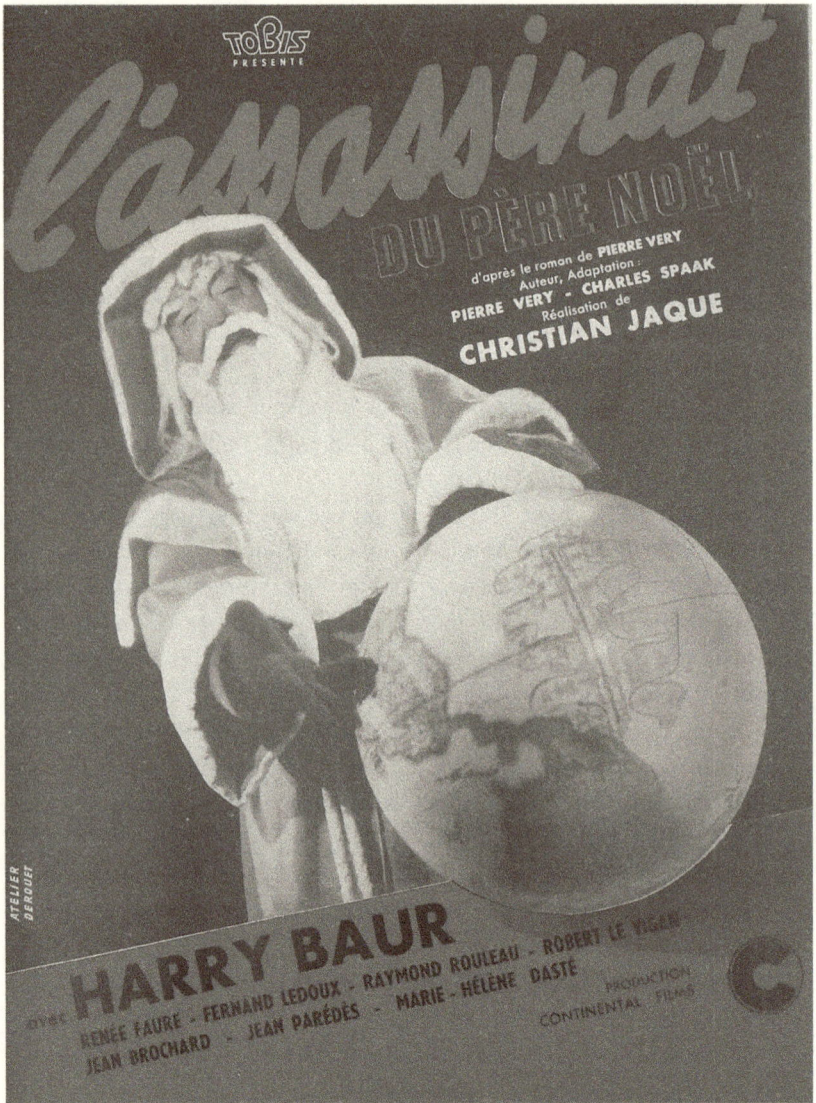

Ad for *L'Assassinat du Père Noël* (1941) (Fondation Jérôme Seydoux-Pathé)

you decided to replace me after the beginning of the shooting, I reserve the right to ask for the removal of my name from the credit title, the trailer, and the film posters.[1]

L'Assassinat du Père Noël was characterized in the corporate press as a "fantasy police mystery" by Continental.[2] The cast was prestigious; it had Harry Baur in the title role and featured Renée Faure, Fernand Ledoux, and Raymond Rouleau. Christian-Jaque insisted on hiring Robert Le Vigan for a small part, and he contacted the actor. He offered him a fee of 65,000 francs for a period of two and a half or three months.[3] Unlike most of his colleagues, Le Vigan was delighted to work for a German company and wrote an impassioned letter to Greven:

Regardless of the personal thanks I owe you, I want to express the gratitude aroused by your initiative with regard to our community. . . . When I was discharged, while no particular interest called me there, I went back to Paris with my family because I wanted to be one of the factors involved in the new order of things between white men like us! . . . Today, sir, thanks to you, I am pleased I followed my judgment and my feelings, as I am now at the stage of benefiting from the collaboration you are welcoming me to.[4]

If Le Vigan welcomed collaboration with open arms, Harry Baur's attitude was far more complex. He was one of the biggest stars of the screen and of the Paris theaters and one of the highest paid. Yet persistent rumors were being spread about him. In an antisemitic pamphlet written by Third Reich civil servant Heinz Ballensiefen, titled *Juden in Frankreich* and published in 1939, he was described as being Jewish. This accusation probably owed to the fact that he had played the role of a Jewish banker in Julien Duvivier's *David Golder* (1931) and Marco de Gastyne's *Rothchild* (1933). According to the new laws created by the Vichy government, he might not be able to get a work permit. The German authorities were also on the lookout for such rumors and allegations. Baur had to prove that at least two of his grandparents as well as his spouse were not Jewish to be considered Aryan.

The Germans were quietly monitoring him because they did not wish to upset the French authorities. A note from the German services reveals this cautious attitude: "In the event Mrs. Baur is Jewish, Baur must be treated as a Jew. It's critical that the case for allowing his public appearances be taken up, as French artists and audiences are used to regarding him as a Jew. We mustn't ignore the fact that a work permit for Harry Baur could be seen as surprising and may arouse questions about our attitude regarding the Jewish question."[5] Baur managed to prove that his paternal grandparents were Catholic, but he couldn't prove that his wife, actress Rika Radifé, was Aryan. She was born in Istanbul on July 14, 1902, of Turkish parents, and the birth certificate she provided the French and German authorities proved unsatisfactory.

Finally, in November 1940, Baur managed to provide evidence proving that his maternal Alsatian ancestors were also Catholic. On November 18, he was informed he would be allowed to work on the stage and for the screen. But Baur was nevertheless still the object of various denunciations. In July 1941, Mrs. Baur's hairdresser, who was an informer for the German authorities, claimed that the actor had said, "We Jews are the best artists in the world."[6] This accusation was worrying enough to the Germans that they decided to reexamine the documents related to his grandparents and to ask more questions about the status of his wife. We can imagine that by signing with Continental Films, Baur was trying to put a stop to these investigations. He no doubt thought that by working for the German company, he would no longer come under suspicion by the occupying authorities. He was unfortunately wrong.

After the war, while being investigated as screenwriter, Pierre Very explained how the adaptation rights for his novel were purchased by the company:

> In December 1940, in agreement with my publisher La Nouvelle Revue Fran-çaise, which had a mandate for this kind of affair, I sold the film rights of my novel *L'Assassinat du Père Noël* to the film production company Continental (which, at that time, I swear on my honor, I didn't know was German). It paid sixty thousand francs, from which after a 50 percent deduction for my publisher and 10 percent for my agent, I received in total twenty-seven thousand francs. My novel *L'Assassinat du Père Noël* was published in 1934. In selling the film rights to Continental, I therefore acted as a novelist and not as a screenwriter.[7]

The novel was adapted by Belgian screenwriter Charles Spaak, who also wrote the dialogue. He worked on the script with the director without any interference from the company. He never even met a company executive.

If Greven was keen to employ the cream of the crop among filmmakers, he also had strict standards regarding technicians. The head of Continental summoned cinematographer Armand Thirard to offer him an annual contract. Thirard was one of the few cinematographers in the French film industry who had an agent, in this instance, Jean Dewalde, who also represented actors Louis Jouvet and Edwige Feuillère. Immediately after Marcel Carné had been hired, Thirard was called up by Greven. Recently discharged and out of work, Thirard agreed to discuss a possible contract with the company. But he stated his conditions regarding his salary; he knew his value in the film industry. He acknowledged that discussions lasted for months. In his defense, he said that his colleague cinematographers were able to profit from the precedent of his contract and ask for better salaries from French producers.

Guy de Gastyne was recruited as art director for *L'Assassinat du Père Noël*. He had worked on Julien Duvivier's last picture in France, *Untel père et fils* (1940), shot at the Victorine studios in Nice, shortly before the director left for the USA. Gastyne was summoned at Continental—like Thirard—and, as he was without work, he signed for one picture: "All right, we're going to agree. We'll see. We'll try to do something worthwhile in spite of all, to show that we know how to make a picture."[8]

Thirard and Gastyne were not aware at that time that they would become pillars of the Continental style. Thirard brought his chiaroscuro lighting effects and his skill for lighting a set quickly and efficiently, while Gastyne brought his talent as set designer able to recreate the past as well as a contemporary atmosphere.

Christian-Jaque took advantage of the complete freedom offered by Continental to skillfully introduce hidden allusions to an occupied France waiting to be liberated by a savior. The filmmaker claimed that he was directly referencing General de Gaulle. It is difficult to confirm his claims, but it is true that the final sequence of the film offered a vision of hope to a humiliated and wounded France. In this sequence, old Cornusse (Harry Baur) dressed as Santa Claus, brings a globe with a world map to little Christian, a sick child. The boy asks, "And the little Chinese kids, what are you telling them?" Cornusse replies, "I tell them about France and the little French kids and also about a certain beautiful princess who was asleep in her little armchair. She had been asleep for a long, long time. Some thought she was dead. Some even believed it. But they were wrong. She was alive, perfectly alive and, in her sleep, she was having a dream, a beautiful dream, always the same dream. She was dreaming of Prince Charming, who would come wake her up, wake her up and bring her happiness."[9] Even if that sequence could be understood as a simple reference to old Cornusse's daughter, played by Renée Faure, Continental executives asked for explanation on the phone. Christian-Jaque managed to convince them of the harmlessness of the sequence as it was finally shot.

After the shooting on location in Chamonix in the French Alps, the picture was shot at the Neuilly studios starting on March 24, 1941. Production of *L'Assassinat du Père Noël* was completed without a hitch on April 25, 1941. Christian-Jaque had hired René Le Hénaff to edit the film. It was a thankless task for him but necessary, as he was without resources since having been discharged. "I reluctantly accepted the job offer. In addition to my having no desire to work for the Germans, it was hard for me who had been editor for many years and started as a film director before the war to go back to my former job. I could not show enthusiasm, that goes without saying, for going down the ladder for a salary, moreover, well below what I was earning several years before the war for that same technical job!"[10]

The German distribution company Tobis was in charge of the advertising campaign for the film release. It just so happened that the employee in charge of advertising was none other than journalist and future film historian Maurice Bessy. He helped create the poster for the film, which aroused the anger of the German authorities, as an inflammatory letter he received from Tobis indicates:

> The military governor in France strongly reprimanded us regarding the ad for *L'Assassinat du Père Noël*, whose size, color, and writing resembles that of the posters affixed on Paris walls regarding the reward offered to find the murderers of German army soldiers. It's only through a personal request that I was able to avoid your immediate arrest. Within twenty-four hours all those posters must be scratched out or covered. I urge you to do what is necessary because after this time I will not be able to intervene in your favor. As you know, Mr. Greven already asked for your dismissal several times, stating he had information allowing him to consider you an enemy of the Third Reich. It's certain that incidents like these are very serious, and it's difficult for me not to agree with him.[11]

While *L'Assassinat du Père Noël* was the first film Continental produced, it was not released until October 16, 1941. For the first release, Greven preferred a comedy with Danielle Darrieux directed by Henri Decoin that must have looked more commercial than the Christian-Jaque picture. Moreover, he had known Decoin for many years.

CHAPTER 5

Decoin and Greven

Among all the French filmmakers who had worked in Germany before the war, Henri Decoin knew Alfred Greven the best. However, his relationship with the Continental big boss was always extremely tense and ended with a lawsuit.

Decoin, like his colleagues, was in the south of France when he first heard about the creation of Continental Films. He remembered:

> It was in August 1940, in Cannes, when Jean Renoir, returning from Vichy where he had gone to apply for his passport to go to America, told me that the government commissioner in charge of cinema, Tixier-Vignancour, had ordered me and Danielle Darrieux to go back to Paris to work for Continental, a French company managed by Alfred Greven. Then, a month later, Mr. Loureau asked me to dinner and informed me that Mr. Guy de Carmoy was the head of cinema in Paris and that it was in the interest of the film industry to accept him as chief and to follow his instructions. . . . In October, still in Cannes, I received a phone call from Mr. Chemel, who happened to be in Marseille on behalf of Continental. Mr. Chemel notifies me that he has been put in charge of Continental productions by Mr. de Carmoy and that in the interest of French cinema, we—Danielle Darrieux and I—must go back to Paris and resume our artistic work. He informs me that directors Carné, Christian-Jaque, Tourneur, Lacombe, Joannon, and Gleize have already been hired by Continental and that filmmaking is going to resume and all film stars are going to make a film! . . . I don't go back to Paris immediately. I think about it. I ask my friend Pierre Maréchal, production manager with [Joseph] Lucachevitch, to go to Paris and make inquiries and then report back to me. A few days later, I receive a letter from Pierre Maréchal in which he writes "French cinema is going to be revived. Continental, a French company with foreign capital, is going to make films with Carné, Christian-Jaque, Joannon, Lacombe, Tourneur, and Gleize. Alfred Greven, whom you know, will give French

producers the authorization to make films if film stars do not boycott his productions . . . etc., etc." I show Grégor Rabinovitch—my producer for *Battement
de cœur* (1940)—this letter, who advises me to work for Continental till something better comes along. We leave for Paris, arriving on November 1.[1]

And just like his colleagues, Decoin needed to be reassured before signing a
contract with Continental. But, unlike his colleagues who had appealed to those
in power in the absence of other options, he asked the opinion of producers
he had already worked with. He was conscious that they would be barred from
filmmaking by the new antisemitic laws. Decoin, unlike others, did not at all
support these race laws, and he would even continue to work with his screenwriter Max Kolpe in spite of the fact that he was Jewish and therefore not
allowed to work.

During the 1930s, French cinema had undergone several serious crises with
the successive bankruptcies of Gaumont and Pathé. The film industry had
been thereafter only financed by independent producers who happened to be,
in most cases, from Central Europe. The significant number of Jewish producers had led to hostile comments and xenophobia among some filmmakers.
When Adolf Hitler came to power in 1933, a number of talented German-
Jewish technicians and directors also had fled to France. Some members of
the industry took a dim view of this competition in a time of crisis in French
cinema. Yet Robert Siodmak, Max Ophüls, and brilliant cinematographer
Eugen Schüfftan all enriched French filmmaking thanks to their talent.

In addition to the antisemitic laws making it impossible for Jewish people
to work in cinema that came into effect on October 3, 1940, a 1939 law forbidding racial defamation was repealed on August 16, 1940. The most vicious
antisemites and racists could therefore spread their hatred in the press without any limits. In April 1941, the extreme-right film critic Lucien Rebatet
published an incredibly violent pamphlet titled *Les Tribus du cinema et du
théâtre* in which he explained that French cinema had to be "de-Jewified." The
book was celebrated in the trade press, as in an editorial by journalist Paul-
Auguste Harlé, who remarked that "Rebatet's book is violent. . . . But this
violence is necessary. We must *put the situation right*, we film people who have
been perverted by twenty years of living under the same roof with mostly
foreign Jews who have only recently left the ghetto, with dubious commercial
practices, shady schemes, and risky swindles. . . . Those films, some of which
we had to realize were revolting, dangerous not only for young French people
individually but for the country's mentality as a whole, we were spineless

enough to buy them, screen them, and proclaim them beautiful with promotional hype."[2]

It was in these circumstances that Henri Decoin met Alfred Greven after he had made a brief visit to Guy de Carmoy.

A few hours after that lunch, I go to rue de La Baume where I meet Greven. I had known the head of Continental since 1933. I worked several times in Berlin, at UFA under the direction of Greven, Rabinovitch, and Ploquin. Across a six-year period, either in Berlin or in Paris, I, like many other directors, encountered Greven. In Berlin, in 1935, while I was shooting *Le Domino vert*, Greven was present at my engagement to Danielle Darrieux. Therefore, the head of Continental was not unknown to me when I met him. Immediately, in his first sentences, I notice that nothing has changed in him. He is not triumphant. He will make up for it later. . . . We discussed the contract we were to enter into, then I left him.[3]

This was the beginning of November, and Decoin was in no hurry to sign up. He made inquiries with those of his colleagues who had already signed the contract. Greven began to lose patience and sent him letters and called him on the phone. In the end, Decoin asked for another appointment on December 15 to clarify some points. "The director working for Continental will remain in control of his work, free to refuse a subject, to correct dialogue, etc., etc.," Greven and Aimé Chemel reassured him. He and Danielle Darrieux finally signed their contracts in February 1941.

At the beginning of February 1941, the Continental script department had only one staff member, Pierre Léaud, who worked with production manager Aimé Chemel. He was actor Jean-Pierre Léaud's father, and before the war he had been assistant director at UFA and at Alliance Cinématographique Européenne. This was why he had been summoned by Continental and offered a job to write screenplay synopses and translate them into German. He was offered a monthly contract and worked there from February until October 1941. He was not the only person working for Continental at a job unrelated to what he did before the war, despite his having a trade card as an assistant director.

Decoin refused all the scripts offered by Léaud and Chemel. He had his own ideas.

I am in contact with Max Colpet [Kolpe], Israelite, deported from Germany, in hiding in Paris, who is the coauthor of my last film, *Battement de cœur*. Max

Colpet is working on a story, *Premier Rendez-vous*. He would like to sell it while remaining incognito. The story is not quite ready yet, but the subject interests me. I work with Colpet, sometimes at my place, sometimes at his hiding places. We write a continuity script, he in German, me in French. For several weeks now, Greven has believed that I have been working on a script of which I am the author. Finally, I present him the two continuity scripts: the German and the French one. As I expected, Greven reads the German one and agrees to make *Premier Rendez-vous* by Henri Decoin.[4]

Decoin sold Greven the script for 100,000 francs. He gave half to his coscreenwriter, which made it possible for him to cross the demarcation line and to seek refuge at the Grand Hotel in Cannes with Mr. Gendre, the father of actor Louis Jourdan, who received him like a friend on the recommendation of Decoin. Later, Colpet would manage to flee to Switzerland, again thanks to Decoin's help, where he would join filmmaker Jacques Feyder.

Decoin had wanted to hire Louis Jourdan for the romantic lead opposite Danielle Darrieux. Greven refused on the pretext that his father was rumored to be a freemason. Decoin in the end prevailed and left for the south of France to hire Jourdan. Further difficulties cropped up when Jourdan asked for 50,000 francs for the part but Greven didn't want to go over 30,000. In the end, they agreed on 30,000, and Robert Beunke had him sign a contract.

Back in Paris, Greven organized a dinner with all the Continental filmmakers in his Paris flat on rue Beaujon to celebrate the start of production. Christian-Jaque was preparing *L'Assassinat du Père Noël*, Maurice Gleize *Le Club des soupirants*, Georges Lacombe *Le Dernier des six*, Marcel Carné *Les Évadés de l'an 4000*, Léo Joannon *Caprices*, and Decoin *Premier Rendez-vous*. Decoin remembered that "Greven presided over the table with Carné at his right and Christian-Jaque at his left. The evening was spent in technical discussions during which Marcel Carné never agreed with Greven. I must say that Marcel Carné never demeaned himself and spoke his mind with the head of Continental. . . . His attitude made a strong impression on me."[5]

The shooting of *Premier Rendez-vous* started on April 22, 1941, at the Billancourt studios. This romantic comedy was the perfect follow-up to *Battement de cœur*, which had been released in February 1940. It had the same steady pacing and the same sparkling charm that its lead actress exuded. Inspired by contemporary American comedies, Decoin brilliantly managed to transpose the delicate mechanics of the romantic comedy to a French context. Darrieux sang two songs—"Premier rendez-vous" and "Chanson d'espoir," with music

Ad for *Premier Rendez-vous* (1941) (Fondation Jérôme Seydoux-Pathé)

by René Sylviano. She dubbed herself for the German version of the songs. Greven had indeed decided that the film would also be released in Germany.

Although the budget looked sizable, Decoin hired a number of young people studying acting at Cours Simon as film extras. Among those, a young actress named Jacqueline Desmarets (who would soon change her first name to Sophie) got the small part of Henriette, one of the orphans who befriends Danielle Darrieux. She wore her own clothes to shoot a scene and managed to stain her dress. Her mother sent her dress to the cleaner, and so the next day she arrived wearing a suit, which created a continuity error, as she gets on the bus wearing a dress but gets off wearing a suit.[6]

Among the young actors from Cours Simon making their first appearances in a film were Rosine Luguet, the daughter of actor André Luguet, also hired by Continental, Françoise Christophe, Simone Valère, Daniel Gélin, Georges Marchal, and Jacques Charon.

Decoin liked to name his characters after his acquaintances. For *Premier Rendez-vous*, he made the mistake of naming one of the pupils in the college, played by Georges Marchal, Jean de Vaugelas. Decoin had known an aviator called de Vaugelas in his squadron during the war. Unfortunately, the real Jean de Vaugelas did not like being portrayed on screen as "a young heir of a good family who in taking pleasure in torturing his teachers thereby discredited the name de Vaugelas."[7] He sued Continental Films as well as Decoin and his screenwriter Michel Duran in 1941, seeking a modification of the film and requesting 500,000 francs in damages. In March 1944, he was awarded 20,000 francs, but his request that the film be modified was not granted. Ironically, Jean de Vaugelas was also a member of the notorious "Milice," a paramilitary organization that collaborated with the Germans against the Resistance.

Decoin noted bitterly, "I realized during the shooting of *Premier Rendez-vous* that it was going to be difficult for me to get along with the Germans artistically speaking. But I had signed for three films, and the first one was not yet finished!" His marriage with Danielle Darrieux was also in bad shape. They divorced on October 6, 1941, although they remained good friends.

Premier rendez-vous was the first Continental Films production, released on August 14, 1941. The Normandie cinema on the Champs-Élysées was stormed by Parisians, who queued for long hours before opening time. In the press, the film was cheered as quality entertainment allowing the audience to forget everyday problems. The collaborationist press was quick to underline that the film was in line with the new standards of the Vichy regime: "*Premier Rendez-vous* marks both a brilliant renewal of French cinema and a noble return to a healthier idea of filmmaking. It was about time! Our cinematographic art was used too much as propaganda by agents of social disintegration whose origin is not difficult to guess."[8] This criticism becomes amusing when one knows the film was written by Max Kolpe.

Reviewer Jacques Audiberti captured perfectly the audience's impression during that summer of 1941 when people were still trying to cope with the defeat of June 1940: "*Premier Rendez-vous* is a masterpiece. These two terms don't look as if they go together. However, do not doubt it, this film erases and covers over those stale melodramas, those unusable comedies that we weakly applauded together in recent weeks. If this film is also the first rendez-vous of French cinema and its public after the strange war in which we died without quite perishing, let's say right away, without exaggerating its symbolic impact, that the success of this first rendez-vous with a double meaning can bring some comfort."[9]

Henri Decoin then started working on his next film, *Les Inconnus dans la maison*, an adaptation of a Georges Simenon novel, a far more disturbing work than *Premier rendez-vous*.

CHAPTER 6

Henri-Georges Clouzot, Screenwriter

Filmmaker Georges Lacombe began shooting a comedy mystery, *Le Dernier des six*, on February 28, 1941, at the Billancourt studios. The script had been written before the war and was an adaptation of a novel by Belgian novelist Stanislas-André Steeman titled *Six hommes morts*. Lacombe found the dialogue mediocre and suggested that production manager Aimé Chemel hire a dialogue writer to rewrite it.

In December 1940, Henri-Georges Clouzot had been hired for the work. "They asked me to rewrite the dialogue of *Le Dernier des six*. I found the script extremely weak. I entirely rewrote the screenplay and dialogue."[1] At the time Clouzot was a little-known screenwriter who was just coming out of a long period of inactivity because of a serious illness. His work on the screenplay was very much appreciated by Alfred Greven, and he asked him to join the Continental script department. Clouzot told him no. "At that time, I thought I wanted to stay free. But as it happened, I didn't get any offer from a French company, and as I was literally starving, I joined Continental."[2] Clouzot mentioned the offer to his friend Pierre Fresnay, an actor, who advised him to accept the proposition, "feeling that at his age, it was extraordinary to have at his disposal such an instrument and such important means."[3] Fresnay was right to believe in such an opportunity to climb the ladder, as Clouzot became the head of the script department for the company.

Clouzot gave a new style to the story, inspired openly by the delicious American comedy mystery series *The Thin Man*, in which William Powell and Myrna Loy played a couple of humorous detectives. American films being absent from the screen during the occupation, production companies were looking to create detective stories, musicals, and gangster pictures to provide the public with the entertainment they had enjoyed before the war. Continental followed suit. Clouzot gave Inspector Wens a lovely deadpan humor opposite his girlfriend,

Ad for *Le Dernier des six* (1941) (Fondation Jérôme Seydoux-Pathé) the irritating Miss Mila Malou. According to Clouzot, Pierre Fresnay had not been the first actor chosen to play Wens, but he managed to embody the part with such talent that it looked as if it had been written for him. As for the character of Mila Malou, Clouzot wrote it specifically for his girlfriend, actress Suzy Delair. Like for her partner, working at Continental gave her the opportunity to become a star; up until now, her career as an actress had been limited to bit parts, like that in *L'Or dans la rue* (1934), where she had been an extra playing a friend of Danielle Darrieux.

Continental had wanted a bigger star and had contacted Arletty. But she had refused outright. "I want to specify that I never at any time during the occupation showed any hint of collaboration. Although I had been approached many times, I always refused to make a single film for a German company and particularly for Continental. . . . This was an opportunity to earn a lot of money. I estimate that for the films I was offered I could have earned several million if I had accepted them."[4] In spite of her refusal, Greven would go on asking her to take numerous other parts.

Georges Lacombe seemed to have difficulty establishing his authority on the set. Deputy stage manager Paul Olive, who had been chief stage manager before the war, chomped at the bit during the shooting and observed that if "[he] had been chief stage manager of *Le Dernier des six*, there would have been only one director instead of three, because Mr. Fresnay and Mr. Clouzot would have been asked—politely but firmly—to do only their job."[5] There wasn't any doubt that Clouzot already had a burning desire to become a director. As for Pierre Fresnay, he had already directed a film—for the first and only time in his career—titled *Le Duel* (1940), the dialogue for which had been written by Clouzot.

Alfred Greven was unhappy with the result and asked for an extra music-hall sequence. To that end, Lacombe was dismissed, and Jean Dréville, who was on the verge of signing with them, was asked to direct a new scene. He was shown the two reels between which this new sequence had to be inserted. Dréville recalled: "I phoned Lacombe and told him, 'They asked me for an idea for your extravaganza. I submitted one to them.' I also submitted it to Lacombe. . . . At Continental, they told me, 'We would like you to be present at the shooting.' I answered, 'On one condition, Lacombe must be there too.' So, Lacombe was there. . . . I directed the small extravaganza, and Lacombe, on the same day, shot other retakes for other parts of the film."[6]

Jean Dréville's story was not corroborated by Henri Decoin's testimony. Decoin remembered that "within the first two weeks of shooting of *Le Dernier des six*, Lacombe was in the company's bad graces. Not knowing how to defend himself, Lacombe was forced to abandon the film. He was replaced by Jean Dréville, who created new scenes. When the film was finished and released, we could see for ourselves that in spite of all the slander dumped on Lacombe, the success was entirely his."[7]

Le Dernier des six was released at the Normandie cinema on September 16, 1941, and was showered with praise in the press. François Vinneuil, aka Lucien Rebatet, particularly enjoyed the work of the screenwriter. "His dialogue is as lively and caustic as Jacques Prévert's, but with less artifice and indulgence in witticisms and literary effects. It's written rather than hurled like the appalling chattering we are used to hearing at the cinema, and that doesn't prevent it from being natural, easy. It adds pleasure to the film without weighing it down. In short, we would be pleased to listen to it on its own, and yet we find the sense of cinema in it as much as in the images of Georges Lacombe."[8]

Aimé Chemel, who had participated in the production of *Le Dernier des six*, left Continental for good in April 1941. From now on, it was Rudolf Hans Bauermeister who would be the company production manager. If Greven rarely came to visit the sets, Bauermeister was omnipresent and managed productions with an iron rod. Greven's righthand man was little appreciated by technicians and filmmakers. Actress Ginette Leclerc remembered that when he came on the set, everybody, actors and technicians, stood up because it was forbidden to sit down on set.[9] There was no doubt he imposed a reign of terror on the company.

Georges Lacombe also left Continental immediately after the end of the shooting of his first film, even though he had signed a contract for two productions. Greven decided he probably didn't need him anymore after their disagreements during the shooting and after hiring several other directors. Seasoned filmmaker Maurice Gleize was hired to direct *Le Club des soupirants* (1941), starring Fernandel, at the Marcel Pagnol studios in Marseille. As for Jean Dréville, after his work on *Le Dernier des six*, he signed a contract for one film at Continental.

After the release of *Premier Rendez-vous*, another project was offered to Henri Decoin: "Bauermeister, who had become Greven's eminence grise, gave me Simenon's novel *Les Inconnus dans la maison* to read. I found this detective story exciting. I saw an opportunity to work with Raimu, to offer him a part worthy of his talent."[10] However, Decoin was extremely uncomfortable with one element of Simenon's novel. "One of the main heroes of the novel, Luska, the murderer, was Jewish; I asked for Luska not to be Jewish in the film.

Pressbook cover for *Les Inconnus dans la maison* (1942) (Fondation Jérôme Seydoux-Pathé)

Bauermeister confessed that if Greven had bought the rights to Simenon's novel, it was because of Luska's character, this dirty little Jew, and that he would never allow Luska to be renamed."[11]

It was, of course, Clouzot, now the head of the script department, who was put in charge of the adaptation and dialogue. Decoin went to see him.

> I told him how sick I felt at the idea of putting a little Jew in an unpleasant part, the part of a murderer, on the screen at the time when, in France, all Jews were tormented. Then, I waited for the decision about the Luska case. Bauermeister informed me a few days later that Greven would do without me directing *Les Inconnus dans la maison*. I was upset by this decision. . . . I met with Raimu. He agreed with me. He decided to try to make the head of Continental change his mind. He succeeded, as Greven agreed to change Luska's name, although he called me "king of the Jews." From that time on, following the Luska incident, my clashes with Greven became more and more frequent.[12]

If Decoin had qualms about promoting antisemitism inside a German company, Georges Simenon, on the other hand, was absolutely delighted to be able to sell the film rights of his works to Continental. In August 1941, he wrote to Pierre Léaud, then still in charge of scripts, to offer his services to the company. "Your letter, which I received this morning, gives me great pleasure. In general, I have good confidence in my first impressions. After the visit of the so nice Mr. Keller, I felt we were going to do good work; my travel to Paris and my communication with Mr. Greven, Mr. Bauermeister, and yourself reinforced this impression."[13] As a Belgian citizen, Simenon couldn't leave his residence at Fontenay-le-Comte (in Vendée in the west of France) because he lacked a visa. "I'd like to go to Paris if I'm authorized to do so. I think moreover that it would be justified that this authorization be more general, and I know that Jean Luchaire, director of *Nouveaux Temps*, wrote to the German Propaganda Office for that purpose. It's true it was more than a month ago, and I do not see anything coming of it. I think a Continental intervention would speed things up. There are days when I go mad, imprisoned in Fontenay where I go in circles, while any Gaulist [*sic*] can move about freely."[14]

Simenon wished to sell the film rights to a series of novels featuring Inspector Maigret, even though he had already sold those same rights in Hollywood before the war. But because he had had no news from the United States, he had no qualms about selling the same titles in France while excluding the United States from the contract. He offered to write the screenplay, the shooting script, and the dialogue himself for 150,000 francs per film. Obviously, Continental did not need his services as a screenwriter, but the company nevertheless bought the film rights to five novels, the first being *Les Inconnus dans la maison*.

Simenon's attitude was dramatically different from that of novelist Pierre Benoit. Greven had contacted him in October 1940 to buy the film rights of his novel *Alberte* for 3 million francs. Benoit flatly refused.[15] Yet that same writer was an eminent member of the "collaboration" group, made up of former members of the France-Germany committee.

Clouzot finished the adaptation and dialogue of *Les Inconnus dans la maison* and then sent the screenplay to Decoin, who produced the shooting script. Raimu, still in his house in Bandol in the south of France, was growing impatient in July 1941, as he still had not received the shooting script or dialogue continuity script of the film: "Here I am again in my Provence until Sunday after Cannes, because I've been called for regarding dough. So, I hope to see you there with Mr. Greven. In any case, if you still want me at the beginning of November, be kind enough to let me know, because I'll be very pleased to work with you. Greetings to Mr. Greven."[16]

Decoin left for the south to see Raimu on August 10, 1941. He met him in Nice, where he was staying at the Negresco Hotel, and gave him the shooting script. Greven joined them there. Decoin was delighted. "Raimu, for the first time in his life, admits that he likes the shooting script, that it's a masterpiece, and that he is happy to play the part."[17]

The shooting of *Les Inconnus dans la maison* got underway on November 15, 1941, at Neuilly studios.[18] Decoin recalled the details.

> The atmosphere is heavy. My schedule for shooting has been set at twenty-six days. If I manage it, it will be an acrobatic feat. But I must succeed in making this film because I love it! I am the only one who has so few days to shoot. I feel hostility toward me. They are waiting for the first opportunity to replace me with another to finish the film. I ask Clouzot. According to him, Greven blames me for making Germanophobic remarks on the set and in bars. I say that it seems that the Germans have had it! To catch me out, they posted a certain Mr. Keller at the Neuilly studios, as a representative of Continental for the production of my film. In fact, this Keller has a mandate to catch me in the act of talking against the Krauts. The grips warn me as soon as Keller arrives on the set. And yet, despite my patience, altercations crop up between the spy Keller and me. I call him a dirty Nazi; he threatens me with the Gestapo! One day, at noon, [Jean] Rossi, my production manager, informs me that I mustn't cease work but

go on shooting because Greven is coming, and they gave the order to wait for him. The grips are hungry; it's very cold. And after one o'clock, restaurants have nothing left to eat. I stop work. It's half past twelve. We evacuate the set. We are going out for lunch. At the restaurant, half an hour later, Rossi comes to fetch me. "Mr. Greven is at the studio! He is waiting for you; he is furious!" I reply, "Let him wait! We are having lunch!" Wild, foaming with rage, Greven goes back to his office and writes me. I answer him tit for tat, and I decide not to go back to work, in spite of the important number of extras on that day, before I get his answer. Greven phones Keller, telling him to order me to restart work! I refuse. One hour later, a car arrives with Greven's answer; he has given in! So I go back to work. And it's in that atmosphere that I finish *Les Inconnus dans la maison*. It's been exactly eleven months since I joined Continental. I do not see Greven anymore. It is only through letters from office to office that we speak.[19]

The constant fear of informers and surveillance at the Neuilly studios described by Decoin was fully corroborated by studio manager Jean Rossi, who remembered having gone through a similar experience during the shooting of *Défense d'aimer* (1942), directed by Richard Pottier. Only five minutes after Pottier had decided to redo a scene, Bauermeister called Rossi on the phone to ask for the reason.

Maurice Tourneur's recollections about the general atmosphere on set were similar: "There were extremely unpleasant people in the firm, apart from Greven whom we never saw! We had to make films in twenty or thirty days. We had endless discussions. It became impossible."[20]

Whether the director was a beginner or a seasoned professional, he was closely watched and each of his decisions to retake a scene was checked. Henri Decoin had only one dream: to leave Continental for good.

CHAPTER 7

Les Inconnus dans la maison

Les Inconnus dans la maison as well as two other films produced by Continental, *Le Corbeau* (1943) and *La Vie de Plaisir* (1944), were controversial; all were considered "antinational" films according to the term used at the time. More than their content, it was the context in which they were produced that distinguished them among other works of entertainment.

As we have seen, Henri Decoin was at once sensitive to the fact that Simenon's novel had a distinctive antisemitic bent, and he had tried from the start of the production to eliminate as much as possible what to his eyes was a disturbing element, while, on the contrary, Greven appreciated that the novel's murderer was a Jew.

To play the part of Luska, manager Jean Rossi had called a young actor whom he had met in Italy before the war, Marcel Mouloudji. The nineteen-year-old actor, who had appeared in prestigious productions like *Les Disparus de Saint-Agil* (1938), directed by Christian-Jaque, was completely destitute by then. He welcomed this opportunity with relief: "What a godsend for me! I was becoming a tramp. Of course, it was the part of a murderer."[1] At the time, however, Mouloudji was unaware of the xenophobic dimension surrounding his character. He was the son of a Kabyle and his mother was from Brittany. He unwittingly gave the impression of a corrupting stranger in a French middle-class environment. Simone de Beauvoir, who knew the young actor and saw the film when it was first released, immediately noticed this disturbing aspect: "Raimu was remarkable in *Les Inconnus dans la maison*, but the script made unpleasant concessions to racism; the murderer played by Mouloudji was not expressly identified as a Jew, but he was a metic."[2] The offensive term "metic" was widely used in the extreme-right press and referred to all foreigners living in France, whether they were Jews from Central Europe, people from North Africa, or from elsewhere. As de Beauvoir indicates, it was a time when xenophobia was endemic.

Pressbook cover for *Les Inconnus dans la maison* (1942) (Fondation Jérôme
Seydoux-Pathé)

Gennaro (known as Jean) Rossi, the studio manager who had hired Mouloudji, was himself a foreigner. He had been born in 1883 in Naples and had worked on many French films as production manager before the war. He was hired by Continental in March 1941 as chief stage manager with a lower salary than the one he had earned before the war. It was in that capacity that he worked on *Les Inconnus dans la maison*. From October 1942 on, following a denunciation, Bauermeister demoted him to simply stage manager.[3] Rossi would have liked to leave the company, but his wife, who happened to be French, pointed out that as a foreigner he would have difficulty finding a new job. He bit his tongue and stayed at Continental until June 1944.

The screenplay was written by Clouzot, but Decoin, the director, took full responsibility for its contents. He reread it and approved the dialogue and even helped write Raimu's long final monologue. The allusions to sport were certainly his. As a former sportsman, he believed in the virtue of physical exercise.

The film has a murder mystery plot that is typical of Simenon's novels. Mr. Loursat (Raimu), a lawyer who has been drowning his sorrows in alcohol ever since his wife left him, discovers a dead man in his house. The boyfriend (André Reybaz) of his daughter, Nicole (Juliette Faber), is charged with the murder. She had been mixing with a group of young men committing petty theft. Loursat comes out of his alcoholic stupor, defends the young man, and manages to unmask the real murderer during the trial. Apart from the traditional murder mystery plot, the film offered a particularly savage portrait of the provincial middle classes, not unlike that of other Simenon novels such as *Le Voyageur de la Toussaint*.

Yet Decoin and Clouzot had fun with Raimu's monologue, an acerbic criticism of the well-to-do as well as the government. It was this tirade that created waves:

> Well, gentlemen of the jury, you know our city: show me the way to the stadium, the way to the swimming pool! You're mumbling, you know very well there isn't any stadium, nor any swimming pool. There are one hundred and thirty-two cafés and four brothels; for those, there is no need to point them out, everybody knows them. That's what our leaders of yesterday did for our youth. When kids cannot get drunk on fresh air and speed, they must let off steam somehow, they go to the movies. And one day, one night, from spectators they become actors. They cover themselves with blood. Well! That bloody cloak, it's you, it's us, who threw it on their shoulders.

Decoin took full responsibility for this indictment of an unstable parliamentary republic. "I'm against Munich, against the Third Republic of the 1938–1939 period."[4] Of course, this criticism of the negligence of an unstable regime that procrastinated too much in the face of a dictatorship seems perfectly valid to us in retrospect. However, it was conveyed by a film produced by a German company. Criticizing the prewar parliamentary regime in this context looked like agreeing with Pétain supporters and collaborators who execrated the French Republic. This was not Decoin's intention when he wrote the text with Clouzot, but it was how it was interpreted in the clandestine magazines that first began appearing in 1943, in particular *L'Écran français*: "In a detective movie, *Les Inconnus dans la maison*, French youth is portrayed by louts; the French middle class is held responsible for these young hoodlums. 'Ah, there weren't any swimming pools and stadiums . . . ,' the lawyer exclaims. We immediately recognize the lingo of Nazism."[5]

At the time of its release in May 1942, the racist aspect of the film was not mentioned in the press. Only Jacques Audiberti mentioned "the small curly-haired Mouloudji" in the role of the murderer.[6] On the other hand, the social and political criticism was noticed: "For the first time, during a critical scene, a film raises the problem of the moral education of youth and the responsibility of the parents as well as the long-standing neglect of the authorities."[7] Even film critic Lucien Rebatet, who was always the first one to launch into antisemitic or xenophobic diatribes, made no references to Mouloudji's character. On the other hand, he very much liked Raimu's speech: "This diatribe against middle-class foulness has an almost Celinian ring, which has the fortunate effect of upending our usual moral standards and is perfectly suited to our present times."[8]

But, overall, film critics praised Raimu's extraordinary characterization as a mute alcoholic lawyer who comes to his senses in criminal court, where he delivers a brilliant speech for the defense that leaves the jury and the audience speechless. "Raimu—our greatest artist—delivered an admirable performance in carving out an extraordinary character with this equivocal lawyer, expressionless, drunken faced, who becomes aware of his decline and is suddenly clear sighted, putting on the dock the whole of the corrupt middle classes, in a pathetic spurt of effort."[9]

Decoin not only had shot the film in difficult conditions but was also unable to use the crew of technicians he wanted. Alexandre Laurier was "my assistant on *Premier Rendez-vous*. Subsequently, they asked me to make *Les*

Inconnus dans la maison; I asked for Robert Le Febvre, who was my cinematographer. Greven said, 'No.' I asked for Alexandre, he told me 'No.' He was afraid of teams. . . . They took Alexandre away and gave me the son of Metchikian. And everybody was saying, 'Be careful, it's the eye—not of Moscow—but of Berlin . . .' I was careful, and from day one, I had a bone to pick."[10] Nevertheless, Decoin was very pleased with his film. And he was not the only one.

In June 1942, Greven sent a copy of the film to Georges Simenon so that he could screen it in Vendée. The author was still under house arrest in Fontenay-le-Comte, and he effusively thanked the producer.

> Dear Mr. Greven, I have been very touched, believe me, by your so elegant and so exceptional gesture. Thanks to you, I was able to watch *Les Inconnus dans la maison*, which Continental has made a masterly production of. I am happy, in thanking you, to be able to express my complete satisfaction. What struck me the most was the perfect cohesion of the whole, and, besides the admirable Raimu, the judicious choices with respect to the more minor actors. The group of young people, among others, is more than remarkable. As soon as I am able to go to Paris, I'll be sure to visit you and to shake your hand. In the meantime, Mr. Greven, I beg you to accept my devoted and friendly sentiments.[11]

There was no doubt that Greven was particularly pleased to have obtained the rights to Simenon's works, and he thanked him with unusual generosity.

Looking back at the controversies after the war, Decoin pleaded in front of the purge committee that "his film would have gone quietly unnoticed; it was a clean picture. Nobody would have said a word about it. But somebody, I don't know who, in Algiers, or in England or in America, or in France, said that *Les Inconnus dans la maison* was released in Berlin under the title *French Youth*. It's not true."[12] Indeed, when the film was dubbed and screened in Germany, it was under the title *Das unheimliche Haus*, that is, *The Mysterious House*. It was a work of entertainment, and as contemporary reviews showed, nobody saw it as Vichy propaganda or as a pro-German film. But it was produced by Continental films, which made it dubious to the purge committee.

CHAPTER 8

Greven's Empire

From the moment he arrived in Paris, Alfred Greven had only one goal: to control the French film industry economically and artistically. The recruitment of filmmakers and film stars for Continental Films was merely the visible part in his efforts attracting media attention. He had an extremely ambitious plan: to create a vertically integrated company that would not only produce films but also acquire studios, have its own laboratory for printing copies of the films, and distribute them itself in its own circuit of cinemas as well as abroad.

Of course, this plan was not advertised in the least in the press. Greven organized all this in the greatest secrecy, using shills, a Spaniard and a Frenchman, so that no word would get out. As early as August 1940, Greven got in touch with José Bosch, a Spanish national and former department head, authorized representative, and then administrator of Tobis. Bosch remembered,

> He told me he wanted to buy a few cinemas to screen movies in and to create a film production company with Gaumont and Pathé. He offered me the job of overseeing the production department. I refused. Later, he asked me to create a company. Greven gave me the funds (one million), and then I went to see Mr. [Serge] Dairaines, who agreed to establish this company. If I wanted to remain in the shadows in this company, it's because we wanted to buy cinemas, and as the funds were German, we would have encountered difficulties. I should add that Mr. Dairaines could not have been unaware that the capital was German; I told him it was provided by Greven. In March 1941, there was an increase in the funds, also provided by Greven. . . . In March 1941, I took the position of director-manager of the company, and Mr. Dairaines stayed on as legal adviser of the company.[1]

Serge Dairaines managed a law firm and had all the qualities of a perfect collaborator for the occupying forces. A former member of Action Française, he had become a fervent supporter of fascism inside the French Popular Party led by Jacques Doriot.[2]

Thus, Greven bought out several circuits of film theaters with his collaborators and created the Society for the Management and Operation of Cinemas on November 1, 1940. If originally Dairaines seemed to be main shareholder, he quickly passed the baton to Greven, who in January 1942 held 99.4 percent of the shares through Continental Films. Greven was voracious and took advantage of the new antisemitic laws forbidding Jews to own cinemas. During the "aryanization" of properties, the producer bought out the Siritzky circuit, which consisted of a large number of cinemas in Paris as well as in Le Havre, Bordeaux, Toulouse, Nancy, and Lyon. He also later bought the Bel circuit, which included twelve theaters in the south of France.

Greven was now running a total number of forty-three cinemas. It was easy for him to congratulate himself on his management while replying to the criticisms of Raoul Ploquin, who ran the Organizing Committee of the Cinema Industry and maintained that the competition was unfair. Greven explained that of the theaters the company owned Le Normandie had been "the least attended theater in Paris since its opening" and that on top of that the Olympia and Moulin Rouge were "in the worst areas," and yet through its movies, "that is, German films and Continental films," and "after investing about 10 million francs to transform and improve" these theaters, the company had "succeeded in making the Normandie, Olympia, and Moulin Rouge the best theaters in Paris."[3]

Greven had selected a laboratory for developing and printing copies of his films, Cinéma Tirage L. Maurice, which had already worked for two German companies, Tobis and Alliance Cinématographique Européenne, before the war. The company had been created in 1919 by Léopold Gratioulet, known as Léopold Maurice, who was from a family of motion picture pioneers. In fact, his father, Clément Maurice Gratioulet, known as Clément Maurice, had been a Lumière operator. Before the war, Cinéma Tirage L. Maurice was not the leader in the field of printing copies; rather Éclair was number one. But, thanks to Greven, Cinéma Tirage L. Maurice was going to dominate the film printing market.

At first, Greven was content to rely on the company, even as he expressed dissatisfaction over the speed of delivery. In August 1941, he wrote the following threatening letter: "I must note with great surprise that we are badly served by your house. If, in the future, our orders are not executed more quickly, I must warn you now that we will have to withdraw the negatives from you. It is absolutely unacceptable that you are making us wait for five days for a copy of *Le Dernier des six*."[4] The strategy of intimidation went on in October 1941 with a new letter from Continental Films:

> We regret to inform you that our orders are still not executed as they should be in your factories. Negligence, omissions and mistakes are frequently happening. Awhile back, we had to postpone a very important screening for two days in a row, as you didn't deliver the reels in time (*Péchés de jeunesse*). The trailers are regularly delivered late. Finally, recently for two documentaries, we worked late into the night at the studio so that we could deliver this work to which Mr. Greven attached a particular importance. Although you had been warned a week in advance, your plant did not execute the necessary work on the negatives. Your management, which had been informed, did not seem to attach a great importance to this and promised to deliver the work one day later. We cannot accept such ways of doing things under any circumstances. With each order, we are told about too short lead times and delivery difficulties. The management of your plant is a matter for you, but we cannot be satisfied with such methods. From now on, for all works we will give to your plant, Mr. Chapot, who is in charge of all these questions, will give you very precise instructions in writing. We ask you to make sure they are strictly observed; otherwise, we will entrust our work to another laboratory.[5]

Léopold Maurice subsequently received demands from the German authorities that he sell part of the shares in the company that he owned. He refused, and so he was threatened with a closure of his plant and the transfer of the orders to a competitor. He was then encouraged to sell a number of shares that would be compensated by a commercial contract with Continental Films. In June 1942, he finally signed this contract, giving Greven a preemptive right to 21,700 shares for five years. In addition, Cinéma Tirage L. Maurice would receive all the printing work from German companies at a preferential rate. Continental would also receive a percentage on the profit generated by Cinéma Tirage L. Maurice. If Greven decided to act on the preemption, Maurice would receive a comfortable pension funded by Continental. Gratioulet justified his signing of such a contract on the grounds that it would safeguard his company and its employees.

Greven selected two studios for the production of his movies: those in Neuilly and in Billancourt. The owner of the Neuilly studios, Marcel Chavet, had gotten in touch with Greven as soon as October 1940 to offer to rent him his studios. In the 1910s, the city of Neuilly-sur-Seine (west of Paris) had been one of the main filmmaking locations in France, the Film d'Art studios being located on the rue Chauveau, before the opening of the Neuilly studios in 1931 located at 42 bis boulevard du Château near the American Hospital of Paris. Chavet touted his studios, where several prewar masterpieces such as Julien Duvivier's *Un Carnet de bal* (1937) and *La Charette fantôme* (1939) as well as Jean Grémillon's *Remorques* (1939, released in 1941) had been shot. Chavet sang the praises of the facilities: "We take the liberty of reminding you that we have at our disposal three independent sets, a large backlot on which outdoor sets can be easily built—this backlot can even be extended according to your wishes— and just as important, our technical equipment."[6] He offered to rent his studios for three years at the rate of 4,500 francs per day. He would not only set Continental up with the necessary technical equipment (stock of sceneries, electrical equipment, and set equipment) but would also "provide them with our staff, which is first-rate and well-trained and of which you will have complete satisfaction."[7]

Chavet said he offered to rent his studios to Continental to avoid their requisition. According to him, there was already a notice of requisition on the door. There was no doubt that Greven had considerable powers for achieving his aim. Chavet was worried for his company: "I saw my entire firm, which I had created, vanishing. All my equipment would have disappeared as happened for a time even under Continental. My scenery stock was reduced by 50 percent to the benefit of Billancourt, which was full owned by Continental."[8]

The Billancourt studios at that time were managed by Paris-Studio-Cinéma, a company run by Marc Lauer. A first tenancy agreement was signed between Continental and Lauer's firm on November 29, 1940, for the rental of the studios and all its equipment for the whole of 1941 at the rate of 1.1 million francs. In June 1941, Lauer was accused of being a Jew, and a new commissioner manager was appointed to run the company. Lauer, however, managed to procure documents proving he was Aryan and recovered his studios. In January 1942, he signed a new tenancy agreement for five years with Continental Films at the rate of 10 million francs per year that waived and temporarily transferred its rights to its Western Electric equipment.

This contract meant that studio staff had to work for the German company. It is also ironic that Continental Films would end up using American sound equipment for the duration of the war in Billancourt.[9] The American firm was perfectly aware that Continental was using its equipment, as it directed one of its employees, engineer Jean-Armand Anderlé, to go work for Continental.

Anderlé recalled that he "went to Continental, as the Western company administrator forced me to do so. I had a letter, as I refused to go to Continental without a letter certifying that I wasn't approaching Continental myself and that it was necessary for Western." His job at Continental was to "to keep watch over this equipment."[10]

Although he was already leading an empire, Greven did his best to stamp out competition. Pathé and Gaumont, the two historically great French film companies, were in a sorry state in 1940 following their respective bankruptcies in the mid-1930s, but Greven didn't want to give them any opportunity to recover. The Germans banned the distribution and exhibition of small-gauge formats such as Pathé-Rural (17.5 mm) and Pathé-Baby (9.5 mm), which provided an important source of income to Pathé, to the benefit of 16-mm and 8-mm formats. Greven welcomed this ban: "If the propaganda service banned this gauge that is only available in France, the [Organizing Committee of the Cinema Industry] as well as the French government ought to thank us for this measure, because France is now no longer an island but in sync with the rest of the world regarding small-gauge film."[11] Greven also wanted to take over theaters belonging to Gaumont as well as purchase shares made available through aryanization. The company did all it could to rein in this greedy competitor.[12]

As head of Continental, Greven had reasons to be jubilant. He saw himself as a sort of American-style movie mogul, and his ambition was reflected in the growth of the company's capital. By May 1941, the company's net worth had increased from the 1 million francs it had started with in October 1940 to 100 million and reached 200 million by January 1942. In keeping with this rise in its fortunes, the company moved its headquarters from the anonymous rue de La Baume to the prestigious 104 avenue des Champs-Élysées in April 1941.

From his office, Greven could watch the daily military parade of German soldiers on the most beautiful avenue in Paris. Henri Decoin remembered that "in 1941, several filmmakers met in Greven's office on the Champs-Élysées, including me. We chat about filmmaking. Then, suddenly, at noon, the German fanfare passes by the Champs-Élysées. Greven gets up, opens wide the window, and invites us to come on the balcony to admire [the parade]! I leave! The afternoon of the same day, Bauermeister sarcastically said to me, 'You don't like music, Mr. Decoin?' I reply, 'I like music, especially when it's played by French soldiers.'"[13]

CHAPTER 9

Leaving Continental

Among the first filmmakers hired by Continental, Decoin was not the only one who dreamed of leaving the company as soon as possible. Marcel Carné, Christian-Jaque, and Decoin each used different means to achieve their ends.

Marcel Carné had joined the company when it was first created. He suggested various possibilities for film subjects. "I proposed something about kids in Montmartre from a short story by Marcel Aymé. I offered them *Juliette ou La Clef des songes*: they told me it was communist. Then I proposed *École communale*. [Screenwriter Henri] Jeanson came. There was a fuss with Jeanson in which a director was mixed up. I cannot tell you the name—a person who apparently had given Greven Jeanson's article" (Jeanson had published an article in 1939 in which he praised Herschel Grynzspan for assassinating German embassy official Ernst vom Rathe).[1] In the end, he chose to direct the company's most ambitious film project: *Les Évadés de l'an 4000*, adapted from a novel by Jacques Spitz, a science fiction film with a plethora of film stars, including Danielle Darrieux, Arletty, Charles Vanel, Jean Marais, Pierre Renoir, and Pierre Larquey. He asked Jean Anouilh to write the dialogue. In June 1941, *Le Film* announced the future blockbuster in a double-page display, the text for which reflected the occupation period: "Our world has become so cold that men are living underground . . . the human race wants to survive. But where? On another planet. In a final effort, before disappearing, humankind sends one couple toward the stars and a new earth. A GIANT SCIENCE FICTION FILM. A superhuman work!"[2] The shooting was scheduled to start at the end of July 1941. Carné had already received the dialogue continuity script from Anouilh; he worked on the shooting script while art director André Andrejew took care of the model sets. Greven gave him an unlimited budget. A set with crossing streets was too big for the studio? No problem! They will rent the huge exhibition hall Grand Palais and build this set in the central nave. And yet, as the project got closer, Carné was assailed by doubts. "So, on the verge of directing a very big movie of unusual scope, I realized to my great alarm that I had only one desire: find a legally valid pretext to break off my contract."[3] He then devised a strategy for escape. He proposed that Jean Cocteau, whom he knew Greven didn't like, be hired to design the costumes. The next day, he used the excuse that the contract with Cocteau had not yet been signed to fly into a rage and leave Continental.

That was at least the version given by Carné in his memoirs written several decades after the events. In front of the purge committee in 1944, he didn't go into details as to how the project collapsed. However, he mentioned rows with Greven. "It was a constant battle. . . . I said, 'You are a pain in the neck with all your talk. I'm not working with you anymore.' I left slamming the door." We shouldn't forget that in 1940 Carné was at the height of his career, having directed a succession of masterpieces such as *Quai des brumes*, *Le Jour se lève*, and *Hôtel du Nord*. As Decoin pointed out, he remained outspoken with Greven; because he was conscious of the position he occupied within the French film industry, he had no intention of holding back. On the other hand, he clearly had not undertaken such a project while hoping it would collapse at the last minute. Rather, it seems he couldn't work with Greven, who interfered too much for his taste in his decisions. Carné was too fond of his independence.

In any case, his departure from Continental immediately created trouble for him. "They asked me for three hundred and fifty thousand francs in counterclaim damages. I asked for four hundred thousand francs. We settled out of court. It was all their fault. I had terminated the contract verbally by slamming doors. As for them, they sent me a letter breaking off the contract. Legally, they were in the wrong. That's what the lawyer told me."[4] Carné managed to escape at very little cost. But he had to take into account Greven's persistent grudge. He would try to thwart him. Greven went to see producer André Paulvé and told him, "If you make a film with Carné, this film will never be released."[5] In spite of these threats, Paulvé went on to produce two of Carné's greatest films, *Les Visiteurs du soir* (1942) and *Les Enfants du paradis* (1945).

Christian-Jaque was remarkably skillful in the way he managed to get away from Continental. He waited for the right moment to implement the special clauses he had demanded as part of his contract. After shooting *L'Assassinat du Père Noël* from February until April 1941, he temporarily left the company to make *Premier Bal* (1941) for producer André Paulvé. In October 1941, he was back at the Billancourt studios to start on his biopic about composer Hector

Berlioz titled *La Symphonie fantastique* (1942). He had an option in his contract whereby Continental could hire him to direct "two more films . . . in France," after he had completed *La Symphonie fantastique*. This option was "valid until the tenth day of the shooting" of *La Symphonie fantastique*.[6]

He started shooting his second feature and discreetly prepared his departure from the company. He later described how company executives came to exercise the option on the thirteenth day of shooting (he misremembered the details and recalled the option as being valid until the twelfth day rather than the tenth day):

> I said, "No, it's too late. The twelfth day ends at midnight. It's now nine o'clock in the morning, it's over." . . . Bauermeister came to see me saying, "You're sending me to Russia!" I replied, "I absolutely don't give a damn. You signed a contract; you required that we followed that contract. There is absolutely no reason why you should not follow it as well. The twelfth day is over; the date has passed." . . . Needless to say, weeks of shooting that followed were dreadful, humiliations of all kind. I held out, though, and one day I told Greven, "After all, you're only a tourist here . . ." He couldn't stand it. He told me I was like a Jew, and so on. I replied, "I never lost any money with Jews. With pure Aryans I did." The tension was constant, and then it was over.[7]

Christian-Jaque left the company for good in December 1941. In retaliation, Greven thwarted him for several months in his attempts to obtain authorization to go to Italy to shoot *Carmen*.

As for Decoin, he was chomping at the bit as he enviously observed how his colleague had managed to escape Continental: "Christian-Jaque, who is finishing *La Symphonie fantastique*, calls me on the phone and happily announces to me that Greven has missed the expiration date to exercise the option for three more films and so he is free! He is jubilant on the phone!" He was thinking of doing the same, but it was too late. "As the date to exercise my option is coming in a few days, I hope . . . But Greven, furious about what was happening with Christian-Jaque, called me in his office and shouted at me, 'Mr. Decoin, I warn you, I am exercising your option! Tomorrow, you'll receive a registered letter! You owe me another three films!'"[8] Decoin showed his contract to his lawyer, Mr. Starck. To no avail; his lawyer explained he would have to make the films.

He would therefore have to use another method:

Pressbook cover for *La Symphonie fantastique* (1942) (Fondation Jérôme Seydoux-Pathé)

I open hostilities. I begin by suing Continental, which didn't include my name
on the publicity billboard of the Normandie theater where *Les Inconnus dans la
maison* was being screened. Bailiff's report and summons to Continental and
Tobis to rectify within twenty-four hours or the contract is automatically invali-
dated. I hope, because I am pretty sure that Greven will refuse to bend and
therefore our agreement will be void. Vain hope! The next day, a painter perched
on a scaffolding writes my name on the Normandie billboard.[9]

On April 27, 1942, Decoin with a heavy heart, began work on his third film,
a comedy titled *Mariage d'amour* at the Neuilly studios, starring François
Périer, Juliette Faber, and Paul Meurisse. The screenplay had again been written secretly by Max Colpet and sold at Continental under the pretense that it
was by Decoin and Jean Lec.

Decoin then made a decision with far-reaching consequences: "I decide,
during the shooting of *Mariage d'amour*, to put an end to my association with
Continental. I'm looking for a pretext. It crops up. The day before we start
shooting and during the shooting, Greven decides to change the dialogue, to
modify scenes, and to add extra ones. I am up in arms over this, which violates
the terms of my contract. I refuse cuts and additions, and in agreement with
my lawyer, I inform Greven by registered letter that I won't put my name to
the film."[10]

Greven indeed had made drastic cuts in the script. The film was supposed
to be 2,500 meters long (ninety-one minutes) but it ended up being reduced
to 1,800 meters (seventy-five minutes). On June 2, 1942, Decoin wrote Greven,
"The cuts you made in my script and my dialogue are incompatible with the
style of the film. I went out of my way to remedy those cuts that made in
contravention of the most elementary technique, but I don't think I managed.
We'll judge, you and I, when the film is definitively edited."[11]

Following Decoin's decision to challenge Continental in modifying his picture, Greven refused him access to the studio while the film was still being
edited. Decoin's editor, Charlotte Guilbert, was fired after editing the first two
reels of the film and replaced by the formidable Marguerite Beaugé, who
didn't know the film at all. Decoin disowned everything done by Beaugé. In
an attempt to salvage the film, the company asked Richard Pottier to shoot a
few extra scenes. But the effort was wasted. The film would not be released
until December 1942 and without any director being credited.

Continental considered Decoin responsible for the failure of the film and
sued him for 400,000 francs in damages. After twenty months of litigation,

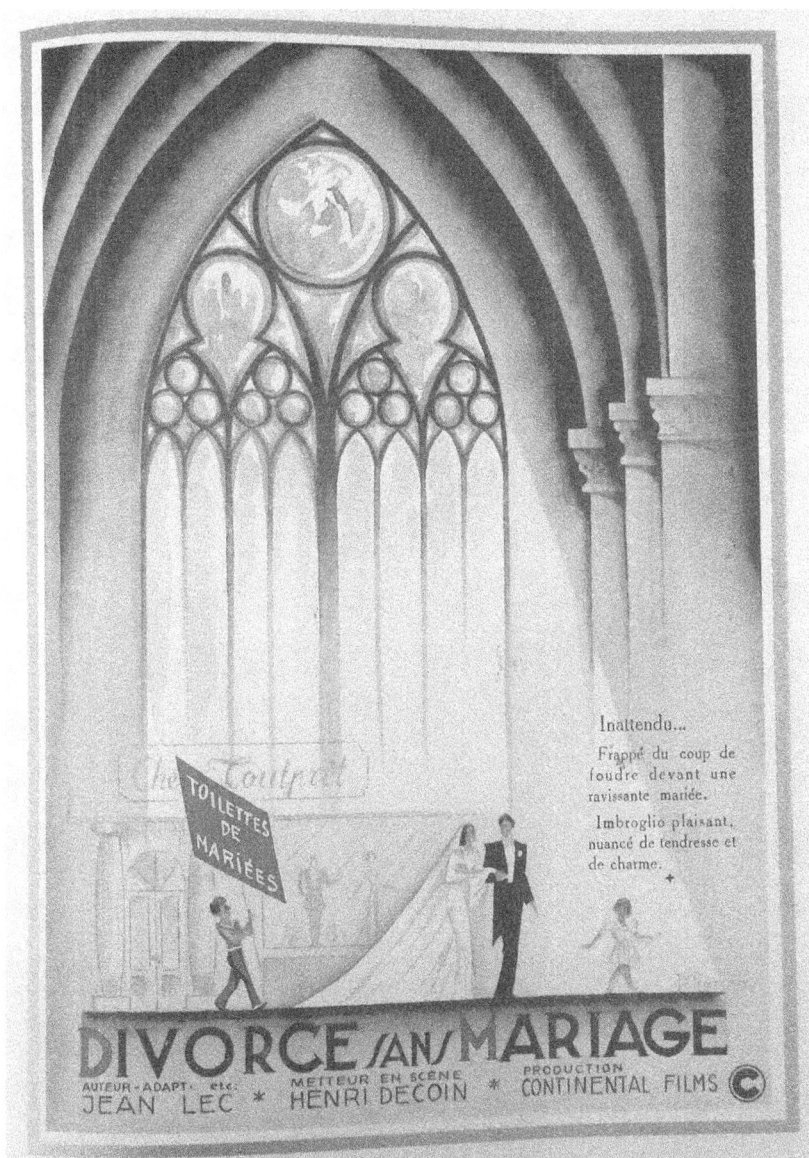

Ad for *Mariage d'amour* (1942) under the working title *Divorce sans mariage* (Fondation Jérôme Seydoux-Pathé)

the commercial court sentenced Continental to pay the 60,000 francs owed to Decoin for his last film. Greven swore he would get his revenge. According to a clause in his contract, he was able to force Decoin to work for the firm Société de production et de doublage de films under Continental license. He subsequently shot *L'Homme de Londres* (1942), yet another Simenon novel adaptation, for that company.

These three directors managed to break free from Greven's clutches mainly because they had no weak spot. The Continental big boss couldn't put pressure on them by threatening their family, for example. Carné was a bachelor. Decoin had recently divorced from Darrieux, and Christian-Jaque was married to Simone Renant, who worked only briefly at Continental. Many other workers in the German company were not so fortunate owing to their personal situation. However, we mustn't underestimate the courage it took Carné, Decoin, and Christian-Jaque to confront their German boss during the occupation. It took considerable sang froid to do what they did.

CHAPTER 10

The Russians at Billancourt

We might think that the Continental staff that worked under the German managers was completely French. In fact, there were employees of several different nationalities within the firm. If during the prewar period, there was a marked xenophobia among film critics and some filmmakers, we shouldn't forget that the French film industry had been shaped since the 1920s by foreigners. Some of those technicians were nobodies whose names often did not even appear in the credits. This chapter is a tribute to these men who brought their many talents to French film.

The Russian Revolution in 1917 had led to an influx of remarkable artists into France. Their figurehead was the brilliant actor Ivan Mosjoukine. He was surrounded by a group of actors, operators, and filmmakers who gave new life to French cinema during the last decade of silent film. At first established in Montreuil-sous-Bois (east of Paris) with the Albatros company, they later migrated to the Boulogne-Billancourt studios situated at 49 quai du Point-du-jour, where they filmed two blockbusters starring Ivan Mosjoukine—*Michel Strogoff* (1926), directed by Viatcheslav Tourjansky, and *Casanova* (1927), directed by Alexandre Volkoff—as well as for the internationally renowned masterpiece *Napoléon* (1927), directed by Abel Gance.

In 1940, a number of them were still working at Billancourt, and Continental was set on taking advantage of their skills. The feelings of these men, who were mainly white Russian émigrés—that is, opponents of the Soviet regime—toward the Nazi occupiers were more complex than it seemed.

Among the first staff members hired in December 1940, there was general stage manager Grégoire Metchikian, who would become one of the pillars of the firm. In fact, he was not Russian by birth, as he was born in Adrianople (now Edirne) in western Turkey, on June 13, 1885, of an Armenian family. During World War I, he refused to wear a Turkish uniform and fled to Russia. It was during that period that he joined the film industry in Moscow, where he began calling himself Metchikoff to give his surname a Russian ring. In 1918, he married a Russian woman also of Armenian origin. In May 1920, they both arrived in France with the group of Russian filmmakers and actors of the Ermolieff company, which became Albatros in 1922. In December 1920, in Vincennes, his wife gave birth to a son named Georges, who having been born in France was thereby a French citizen. He worked as general stage manager for the Ermolieff-Albatros company from 1920 until 1924 at the Montreuil studios. Then, in 1925, he went to work for Ciné-Alliance, Films de France, and Société Générale de Films, all of which used the Billancourt studios. During the shooting of Abel Gance's *Napoléon* from 1925 to 1927, he was not only one of the main stage managers but also an actor. He appears in the final scenes of the film playing General Augereau. Small, stocky, and bald, he protests the idea of the "small general" leading the army into Italy. His acting creates the impression of person who had quite a temper in real life, and indeed, testimonies confirm this stage manager could be difficult.

In 1927, after several attempts, both he and his wife obtained French nationality. At the end of the 1920s, French film production was going through a bad patch; many Russian artists went to work in Germany, while others tried their luck in America. He appears to have worked for a time in Germany for Russian producer Noë Bloch (he was perfectly fluent in German). With the arrival of talkies, he resumed work back in France. He also reassumed his surname Metchikian and was stage manager for prestigious productions such as Anatole Litvak's *Mayerling* (1936) and Jean Renoir's *La Bête humaine* (1938). He therefore already had quite a magnificent curriculum vitae by the time the Germans arrived in Paris in June 1940.

In September 1940, Metchikian heard about the creation of Continental Films and wrote a letter in German to one of his contacts in Berlin to obtain a letter of recommendation: "As for me, health and morale are good. But unfortunately, there isn't any work because nothing has been shot for months. And now, everything is at a standstill. I learned that UFA and Tobis (Greven production) want to make movies here, and I would be extremely grateful if you could recommend me for these productions, as I am really suffering from the current unemployment situation, and I need to work."[1] The recommendation seemed to have worked out well, as in December 1940, Metchikian confirmed to Greven he would accept a one-year contract paying 6,670 francs per month as general stage manager for Continental Films.[2]

As general stage manager, Metchikian had to refer regularly to his immediate superior, who happened to be Bauermeister, the production manager. He was put in charge of the company's first production, *L'Assassinat du Père Noël*, and left for Chamonix (in the French Alps) with the film crew and cast of actors. He had to make sure that everything went smoothly on location and that they did not go overbudget. There was a certain suspicion toward him, as he himself acknowledged: "I kept my usual curt manners and toughness at work. As I was working for a German company, my system always seemed excessive for some people," to the point that they began spreading "misleading rumors of antisocial behavior."[3] The simple fact of wanting to be stage manager who strived for perfection and was budget conscious was obviously perceived as the attitude of an enthusiastic collaborator with the German managers. Metchikian may not have paid attention to these rumors; indeed, he may have showed even more eagerness to please Bauermeister, as Bauermeister had hired his son, Georges, as an intern at Continental.

During the shooting of *L'Assassinat du Père Noël* in Chamonix, he sent regular letters in German to Bauermeister to keep him up to date regarding the shooting and the weather hazards.

> Today, it's the ninth day of shooting. Because of the bad weather, we shot only forty scenes so far, but, fortunately, all the scenes are excellent. The communication between Chamonix-Argentières, etc, was very difficult until yesterday. Cars couldn't get through until the day before yesterday because of the two meters of snow, and commuting by train has been interrupted for four days because of avalanches. So, we have had to go eight kilometers on foot every day with two cameras (a good sport). We have had a bus since the day before yesterday, and it's going better. Apart from these difficulties, everything is going well. People are working well, and everybody is happy. Mr. Christian-Jaque is always in a good mood and very happy with what we have shot so far. . . . I hope we can lower our quote.[4]

Always concerned about the budget, Metchikian suggested cutting the fees for film extras: "If you are offering employment contracts, it is extremely important to reduce the fees. For example, secure the priest for three days instead of four and pay less to all the others."[5] He added a friendly postscript: "The smoked ham is waiting for you."[6]

There was no doubt that Metchikian thought he was doing his job conscientiously, just as he had done before the war. But he forgot that he thereby became the loyal servant of a German-owned company, although we should remember that Metchikian was in a difficult position as general stage manager. He also too easily forgot that many technicians and extras also needed to earn a living. And he knew as well that if they remained within the budget or if the costs ended up being lower than in the estimate, he might receive a bonus. For example, he was promised a bonus of 10,000 francs for *Caprices* (1942) "in the event that the estimate and deadline set for the production of the film have not been exceeded."[7] Metchikian was delighted: "Your letter of July 25 touched me deeply. Rest assured that even without your generous offer, I would have continued to do my best to scrupulously safeguard the interests of your company."[8]

If Metchikian seemed to appreciate his bosses more than he should have, he did have an Achilles heel, his son, Georges. In February 1941, he had been hired as trainee by Continental Films, thanks to his father. He worked on *Le Dernier des six* (1941) and *Péchés de jeunesse* (1941) even though he didn't yet have the Organizing Committee of the Cinema Industry trade card. After working on four films, he became first assistant under the pseudonym Georges Demet. However, at 1,000 francs per week, his salary was pitiful. In spite of his protests, he didn't get a raise. During the shooting of *Vingt-cinq ans de bonheur* (1943), directed by René Jayet and, according to him, apparently supervised by Richard Pottier, Georges Metchikian made a mistake that had serious consequences. His father remembered that "he was asked, 'What do you think of the script of *Vingt-cinq ans de bonheur*?' He replied it was crap in front of everybody. . . . Then they came to me and said, 'What? Your son allows himself to talk like that! He is still young, just twenty-two. He takes the liberty of criticizing a script purchased by Continental, which paid for it! He didn't pay it with his own money, we did!' . . . As soon as the film was finished, they sacked him."[9]

A week later, Georges received a summons from the compulsory work service. His father tried everything possible to prevent his being sent to Germany, but Continental remained inflexible and even refused to provide him with a certificate that would have allowed him to go on working in filmmaking. In March 1943, Georges left for Germany to work in a tank factory. Because he spoke a little German, after six months, he managed to get transferred to the Tobis company.[10] In October 1943, during a short leave in France, he went underground to avoid having to go back to Germany.

Following this incident, his father lost favor with his bosses. As he said in his colorful French, "And after that, they didn't give me a raise or any films. I became the tenth wheel of the coach."[11] However, Metchikian remained stage manager until Continental ceased operations in summer 1944, even if Greven and Bauermeister were not speaking to him anymore.

Metchikian's case was emblematic of the difficulties of being stage manager, that is, the pivotal staff member between the French employees and the German leaders of the company. On the other hand, directors appreciated his work, and Henri Decoin, for one, wrote him a letter of support: "I confirm that during my time at Continental from 1941 until 1942, I was able to observe that your behavior as general stage manager was always impeccable."[12]

Another Armenian of Russian nationality was also hired by Continental when the company was created. Born in Erevan (which was then part of the Russian Caucasus) on February 18, 1885, Archavir (known as Archan) Chakhatouny had served in the Russian army during World War I, achieving the rank of major, and had distinguished himself brilliantly by saving his native city. He arrived in France around 1920, following the Russian Revolution. Like Metchikian, he participated in the shooting of several great films at the Billancourt studios in the late 1920s as actor, credited as Acho Chakatouny. In *Michel Strogoff* (1926), he played the part of the dyed-in-the-wool villain Ivan Ogareff with great panache, and in *Napoléon* (1927), he was Pozzo di Borgo, Bonaparte's archenemy. In 1929, he directed a film shot in Bulgaria about the Armenian genocide titled *Andranik*. The advent of talkies was a catastrophe for him as well as for the great Russian actor Ivan Mosjoukine. His strong Russian accent made him undesirable on the screen. But he managed to quickly find a new occupation, that of makeup man. Like many Russian actors, he was thoroughly familiar with all makeup techniques. He worked on prestigious productions such as Jean Vigo's *L'Atalante* (1934) and Jean Grémillon's *Remorques* (1941). He also worked in Austria and Italy. He was lucky enough to go to Hollywood with a French crew; there he improved his technique with Elizabeth Arden, learning the makeup technique for quickly aging a face. He was even offered a job there. But he refused it because he wanted to go back to France.

In February 1941, Continental contacted Chakhatouny. Both Bauermeister and Greven were aware of his skills and were eager to use a talent like his. But unlike Metchikian, Chakhatouny was uncomfortable with the idea of working for a German company. He had not forgotten that the Germans were the allies of the Turks during World War I: "I hate the Germans because they are the enemies of my country. I am Armenian, and my country suffered a thousand times more than others because of the Germans. One million Armenians were slaughtered. In 1918, everything that happened was done following German orders."[13] Then he decided to seek advice from the Organizing Committee of the Cinema Industry, the only French film authority present in Paris. "I went to the third floor of this house. I saw Mr. Bachelet and Mr. Baldet, you can ask them. I told them, 'I am a foreigner. I've been living in Paris for twenty years, and I would like to avoid getting mixed up in any political affair. I am summoned by Continental. Here is a firm I don't know (It said "French public company," but I knew it was not true, that it was German). Before going to present myself, I am coming to ask you if I have the right to do so?'"[14] Of course, the Organizing Committee of the Cinema Industry representatives told him he could go without any problem. Chakhatouny signed his contract, as he was without a red cent, having been out of work for eighteen months.

Chakhatouny ended up meeting Bauermeister to talk about his salary. The discussion was fierce: "For my last picture, I earned three thousand francs per week. He told me, 'No! No! No! You are working for us; we'll pay you five thousand francs per month.'"[15] The firm thus managed to hire a highly skilled makeup man for a salary well below what he was entitled to. This approach was typical of the company. It was aware of people's weak points and used them to obtain their services at the lowest rate possible. Chakhatouny was a Russian refugee who certainly would have had difficulties finding a job in a French production company.

The makeup man proved to be indispensable to one of the main Continental productions, *La Symphonie fantastique* (1942). This fictionalized account of the life of composer Hector Berlioz required actor Jean-Louis Barrault to age from twenty to sixty-five in the course of the film. Chakhatouny's results were magnificent, and his bosses realized that this makeup man had nimble fingers whose secrets they must know. "They told me, 'We need that makeup to be sent to Germany.' I said, 'Listen, this is my professional secret. Why should I give it to somebody?'"[16] Nevertheless, He had no choice but to comply, and so he left for Berlin to work at the Scala theater. However, over there, makeup men did not manage to reproduce his work.

Following that trip to Berlin, his relationship with Greven rapidly deteriorated. He "treated [him] like a dog" and did not hesitate to threaten him directly when he sought to hand in his resignation. "Chakhatouny, if you do not stay here, I'll send you to a concentration camp. Understood?"[17] He also accused him of sabotage. Terrified, Chakhatouny fainted, fell, and developed tremors in one arm.

His skillfulness in aging a face with blush, eyeshadow, and foundation of various colors was also indispensable to actress Renée Saint-Cyr, who had to age twenty years in the superb *Pierre et Jean* (1943), directed by André Cayatte.

Chakhatouny used mauve and brown shades that removed the bloom from her face in black and white.

Continental asked him to set up a makeup school inside the company. Chakhatouny complied. He warned his young students, "My children, you are French. I am not French, but I have lived here for twenty-one years. I eat French bread and I need to remain faithful to France."[18] After the liberation of Paris, he learned his words had had more impact than he thought, when he met a former pupil who had returned to Paris after being wounded: "He came to see me, kissed me, and told me, 'After your words, Mr. Chakhatouny, I understood one must serve France.'"[19]

While he was not a communist, Chakhatouny knew Missak Manouchian and other members of Resistance movements like the Armenian National Front.[20] His feelings of gratitude for what France had done for him were genuine. Inside Continental, he was appreciated by his colleagues, unlike Metchikian. Assistant director Jean Devaivre describes how "at the Billancourt studios, I also become acquainted with an extraordinary character, Chakatouny, the head makeup man. A crowd of young trainees buzzes around him who follow his teachings. This is the 'Chakatouny school.' Many excellent makeup girls will come out of this school after the war. He is a colorful giant, loudmouthed, who can't stop praising his native country, Caucasus, and its famous Lake Sevan."[21] He stayed with Continental until 1944.

One of the most important figures at Continental was an extraordinary art director named André Andrejew. Born in Russia in 1887, Andrejew trained to be an architect before joining the Moscow Art Theater founded by Constantin Stanislavski. In 1921, he was called to Germany to create a Russian theater there. In Berlin, he came into contact with the world of cinema and launched his brilliant career with Robert Wiene's *Raskolnikow* (1923), one of the most shining examples of German expressionism. In 1925, his reputation was so well established that he was offered a job in America. Unfortunately, the laws on immigration prevented this Russian refugee from going there. He stayed in Europe, where he worked with great filmmakers. Among the masterpieces he worked on during the silent era are Jacques Feyder's *Thérèse Raquin* (1928)— a lost film—and Georg Wilhelm Pabst's *Die Büchse der Pandora* (*Pandora's Box*, 1929). The advent of talkies did not impede his career in the least. In 1933, he left Nazi Germany to work principally in France but also in England, Hungary, Denmark, and Czechoslovakia. In Paris, he collaborated with many filmmakers who were refugees from Central Europe like Anatole Litvak in *Mayerling* (1936).

In 1940, he was in France, working for the Regina-Films company on *Paris-New York* (1940) and *Les Musiciens du ciel* (1940). His wife being ill, he stayed in Paris. He was himself in bad health and had to undergo an operation in September 1940. While he was still in the hospital, he got a letter and a phone call from the German Propaganda Office summoning him to its offices at 52 avenue des Champs-Élysées. Once he was out of the hospital, he went there and met Alfred Greven for the first time, who told him abruptly he had to go to Berlin the following Monday for a picture. "Naturally, I mentioned my illness, saying I couldn't leave Paris. After discussion, he told me I would stay in Paris working for Continental, where I would be paid four thousand francs per week instead of the seven to nine thousand francs I received at the time."[22] He was given a yearly contract, with the company retaining the right to hire him out to other companies and the right to terminate him after six months. We should add that Andrejew, as a Russian refugee, held a Nansen passport—a document allowing stateless people to travel between 1922 and 1945—making his situation awkward in relation to the French authorities.

For Greven, Andrejew was a fine catch. He had just hired a world-renowned art director for a pittance, and in addition, the man spoke German fluently. As a result, Andrejew was put in an awkward position with the French studio grips and technicians. He was regarded as an informer working for the German boss, even if reality was completely different. In addition, he had become acquainted with Bauermeister in Berlin when Bauermeister was just a modest studio employee. As a result, Bauermeister showed a certain deference to Andrejew; he knew his reputation, and he appreciated his observations.

The Continental managers always went first to Andrejew, one of the only German speakers in the studio, to get technical information in their own language. On top of that, the new studio manager appointed by the Germans, Mr. Heyraud, was a beginner without any experience. Each time there was a technical glitch, the German managers called for Andrejew, which made Heyraud furious. However, a good number of the studio workers trusted him. They usually gathered in his office to discuss professional or anti-German matters. Andrejew considered Greven "a madman and a lunatic."[23] Fortunately, he hardly ever came more than once a week; Bauermeister was the one in charge of the daily production problems.

One day, Andrejew called the chief grips in his office and warned them "to be careful and to avoid speaking about politics, as there are rumors a traitor is spying on them."[24] Indeed, a list had been sent to the management accusing some employees of being communist. Andrejew was among the names mentioned. At the Billancourt studios, a staff shop chief named André Kuczura, a supporter of the French Popular Party led by Jacques Doriot, sometimes distributed pamphlets at the studio.[25] This white Russian émigré, born in Polish Russia in 1884 and a naturalized French citizen, was violently antisemitic and anticommunist. One of the grips remembered that "we learned he had established a list of forty names of workers and employees. In this list, there was art director Andrejew, whom he accused of being an agent of GPU, the state police of the USSR, and of belonging to the intelligence services. And I must tell you that if this list didn't elicit any reaction from the German managers, it's because a large part of the staff was on it. Bauermeister wanted to keep his job at Continental, but if they had arrested forty workmen and employees, the studio would have been empty."[26] In the end, Bauermeister summoned Kuczura and, as disciplinary action, he was moved to the Neuilly studios. This story, which could have had a tragic end, shows the heavy atmosphere in which the studio workers labored. No one could trust anyone else. Everybody had to be careful when speaking out or risk being denounced as Gaullist, communist, or anti-German.

Andrejew continued to work with a number of his prewar collaborators. One of the most important was Wladimir Meingard, who had been his assistant for many years. Meingard was born in St. Petersburg in 1884 and arrived in France around 1922. He worked mainly with other Russian art directors, including Pierre Schildknecht (known as Schild) on Abel Gance's *Napoléon* (1927); Alexandre Lochakoff, one of the pillars of the Albatros company; and André Andrejew.

A brief article in the newspaper *Le Petit Parisien* revealed the extent of Wladimir Meingard's despair in January 1941:

> While on duty near quai de la Mégisserie, some policemen heard, yesterday evening at around 11.50 p.m., some calls for help coming from the Seine. The police officers Louis Lecomte and Marc Charpentier, of the first arrondissement, ran and saw, clinging to a block of ice, a man drifting away. Without hesitation, the policemen dived into the river, and a passerby followed suit. . . . The three courageous rescuers managed to bring the unfortunate man back to the bank, who was immediately transported to the Hôtel-Dieu hospital. We learned soon that it was an out-of-work engineer . . . who, reduced to poverty, had decided to take his own life.[27]

Andrejew tried to get Continental to hire him as his assistant. But Greven refused to do so because he was a foreigner. In the end, Andrejew decided to give him work by paying for him out of his own pocket. This is how he came to the studio to help him during the preparation of *Le Dernier des six*. Realizing that Meingard was talented, Continental finally hired him officially on June 2, 1941, offering, as usual, a lower salary than what the company gave to a French assistant. Meingard was the art director only on *Annette et la dame blonde* (1942). He remained at Continental until 1944. There was a good reason for that: "One of the main motives forcing me to stay on at the company was the hope of protecting my wife, in case of persecution of Soviet citizens, because my wife had a Soviet passport. And she had to go to register at the police station every week."[28]

Andrejew's team was completed with designer-model maker Nicolas Wilcké. Born in Moscow on December 23, 1897, he also immigrated to France in 1921 and participated in the shooting of Abel Gance's *Napoléon*, for which he was in charge not only of the building of model sets but also of the special effects. During the 1930s, he worked with all the great French filmmakers: Julien Duvivier, Jean Renoir, Marcel L'Herbier, and Henri Decoin. In September 1939, he tried to join the army, in spite of his age, to serve France. But he received his posting only on June 12, 1940, when Paris was on the verge of being occupied.

Wilcké remembered the circumstances under which he was contacted by Continental: "In April 1941, I was out of work, and French cinema was completely paralyzed. I received a phone call from Continental Films asking me to work for the film being directed by Mr. Christian-Jaque, *L'Assassinat du Père Noël*, and for Mr. Carné's *Les Évadés de l'an 4000*. Considering French personalities, whom I knew well had been hired by Continental Films and having been assured that no German propaganda film would be made, I accepted the proposal and signed the contract."[29]

In 1942, being paid a much lower salary than what he deserved, Wilcké tried to leave the company to join a French company. He was immediately threatened with being sent to Germany to work there. He decided to stay at Continental, where they were at least not producing propaganda films.

Interestingly, both Meingard and Wilcké were denounced by Kuczura at the same time as Andrejew. Most of the white Russian émigrés at Continental were faithful to France and had little affinity for Germany. As Wilcké said, "I considered France to be my second country. . . . During this period, I was always opposed to the Germans, and I expressed rather freely my opinions in front of the studio workers."[30]

There were other Russian makeup men present in Paris during the occupation. One of them, Boris de Fast, tried to get hired by Continental without success. Like Chakhatouny, he had been first an actor. Born Boris Fastovitch on June 6, 1890, in Feodosia, in Crimea, he arrived in France in 1922. With his long, emaciated face, he played traitors or spies during the 1920s in France, Germany, and even Hollywood. With the advent of talkies, he became a makeup man. During the 1930s, he was Danielle Darrieux's official makeup man for *Katia* (1938), *Retour à l'aube* (1938) and *Battement de cœur* (1940). Henri Decoin tried to get him hired for *Premier Rendez-vous* without success. De Fast remembered that "when I was called by Mr. Decoin, he told me, 'Bauermeister is against you.' I tried to see him. He said no. Afterward, Mr. Metchikian and Mr. Chakhatouny told me, 'Try to find out why they are not hiring you for this project.' I got no results."[31] Boris's brother, Victor de Fast, who worked as editor for Tobis, wrote Bauermeister a letter to ask for an explanation. Bauermeister's reply was evasive: "I received well your April 9 letter, and I must unfortunately tell you that the hiring of your brother does not depend on me. I would like, however, to mention that I didn't say it would be impossible to employ your brother. I regret not being able to give you any other information."[32] Boris de Fast spent the whole of the occupation period unable to practice his trade as makeup man. Instead, he became a porter in a hotel that had been requisitioned by the Germans.

Russian makeup artist Boris Wichnevetzky (known as Wichné) was luckier than de Fast. Although he likewise didn't manage to secure a contract with Continental, he nevertheless did a few extra jobs there. Called by chief makeup artist Marcel Rey, he was paid 182 times for his work over a period of three years. He was also offered the opportunity to work on Vichy propaganda films. He categorically refused: "In spite of my misery, I won't have anything do with it."[33]

CHAPTER 11

A Trip to Berlin

Paris, March 18, 1942. Four actresses in mink coats and one actor posed for newsreel photographers as they prepared to board the train to Berlin. They smiled happily for the cameras and waved goodbye from the carriage windows as the train pulled away. The photographs of this departure for Germany, a trip that would become a notorious symbol of artistic collaboration during the German occupation, immortalized Danielle Darrieux, Suzy Delair, Junie Astor, Viviane Romance, and Albert Préjean. The newsreel narrator announced that the French artists had been invited to visit Berlin, Vienna, and Munich by Dr. Carl Froelich, the head of the Reich Film Office, part of Germany's Ministry of Public Enlightenment and Propaganda.

Those images are now famous thanks to Marcel Ophüls, who used them in his 1969 groundbreaking historical documentary *Le Chagrin et la pitié* (*The Sorrow and the Pity*). Since then, this footage has been used countless times in documentaries about the German occupation of France during World War II. No one has truly investigated this trip, however, in an effort to understand why those artists agreed to go to Germany or under what circumstances. Too often, this event has merely been considered a symbol of active collaboration, in line with the commentaries published by the collaborationist press. These men and women, however, were not necessarily traitors to their country but were more likely mere playthings in the hands of the occupiers.

First of all, the newsreel featured only five figures in the French delegation. In reality, there were eight people. In addition to the aforementioned actors, the group included actor René Dary; Pierre Heuzé, editor in chief of the collaborationist film fan magazine *Ciné-Mondial*; and screenwriter André Legrand. The head of the film section at the German Propaganda Office, the fearsome Dr. Paulheinz Diedrich, also accompanied the group.

Four of the travelers worked for Continental Films: Albert Préjean, Suzy Delair, Danielle Darrieux, and André Legrand. They had been asked to attend the German premiere of *Premier Rendez-vous* (1941) at the Marmorhaus Theater in Berlin on March 20, 1942. The German Propaganda Office's main objective was to show the general public in France that the nation's artists, along with their German colleagues, belonged to the association of "continental artists" that stood in opposition to the film industries in Great Britain and the United States. The advertising published by Tobis, the German distribution company, mixed French and German actors together as if they belonged to the same family or the same company.

French writers, painters, and sculptors had already been corralled into going on previous propaganda trips to Germany. André Derain, Maurice de Vlaminck, Kees van Dongen, and Paul Belmondo (father of Jean-Paul Belmondo) had gone to Berlin in October 1941 and visited Arno Breker, Hitler's favorite sculptor. Writers such as Robert Brasillach, Pierre Drieu La Rochelle, and Jacques Chardonne attended a congress of European writers in Weimar at the same time. Most of them were staunch collaborators and were thus delighted to participate in such ventures.

In contrast, French film people were not particularly keen to travel to Berlin. Dr. Diedrich was responsible for extending the "invitations." Producer Raoul Ploquin described Diedrich as "a frightening Nazi of whom I have the worst memory."[1] Each of those on the trip had earlier been called to the German Propaganda Office at 52 avenue des Champs-Élysées and told they must go on the trip.

Screenwriter André Legrand was summoned in February and met a stout German officer (probably Lieutenant Hirsch, one of Dr. Diedrich's henchmen) who told him, "We have decided to organize monthly trips to Germany for authors, screenwriters, directors, and French artists. All well-known authors, directors, and actors will participate in turn." When Legrand asked about the reason for such trips, Hirsch replied, "They are not political or propaganda trips. They are study trips during which you'll visit our studios. You'll see German films not released in France and witness extensive experiments in television. . . . These trips are useful for your country." Legrand asked how, and Hirsch replied:

> They are intended to promote the export of French films in Germany and German-occupied countries. Until now, so far nothing has been exported. The

first trip coincides with the first French film to be released in Germany since 1939. Therefore, we have insisted that Miss Darrieux be present, as it's her film we are presenting. On the other hand, we asked Christian-Jaque to come for *La Symphonie fantastique* (1942), which will be the second film released. Christian-Jaque agreed to come but won't go until the second or third trip. As a consequence, we have selected you as the representative of this film, for which we want you to come.[2]

Legrand was indeed the screenwriter of Christian-Jaque's biopic of French composer Hector Berlioz. But his interlocutor was lying about the film's director agreeing to go to Germany. Christian-Jaque had already left Continental Films, thanks to the loophole in his contract, and he had flatly refused to go to Germany. "I told them I had never been to Berlin and that I couldn't go, etc. . . . If I had ever wanted to go to Berlin, I would have gone before the war."[3]

In spite of Hirsch's reassuring tone, Legrand was perfectly aware that the trip was a propaganda exercise. He therefore tried to dodge the unwanted invitation by saying he was currently working on a script for Gaumont. He was immediately told that the company would be called to request the necessary time off for the trip. He then mentioned his bad health. At that point, the tone became more menacing. "I was gently reminded that I was the author of an extremely unfortunate book and that they were very anxious that I could see with my own eyes and on the spot that I had perhaps made a mistake."[4]

Legrand had indeed published a book titled *Prisons nazies* in the spring of 1940 in which he described the horrors the Nazi regime was inflicting on the Jews and occupied countries such as Austria and Czechoslovakia. Legrand had an interesting personal history. Henri André Steigelmann—his real name—was born in Paris in 1896 to Alsatian parents who had fled the province in 1871 following its annexation by Germany. He had therefore been raised to hate Germany.

When France was invaded in June 1940, Legrand was in Bordeaux, where his latest book was being serialized in a local newspaper. He was told he was in danger of being shot by the invaders. Luckily, he met actor and future Resistance fighter Pierre Blanchar, who took him to safety in Royan. In the end, Legrand escaped the firing squad; his book was banned and added to the infamous Otto List (named after Otto Abetz, the German ambassador to France), an inventory of all books banned in France.

As a banned author, he knew finding work with producers would be almost impossible. At the end of 1940, he was back in Paris in a state of utter destitution. It was at that time that director Christian-Jaque presented the script of *La Symphonie fantastique* to Continental Films. Greven was immediately interested and asked Legrand to come see him. Legrand recalled their first meeting: "With his dangerous joviality, he immediately mentioned my book and the fact that I was on the Otto List. He told me, 'We like your script; we are ready to work with you. If you work for Continental, you'll get your work permit from the German authorities. But, otherwise, you won't get it as you can be considered an enemy.'"[5] Greven then offered to buy his script, continuity, and dialogue for 60,000 francs instead of the 150,000 he had earned for his scripts before the war, knowing that Legrand couldn't refuse the offer.

In February 1942, when Legrand was again threatened regarding his book, he realized the risk. "I understood that, as far as I was concerned, it was an 'invitation' between two sentries. I realized I couldn't avoid the situation or, if I did, they might revoke my work permit. They might do even more."[6] He resigned himself to going on the trip. But he decided he would not make a speech, exaggerating the extent of his tracheitis as an excuse.

Thanks to Legrand's account in front of the purge committee, we have an inside account of how this trip took place. Journalist Pierre Heuzé supplied the story destined for collaborationist magazines in which he cites pro-German statements from everyone, which he most certainly made up himself. Dr. Diedrich also asked Legrand to write articles, but he categorically refused.

Danielle Darrieux was undoubtedly the biggest star of the delegation. She had been hired in late 1940, at the same time as her then-husband, director Henri Decoin, to make a comedy. After her amicable divorce in October 1941 from Decoin, she was forced to sign a new contract with Continental. Greven openly threatened her, pointing out that she had a mother and brother and that she would not want to see any harm come to them.[7] Without Decoin's protection, she had no choice but to sign. In February 1942, when she was asked to go on the Berlin trip, her new fiancé Porfirio Rubirosa, a diplomat from the Dominican Republic, had been arrested as a citizen from an enemy country and sent to an internment camp in Bad Nauheim (in Hesse) together with American diplomats.

Her ex-husband Henri Decoin was also asked to present *Premier Rendez-vous* in Berlin. Bauermeister, on behalf of Greven, insisted he made the trip but the director replied, "My contract doesn't specify I should go to Germany to present my films. If that clause had been included, I wouldn't have signed it. The next day, the Propaganda Office asked me, over the phone, for my identity card number for the trip to Germany. I replied that I was not going. The matter was closed."[8]

Darrieux came to Decoin for advice regarding the Berlin trip. His immediate reaction was to tell her to refuse. She then explained that she wanted to see her imprisoned fiancé in Bad Nauheim. "Then, sort something out to go to Berlin," he said.[9] So Darrieux arranged a meeting with Greven, the outcome of which was that she was permitted to visit her fiancé in exchange for her presence in Berlin.

Two other actresses were also subjected to threats to get them to agree to the trip. According to André Legrand, the German authorities threatened to revoke Junie Astor's work permit and to close the three film theaters she owned in Paris.[10] Dr. Diedrich himself interrogated Viviane Romance about her Polish maternal grandmother and her alleged Jewish origins. Various antisemitic collaborationist newspapers, including *Au Pilori* and *Aujourd'hui*, had published articles in September 1941 calling her a Jew. Even if such allegations were false, it was evident that anyone accused was in a weak position vis-à-vis Dr. Diedrich, who was responsible for providing work permits. He could also deny Romance a passport to travel to Italy, where she was to star in an Italian-French coproduction of *Carmen* (1943). Romance thus capitulated and agreed to participate in the trip to Berlin.

Actress Suzy Delair's case was far more ambiguous. She had recently reached star status at Continental thanks to her boyfriend, Henri-Georges Clouzot, who wrote plum parts for her in *Le Dernier des six* (1941) and *L'Assassin habite au 21* (1942). The explanations she offered after the war were unclear: "I went to Germany because I was forced to do it. I was under contract with Continental. I didn't see anything wrong with working for a German company. The nationality of production companies is of no importance to me. . . . I love order, and I said the Germans had order. That's all. . . . I didn't want to go to Germany; but the Propaganda Office called me and threatened to confiscate my work permit. I didn't attend the dinner at the Crillon Hotel, which was hosted by General Stülpnagel before the departure of the troup."[11]

It's an understatement to say that Delair had few friends at Continental among the French employees. We should therefore be cautious regarding comments about her. However, there is a detail that speaks for itself regarding her departure to Germany. André Legrand mentioned that Dr. Diedrich gallantly carried her suitcase as they were boarding the train to Berlin. Screenwriter Michel Duran witnessed her return to the studio after the trip and how she greeted her German boss: "Greven was passing by; she greeted him with a kiss. Naturally, they hugged. And then she threw a fit because she had not been introduced to Goebbels. 'I am furious at Von Eike for not introducing me. I would have liked so much to shake his hand!'"[12] Her attitude shows, at best, a complete lack of judgment.

Albert Préjean was the only actor under an exclusive contract with Continental when he was called to join the trip. In the summer of 1940, he had been discharged from the French Army with the rank of captain. He was in a financially difficult situation and had to sell his property in the south of France. In 1941, he got a commitment to make a film with Calamy Productions. During talks in Nice with the French company, Préjean received a call from a manager of Continental Films who gave him to understand that German authorities did not appreciate the actor's participation in a radio program critical of French journalist and Nazi sympathizer Paul Ferdonnet, who before the war worked on French-language propaganda programs for Radio-Stuttgart. The manager explained to him that it would be better if Préjean joined Continental Films along with other stars of the French screen. He was offered a limited contract for production of the film *Caprices* (1942) and was advised that if he refused, it would only provide further proof of his animosity and could cost him dearly. He agreed to sign a contract on terms decidedly inferior to those he had signed in 1939.

He completed his first film for Continental, after which the plans for the film with Calamy Productions fell through. So in February 1942, Préjean signed an exclusive contract with the German production company. Since he would otherwise be in default of his new contract, he was obliged to make the trip to Berlin. At the time, he commented, "The trip was in no way a propaganda exercise useful for Germany but a commercial trip that could only benefit Continental."[13] Préjean may sound naive, but he knew very well that given his exclusive contract, he couldn't refuse.

Actor René Dary was also solicited for the trip in spite of the fact he never worked at Continental. Born Anatole Clément Mary in 1905, he had been a film star since the age of three when he appeared as Bébé in several Louis Feuillade comedies. He tried to avoid having to go on the trip by explaining that he was currently busy with a production. He was called to the German Propaganda Office, where Dr. Diedrich informed him that his reasons were not valid because his producer had granted him leave. Dary still hesitated but met with the film's production manager, Jacques Vitry, who advised him to accept, since it would be a professional trip. During a second meeting at the

Propaganda Office, Dr. Diedrich proved to be more menacing. Dary finally acquiesced but asked and received as compensation the liberation of a French prisoner of war.[14]

Among those boarding the train on March 18, 1942, one man, journalist Pierre Heuzé, was utterly convinced of the great benefits of the Franco-German collaboration. He was in charge of writing the chronicle of those twelve days of receptions, meetings with Third Reich dignitaries, and studio visits. His purple prose in *Ciné-Mondial* relentlessly praised their fearsome mentor, Dr. Diedrich, and their German hosts, depicting in grandiloquent terms every stage of the journey. He extolled the merits of their redoubtable mentor, who accompanied those he had forced to make the trip.

> Dr. Diedrich, to shorten the hours we are trapped on the railway, watches over us with such friendly devotion that Suzy Delair exclaims, in one of her impulsive moments, "You are an amazing guy, doctor." . . . We crossed the border without realizing it; Dr. Diedrich used his discretion to help us through the customs passport control. . . . During the night, the country toward which we are sailing no longer has very precise boundaries for us, or rather it is a bit like a great homeland that has expanded simultaneously in time as well as in space: it is Europe! . . . Better than a dream, perhaps it is the reality of the future![15]

They arrived in Berlin at dawn and were taken to the Eden Hotel, where numerous French artists had stayed before the war when they worked at the Babelsberg Film Studio. They were then offered lunch—a meager serving of beans and thin slices of beef, the national wartime menu on Thursday—at the Foreign Press Club. Screenwriter André Legrand launched a conversation with the foreigners present at the table:

> I was seated between a Romanian and a Swiss attaché. I created a kind of atmosphere in which trust and mutual confidences were possible. It may sound incredible given the time, but at the end of lunch, the Romanian attaché, who had not drunk, spoke very freely. . . . I have never understood how the Germans could make the mistake of seating us with foreigners, especially the Swiss and Romanians, people we would perhaps agree with—and I got proof of it—without a single German being there. You will say that they surely had spies present, but this did not dissuade anyone. . . . The Romanian managed to tell me, "But, of course, sir, Germany looks victorious right now. But you don't realize that at home, in Romania, Germans are hated, as they are in Hungary and in Norway; they are

hated everywhere as they are in our country." He spoke to me about Austria, Czechoslovakia, and particularly of his own country. And he concluded—in Berlin—"A country that is hated worldwide cannot win a war. One day, Germany will lose because it concentrates the hatred of the world." He said everything in front of the Swiss attaché, who also participated in all this. I took note very carefully. . . . Junie Astor and Viviane Romance, who were scattered among us, had also been able to get other people to express themselves freely, and the lunch ended in a comical manner with us having coffee with these foreigners who, in Berlin, told us of their memories of Paris and the Latin Quarter and ended up chanting at the top of their voices. . . . When you arrive in Berlin, it was all rather funny![16]

The day continued with a visit to a television studio followed by a soirée in the home of the Reichfilmskammer president, film director Carl Froelich. In his purple prose, Pierre Heuzé praised the place: "In this luxurious residence with large picture windows full of flowers, among the precious china, the carefully chosen paintings, the decor recedes, giving way to an intimacy where each soul remembers the nuances of the familiar homeland."[17] It was here that the French visitors met the head of the Reich film department, Fritz Hippler—righthand man for propaganda minister Joseph Goebbels and director of the 1940 antisemitic propaganda documentary *Der ewige Jude* (*The Eternal Jew*)—as well as other German film people, including actresses Marika Rökk and Henny Porten and the director Georg Jacoby. That evening they also encountered the famous French actor Harry Baur, who was in Berlin appearing in a German film titled *Symphonie eines Lebens* (1943).

On March 20, the premiere of *Premier Rendez-vous* took place at the Marmorhaus Theater located on the prestigious Kurfürstendamm, one of Berlin's main thoroughfares. The film had not yet been dubbed into German and so was presented with German subtitles. The Berlin audience was captivated, and Heuzé waxed lyrical about their hosts: "To a great reconciliation! That is, to the future of France! And to think I can write these lines in Berlin in spring 1942, leaving a cinema, while German soldiers keep watch on the outer edges of the steppes for all of Europe."[18] If the collaborationist's enthusiasm bordered on bad taste, the success of the film was confirmed by the reviews published in German newspapers. They praised the return to a moral code in line with Nazi propaganda: "A sample of the present French film production: it renounces the depressing tendencies that prevailed previously in French cinema but not the legacy of the rules and recipes of filmmaking."[19] The comment assumes a particular piquancy when one knows that the screenwriter of *Premier Rendez-vous* was a Jewish-German refugee hiding from the Gestapo in France.

The day ended with a reception at the Maison des artistes hosted by Professor Benno von Arent. His honorific was typical of the obsession of Nazi dignitaries with academic titles, which they bestowed even when the person so designated had not earned a diploma. Von Arent was simply a theater designer who had been upgraded because of his membership since 1931 in the Nazi Party. Heuzé was predictably dazzled once again: "Upon entering this home, I am suddenly aware that, far from losing interest in the various manifestations of creative thought, chancellor Hitler wanted to endow it with an organization where artists feel comfortable and safe in the world, in a climate that suits them best."[20]

The next day, the group visited Babelsberg Studio, where several of them had worked before the war. After visiting different soundstages, they were taken to a factory where a show had been organized for two thousand French workers. French newsreel cameras captured the faces of the stars as they listened to eccentric French singer Marguerite Gilbert entertaining the workers. Although they hoped that Darrieux and Préjean might also come to the microphone to sing, it was not to be. Préjean said only a few words. Even if the compulsory work service did not yet exist, there were already French people working in German factories. Legrand recalled his unease: "It was terribly embarrassing. Do you think I was happy? I could feel how awful it was. We were there talking to workers who had to endure forced labor. Of course, we had to behave."[21] Legrand remained silent and refused to speak in public when he was asked. This most clearly propagandistic part of the trip appeared to be designed as a call for French workers to go to Germany.

In March 1942, the Nazis were about to ask the Vichy government for more French workers. Under this initiative, known as "the relief," one French prisoner of war was supposed to be released for every three French workers who came to Germany. However, this relief initiative would be a failure and would lead the Vichy government into a closer collaboration in its methodical organization of the compulsory work service system.

The climax of the trip was a reception that evening at the home of Dr. Joseph Goebbels. The propaganda minister and his wife, Magda, joined by famous German stars such as Heinrich Georg and Marika Rökk, spared no expense in receiving their French guests. Heuzé said that he spoke almost entirely in French that evening, just like Magda. After the screening of a film starring Rökk, she sang a song for the guests, accompanied on the piano by the propaganda minister. Dary said that Goebbels spoke that evening only about theater with Heinrich Georg. Préjean said that the propaganda minister spoke mostly with German actors.

It is noteworthy that among the many photos published in *Ciné-Mondial* to record this encounter, there was not a single photo of any of the Nazi dignitaries—none of Goebbels, Hippler, or anyone else. *Ciné-Mondial* had no doubt received instructions in this regard, as French readers certainly would not have appreciated seeing their favorite stars next to anyone wearing a Nazi uniform. If Heuzé's deliriously lyrical prose style was unintentionally comic, his intention was undoubtedly to celebrate the rapprochement between France and Germany so that his readership could accept the suggested kinship between artists on both sides of the Rhine without cringing.

As for Goebbels's feelings about the evening, we can quote his diary entry for March 2:

> In the evening a delegation of French film actors' visit, among them Albert Préjean and Danielle Darrieux. The evening goes off very well. I take the opportunity to explain to the French a number of political matters, for which they show great understanding. From their comments I gather that our propaganda in Paris is far from successful. That comes from the fact that no decent propagandists are at work there. Such a business must be learned properly. You cannot just appoint a well-meaning officer to do it. This work has to be done by professionals. If we manage to elicit anti-German and pro-English sentiments in spite of the English bombing raids leaving more than six hundred dead in Paris, that speaks of a complete lack of talent in the leadership of propaganda. I would quite like to work for a few months in Paris myself, to show our people there how such a thing ought to be done.[22]

According to the minister, this trip was not enough to modify the feelings of French people toward their occupiers. It was certainly one of the reasons why no other trip was organized later on.

The next day, the travelers boarded a train for Vienna, minus Danielle Darrieux, who left them to visit Rubirosa in Bad Nauheim. She later went back to Paris on her own. The narrator of the newsreel showing the group's arrival in Vienna nevertheless mentioned her as being present—an excellent example of the accuracy of the collaborationist media.

The stay in Vienna included a visit to the great monuments as well as the Wien-Film studios. The travelers were welcomed by Baldur von Schirach, the

Reich's governor, and in the evening, they attended a special performance of Richard Strauss's *Salomé* at the Vienna State Opera with the composer at the rostrum. They were seated in the imperial box that was now that of the führer. After the performance, they met the composer and his wife.

Again, André Legrand was astonished by the confidences he collected during the various lunches and dinners in the Austrian capital: "I had a woman sitting next to me who didn't know me and during our first lunch in Vienna, after the second course, she said, 'Do you know why the Huns'—some were sitting in front of us—'are not going to cafés here?' I said, 'Why?' 'Because, each time they go to Vienna cafés, somebody picks a quarrel with them. They get beaten up. Then, the Huns are no longer thirsty.'"[23] During the dinner with Richard Strauss and his wife, people started talking again. Legrand recalled that "Dr. Diedrich, who had many failings but who possessed at least one quality—he was not completely stupid—realized that we were making fun of them, that we were sort of colluding with a number of people. I was with Junie Astor at a table with Mr. and Mrs. Richard Strauss. Strauss was very cautious about what he said. But Mrs. Strauss, after some champagne, was no longer careful. She said afterward (Dr. Diedrich overheard her), 'Well, we can say it between us, Huns will always be Huns.' She said it, I can assure you."[24]

Mrs. Strauss's quip sounds unlikely. There are numerous aspects, however, that lend credence to it. André Legrand thought she was Viennese; he was certainly misled by her strong Bavarian accent. Pauline Strauss (née de Ahna) was well known for her frankness and the way she made bloopers. Celebrated conductor Otto Klemperer reported that Pauline had no sympathy for the Nazis. In 1932, as Klemperer was starting to feel the antisemitism that would lead him to immigrate to the United States, Pauline said straight out, "If the Nazis give you any trouble, Herr Klemperer, just come to me. I'll tell those gentlemen who's who." Her husband raised his eyebrows in amazement, saying, "That will be just the moment to stand up for a Jew!"[25] Their difference in attitude is confirmed by Legrand's anecdote.

The Strauss couple's relationship to the Nazi regime was ambiguous. Although Strauss had been appointed the honorary president of the Reichsmusikkammer in 1933 by Hitler, he was demoted in 1935 because of his friendship with writer Stefan Zweig, who wrote the libretto of one of his operas, *Die schweigsame Frau* (*The Silent Women*). His son Franz was married to a Jewish woman and the composer did everything he could to protect her and his grandchildren from persecution. In 1942, he left for Vienna with his wife, his son, his daughter-in-law, and his grandchildren to take advantage of the protection offered by Baldur von Schirach. At the time when he met the French artists, he was therefore in a delicate position. He had kept his prestige thanks to his status as world-renowned composer. But he knew his family was still in danger. The parents of his daughter-in-law, Alice, had been arrested and sent to the Theresienstadt concentration camp. Strauss went himself to the camp to try to get them released to no avail.

In the meantime, Dr. Diedrich was furious that the propaganda trip was not going the way he had hoped. Legrand noted, "As a result, we left Vienna one day earlier than planned because the Germans realized that contact with us was very dangerous. . . . When we left Vienna, I boarded my carriage and, in the corridor, I met a Viennese man, a true stout Viennese. He put his hands on my shoulders and told me, 'We are occupied like you. We are suffering like you; tell them in Paris.' He kissed me on both cheeks as tears rolled down his face."[26]

On their way to Munich, while Legrand had taken note of the rebellious Viennese spirit, Pierre Heuzé was still glorifying the spirit of collaboration: "Some French people, while the entire world is armed—while our victors have not completed their gigantic work, and the French are in an armistice that is only a stopover—travel toward the heart of Germany, toward a town noted for its human potential, toward the city of change, toward Munich!"[27] The last stage in their journey was indeed the Bavarian capital. They visited the Bavaria Film studios, where they met Georg Wilhelm Pabst, a director Albert Préjean and Viviane Romance knew well as they had made pictures under his direction before the war. During their last Bavarian evening, an opera singer sang one lied and two French melodies. "And because Suzy Delair wanted to thank them on behalf of us all, she sang."[28]

When they were finally back in Paris after twelve days, the French filmmakers gathered (without Darrieux) on the roof of the German Propaganda Office for a cocktail reception with the collaborationist press and its figurehead, Jean Luchaire, editor of *Les Nouveaux Temps*. Heuzé concluded his report in *Ciné-Mondial* in a typically rapturous manner:

> Vanquished? Oh, no, conquered, but conquered by the heart! I recall a principle of physics that we may now apply to France, to Germany, to Europe: that of communicating souls. Oh, yes, a propaganda trip! I write only for those souls of good will and to defend the best men in Germany and the best among us. . . .
> I write . . . for isolated souls here who are looking to begin anew. I believe in the future of my country precisely because I have heard the beating heart of

Germany. I write not because ordered to but because, having regained my pride
in Berlin, Vienna, and Munich, I remain at the service of France.[29]

Nevertheless, no other trip was ever organized in spite of the fact that the
Propaganda Office wanted to send numerous other artists to Germany. Actor
and director Pierre Blanchar remembered his meeting with Diedrich for such
a trip:

> Before starting *Pontcarral*, I was summoned by Dr. Diedrich who told me, "Sir,
> would you like to go to Germany? We are organizing trips to stimulate artistic
> relationships between our two countries. So, there is already a trip scheduled;
> there will be one with Miss Darrieux, Mr. Préjean, Mrs. Suzy Delair, etc. . . .
> Would you like to go to Germany?" So, I told him, "Dr. Diedrich, I suppose if you
> intend to receive me in Germany, you'll do it very well?" He said, "Of course,
> you bet! We'll book you in the best hotel in Berlin." I said, "I know it. Which
> one? The Eden, the Esplanade?" He said, "The Eden." Then I said, "Therefore,
> in the morning, you'll serve me coffee with milk, fried eggs, bread rolls, butter
> and jam?" "But, of course, sir." I said, "And probably, lunches will be very com-
> fortable, won't they? And performances at the Propaganda Ministry, lunches at
> the studios, at UFA or at Tobis?" "But, of course, absolutely." I told him, "Well,
> Mr. Diedrich, I would not find it very pleasant to fill myself up in Germany
> while French people are starving. So, I prefer to abandon this kind of sport.'"[30]
> Taken aback, Diedrich said: "Ah! Yes, of course. All right, Mr. Blanchar."[31]

But the reason why the second trip to Germany was canceled was certainly
because in May 1942 Goebbels screened *La Symphonie fantastique* with Fritz
Hippler and was furious to discover that the film did not conform to his criteria for a French film that could be released in Germany.

> In the evening, we viewed a new motion picture produced by our company
> Continental in Paris, after a scenario written about the life and work of Hector
> Berlioz. The film is of excellent quality and amounts to a first-class national
> fanfare. Unfortunately, I will not be able to release it for public showing. I am
> angry to think that our own offices in Paris are teaching the French how to rep-
> resent nationalism in pictures. This lack of political instinct can hardly be
> improved on. But that's the way we Germans are. Whenever we go into another
> country, be it ever so strange to us or even an enemy, our first mission always
> seems to be to put that country back into order without questioning whether

perhaps in several years or decades it may go to war against us. The lack of political instinct among the Germans is the result of their passion for work and of their idealistic enthusiasm. Constant care must be taken in this case to ensure that this does not lead to malicious and negative consequences. I ordered Greven to come to Berlin from Paris to give him absolutely clear and unmistakable directives on this point, the essence of which is that so far as the French are concerned, only light, frothy, and even possibly corny pictures are desired. No doubt the French people will be satisfied with that too. There is no reason why we should cultivate their nationalism. We must, as much as possible, tempt away the most exceptional talents of French cinema for our own German film industry. I do not see any other way to reach a satisfying solution in this area. I worry when thinking of the consequences if we had not intervened. We Germans, we haven't got yet the stature of a people of the world. We have grown up with a mass of juxtaposed states and as a result, we still miss the essential political practice and experience. What we missed for centuries we have to make up for in a few years. We will make again such mistakes repeatedly. The mission of our direction will be to change course and to stay vigilant so that we do not lose by our policies what we have conquered by force.[32]

Goebbels's desire to import French film stars to Germany had already become a reality in spring 1942 with Harry Baur's arrival in Berlin to shoot *Symphonie eines Lebens*. Unfortunately for the propaganda minister, this operation would prove far more dangerous and difficult to manage than he expected.

CHAPTER 12

The Harry Baur Affair

Until now, the departure to Berlin and then the arrest and death of the great actor Harry Baur remained a mystery. Thanks to German and French archival documents, it's now possible to unravel the web of intrigue that led to the death of this distinguished artist.

Baur worked for Continental Films on two films, Christian-Jaque's *L'Assassinat du Père Noël* (1941) and Maurice Tourneur's *Péchés de jeunesse* (1941). In June 1941, while he was shooting Tourneur's film, he was contacted by German emissaries from the Tobis company who had been sent from Berlin. Harry Baur's wife recalled that "these gentlemen told my husband their intention to hire him for a film that would be shot in Germany. They insisted that the German authorities attached great value to this trip and reminded him that as former president of the International Association of Artists, he couldn't object to this artistic enterprise of an international nature."[1]

Harry Baur tried to buy time by invoking his health. The emissaries announced that they would be back a month later. On the set date, they insisted he go, saying they would take all necessary medical precautions. Baur replied he didn't speak German at all. They said he would be provided with a teacher who would help him learn his part. "Faced with his reluctance, his interlocutors specifically mentioned the recent attacks he and his wife had been subjected to and that had been reported in Parisian newspapers. Their statements were clear enough for my husband to understand the danger he incurred in the case of a refusal."[2] Turning threats into action, the authorities summoned Harry Baur's wife to the German anti-Jewish services and kept her for forty-eight hours under the pretext that she couldn't prove she wasn't Jewish.

Rika Radifé was born Rebecca Behar in 1902 in Istanbul of Turkish parents. Her religious status remains unclear. She pretended to be Muslim before the German authorities and gave a birth certificate accordingly. However, the

Ad for *Péchés de jeunesse* (1941) (Fondation Jérôme Seydoux-Pathé)

Turkish consulate couldn't confirm the document.[3] Cornered, Harry Baur signed the contract to free his wife. It was specified he wouldn't be forced to participate in any propaganda. Rika was immediately freed, and the couple received all the necessary documents to travel to Berlin. "The aforementioned documents had been drawn up prior to my summons to rue de Téhéran. The comparison between the dates shows that [my detainment] had been a maneuver designed to elicit my husband's acceptance. Train tickets had already been booked, and a few hours after my release, I took the train to Berlin with my husband."[4] It was September 14, 1941, when Baur and his wife left on their first trip to Germany.

The French press mentioned the trip and his contract. As early as August 1941, the weekly *Comœdia* was reporting that "our great stage and screen star will pack his suitcases and will leave our stages and studios to fulfill in Berlin the twenty-six weeks' contract he just signed. . . . Let's hope that Baur—who is leaving, it is said, with a comfortable salary of six million francs—will do an excellent job propagandizing French art abroad."[5] Needless to say, the news came as a bombshell to the world of cinema and theater. Even the German intelligence services noted "an atmosphere approaching scandal in French artistic circles."[6] For French people who were not aware of his real motivations, Baur was a traitor ready to compromise himself for money.

The shooting of Hans Bertram's *Symphonie eines Leben* was supposed to start at the beginning of November, probably to give Baur enough time to learn his part in German. Once in Berlin, Baur and his wife were installed in a flat and put under surveillance of the Gestapo. By the end of November, Harry Baur still had not started shooting the film. A French actor, Jean Pascal, who happened to be in Berlin under duress like Baur, came to visit him. "Mr. Harry Baur was constantly watched by the Gestapo which had assigned an officer to him on the pretext of improving his German. Like me, Harry Baur had to choose between the Gestapo jails and going to Berlin. . . . Even in Berlin, he spoke his mind and did not shy away from criticizing the Germans or even listening to the British radio in his flat. So did his wife."[7] He was asked to speak to the press, but he stubbornly refused to do so.

During that first stay, Harry Baur went to a public political meeting. On October 3, 1941, Adolf Hitler made a speech in the Sportspalast, a giant arena in Berlin. Germany had attacked the USSR on June 22, and he galvanized the crowds to support the future war effort with propaganda. Rika Baur specified that her husband attended "for information purposes. Like him, nearly all the travelers in Berlin on that day tried to get a seat at the Sportspalast, the meeting being one of the most important of all since the advent of the regime."[8] Unfortunately, a picture of Harry Baur was taken during the meeting and was published on the front page of collaborationist newspaper *Aujourd'hui* in Paris.[9] The actor's reputation took another serious hit.

After two and a half months in Berlin, at the end of November 1941, the couple were sent back to Paris without Baur having shot a single scene of his film. The German authorities were still worried that Baur might not be completely Aryan according to racial laws and couldn't decide if his wife was Jewish or Aryan. Rika was summoned and questioned again about her birth certificate.[10] The French press had received very strict orders not to publish any article about the actor on his return to Paris, no doubt in order to avoid a repeat of the negative publicity the previous publications elicited.

In the end, after Baur had been in the French capital for a month and a half, the German authorities decided to send the actor back to Berlin to quickly shoot the planned film. On January 14, 1942, the Baurs took the train to Berlin, even though Harry was in poor health at that time. According to the head of the German secret services, Helmut Kochen, propaganda minister Joseph Goebbels, "who had in his hands papers proving Harry Baur's Aryan status, asked the German police to suspend the arrest until the completion of the film he was interested in, with the understanding that Baur's case would be clarified later."[11]

On January 16, shooting started. Actor Jean Pascal remembered his state of mind during this period: "At the end of January 1942, Harry Baur told me roughly the following, 'There are people, for whom I did some good and I helped morally and financially, who are now hurting me.' He always tried to help his fellow countrymen and handed out money to prisoners as well as clothes. His wife did the same."[12]

Baur obstinately refused to give any interviews or appear on the radio during the shooting. His wife remembered that "several personalities and Dr. Goebbels himself insisted that he apply for German citizenship, and he refused emphatically."[13] It was obvious at that time that in the mind of the propaganda minister, Harry Baur was a member of the Reich owing to his Alsatian background, and he didn't doubt that he was of Aryan descent.

The beginning of the ordeal for the Baurs came in May 1942, when they returned to Paris. Three days after their return, on May 20, they were both arrested and sent to prison. Harry ended up at the Cherche-Midi prison while Rika was sent to the Santé. They were in the hands of the Gestapo and of Captain Theodor Dannecker, in charge of the Jewish question at the German intelligence services, who was notorious even among the German authorities for his sadistic methods.

We have to back up slightly to understand why Dannecker arrested Baur and his wife. When Baur's picture was published on the front page of *Aujourd'hui* in October 1941, one of his childhood friends, Édouard Bouchez, was outraged, but not for the reasons he should have been: "It is shameful for a newspaper to depict a man so full of defects, so cowardly in all respects, execrated by all his colleagues, besides such a beautiful and moral person as the Führer."[14]

Édouard Bouchez was indeed a childhood friend of Harry Baur in spite of the dreadful terms he used to describe his former friend. Born in 1881 in Paris, Bouchez was the son of an attorney general. However, he decided to become a stage actor. By 1913, he had risen through the ranks, becoming theater director in Mers-les-Bains. But by 1922, his career had stalled, and he decided to leave the stage to become an insurance broker, taking advantage of his address book in theater circles to secure contracts. In 1903, he had married a German woman, and they had had three children. Baur was godfather of two of his children and was also witness at the wedding of his daughter, while Bouchez was also witness at the wedding of Baur's daughter Loëna. Loëna remembered the beginning of their falling out: "Before the war, we had stopped seeing him and everybody in our family circle knew he was madly jealous of my father. Papa teased him about it, further spurring his jealousy with remarks like the ones two childhood friends came make when they are as intimate like my father and Bouchez were. In private, we called him 'Boubou.'"[15]

From jealousy to hatred was quite a step. It seemed to have happened when Bouchez's antisemitism became pathological. In his mind, Baur was not himself a Jew—after all, he held Bouchez's daughter over the baptismal font! But he was "tainted by the Jews" because of his wife, his son-in-law, and his Jewish friends.

In addition, from the start of the occupation, Bouchez associated with German circles, as numerous members of his family were part of the occupying forces, like General Müller, aide-de-camp to General Stülpnagel, who was his cousin. He was often seen at the offices of a notorious organization created in 1941, the Institute for the Study of Jewish Questions located at 21 rue La Boétie. His nephew, Lieutenant Manfred Sellier, who was working for the German intelligence services and saw him leaving the place, told him to avoid any association with the institution if he didn't want to have problems after the war.[16] Bouchez had the handiest explanation: he was going to the institute to help former clients who had been arrested by the Gestapo. Under the guise of helping those unfortunate people, Bouchez engaged in a lucrative business. Distressed families contacted him, and he offered his services for a fee, taking small envelopes containing from 2,000 to 15,000 francs. He scrupulously wrote the amounts on the envelopes, which would be found after the war at his home. We do not know if his "assistance" was fruitful, but it proved certainly profitable for him.

The Institute for the Study of Jewish Questions was established in May 1941. This institution was financed entirely by German funds. However, the Germans employed French flunkies to give it a local color. A young Alsatian, Maurice Müller, who had been appointed interpreter under duress at the institute, explained that it was designed by the Germans "on the one hand, to undermine measures planned by Vichy for the resolution of the Jewish question, which were too lackluster for them, and on the other hand, to coordinate the activities of the Propaganda Office action (anti-Jewish propaganda) and Dannecker's division (police repression). This institute was supposed to serve as pseudo-French cover for the action of the two aforementioned services." Müller noted that the head of the institute was "unquestionably Dannecker; René Gérard as well as Sézille were flunkies" and added that it didn't have its own budget: "It was Dannecker and the Propaganda Office who provided the necessary funds."[17]

The same witness provided an enlightening portrait of Captain Sézille, who was Dannecker's henchman. A member of the colonial army, he was the "founder of the Group of Anti-Jewish Friends, of the Anti-Jewish Brigades and of the Action Committees" and became general secretary of the Institute for the Study of Jewish Questions after Gérard: "Politically speaking, he came from the Cagoule and had been one of Darquier de Pellepoix's agent at the Anti-Jewish Rally of France, where he had a permanently manned office. An inveterate drinker, he was drunk every day from 11 a.m. on. Violent and quick tempered, he was foul mouthed and had no education. He was incapable writing a report without spelling mistakes. His creed, which he repeated many a time in front of me and others, was the following: 'I am 100 percent French and 1000 percent German.'"[18]

Bouchez met Sézille in December 1941 and made the following statements about his former friend:

Harry Baur is married to a Jewess. His marriage took place in Paris at the sixteenth arrondissement town hall. His daughter is also married to a Jew named Mardochée Meyer, an Algerian Jew. Harry Baur's grandchildren have been raised

in the Jewish faith and have been circumcised. In his living room, Mr. Harry
Baur has a inscribed picture of the Jewish lawyer Lévy Oulmann. . . . Baur, who
isn't Jewish himself, is through his Jewish connections, tainted by Jewishness as
much as if he was of the Jewish race. All his previous connections, before the
war, were in Jewish circles. A fanatical trade unionist, he gave his support to the
demonstrations of the Popular Front and to the Spanish Republicans. . . . He
appears here in a newspaper [*Aujourd'hui*] for which Georges Suarez, Abel Her-
mant, half Jews, and a whole line of former notorious Freemasons and profiteers
of the former regime write. There was, in the publication of this photograph of
a filthy person, Harry Baur, and such a beautiful person, Hitler, a clear demonstration of the position Baur has taken, cleared by his stay in Berlin. But, if it had
had all the information, Germany would have never have authorized such a trip.[19]

Sézille sent his report to Theodor Dannecker in December 1941. In January
1942, Sézille was visited by three Germans asking for more information regarding Harry Baur. There was no doubt the report was worrying people in high
places, probably primarily Joseph Goebbels, who was desperate to put Baur
into a film. He was therefore sent quickly to Berlin so that he could fulfill his
contract, even if that meant questioning him afterward.

We should not underestimate the in-fighting between the various branches
of the German army. Theodor Dannecker was at war with the head of the
intelligence services in Paris, Helmut Kochen, who didn't appreciate his overly
personal actions. And as Knochen specified, Dannecker was not endowed
with full authority:

> Dannecker, being in possession of a denunciation toward Harry Baur, no matter
> how precise, couldn't order the arrest himself given the fame of the person con-
> cerned. He had to refer to the Reich Main Security Office in Berlin to which he
> was responsible as well as I. And he had to ask for advice from Goebbels's divi-
> sion, which was represented in Paris by the Propaganda Office. If the German
> police had initiated such an arrest, it would have been immediately overturned
> by Goebbels, who personally took care of stars.[20]

Goebbels was an awkward position. He had to clear up this matter as quickly
as possible or his film would never be released. Further, his enemies could take
advantage of this disaster to trip him up.

Goebbels therefore authorized the Baurs' arrest in May 1942. But as he had no
confidence in Dannecker, he sent an emissary to France, SS Sturmbannführer

Ralf Tiemann, to take part in the interrogations. Knochen clarified this point: "The fact that Tiemann, who was attached to section 3 of the Berlin Reich Main Security Office and charged in Paris to liaise with the Propaganda Office, interrogated Mr. and Mrs. Baur proves that Goebbels's division didn't want the question to be decided by Dannecker's unit alone, that is to say with anti-Jewish blinders but objectively."[21]

Rika Baur was jailed in solitary confinement at the Santé prison where Resistance fighter Marie-Claude Vaillant-Couturier was also detained. She underwent numerous interrogations by Tiemann, with Robert Jodkum from the Security Police and Security Service serving as interpreter. The particularly harsh questioning she had to endure related to racial and political questions:

"The Germans absolutely wanted me to say that my husband was Jewish or at least 'tainted with Jewishness' and that he owed his situation to his Jewish friends. As for the political side, they accused him of being a Freemason, a communist, and a trade unionist. The Germans told me, or tried to make me say, that my husband supported the Republicans in Spain by his actions, adding that the proof was he had supported the department stores strikers in 1936. . . . Finally, I was violently mistreated during the questioning regarding Lévy Oulmann. The Germans showed me a picture of Lévy Oulmann that he had inscribed to my husband with "To my brother in heart and mind." I replied that, in this instance, the word "brother" had nothing to do with Masonic practices.[22]

Interestingly, the questioning exactly mirrored the accusations brought by Édouard Bouchez.

Harry Baur was tortured numerous times at the Cherche-Midi prison. He was questioned by five tormentors: Karl Bömelburg, Heinz Röthke, Helmut Knochen, and especially Theodor Dannecker and Ralf Tiemann. An inspector from the French police headquarters who was transferred to the anti-Jewish division was responsible for fetching him in prison and taking him to the Gestapo headquarters at 72 avenue Foch along with another colleague. He described the physical abuses endured by Harry Baur: "I remember particularly a questioning conducted by Dannecker and Tiemann that was especially harsh and painful and that lasted no less than twelve hours. It's during this interrogation that Mr. Harry Baur told Dannecker 'it will be less cowardly for you to hit a man standing' when Danneker, who was about to hit him while he was seated, asked him why he was getting up. In the prison, Harry Baur was beaten with a stool."[23]

The tormentors asked the Baurs very specific questions regarding their daughter and their grandchildren. Rika was astonished when they mentioned that one of Loëna's children had been circumcised at the American Hospital of Paris by a rabbi whose name they knew when she couldn't even remember it herself. There was no doubt that the Gestapo had been informed on by somebody close to the family. Moreover, during Harry Baur's last questioning, a German policeman delivered this awful statement: "We know you are not Jewish, and we have always been convinced you weren't. When you know the name of the person who denounced you, it will make what's left of your hair stand on end."[24]

The German had indeed sent a French policeman accompanied by an officer of their services in Alsace, to Heimsbrunn, near Mulhouse, to verify once and for all who Harry Baur's ancestors were. After going through the civil and religious archives, they were forced to face the fact that Baur was Aryan. Upon their return, Tiemann remarked, "We blew it; Harry Baur is not Jewish."[25]

Jodkun then told Dannecker and Tiemann that Baur could end up dying in prison given his appalling state of health. If it happened, their division would have to bear the responsibility. They therefore decided to free Rika Baur on September 10, 1942, after 115 days of imprisonment. And they freed Harry Baur on September 20. They went back to their home, 3 rue du Helder, still under close surveillance. Following Dannecker's orders, Jodkun placed two French inspectors outside their home who watched them constantly. But the ordeal was not yet over for Harry. "Although my husband was dying, the Germans came to take him away for further questioning. These continued every day without interruption, in a manner of speaking, until December 20, 1942."[26]

When Harry's physician came to examine him shortly after his release from prison, he discovered a man in a pitiful state: "The patient had been ill-treated, beaten up, kicked extremely violently all over his body, but more specifically on the back of the neck, around the precordial region and on the back, where they were large bruises and numerous external wounds, some that had healed and others were infected."[27] The French film colossus who had brought to life a powerful Jean Valjean was only the shadow of himself; he had lost thirty-seven kilos.

In a menacing tone, the Germans informed Mrs. Baur "that there never was any Harry Baur case," that she "had never been arrested" and neither had her husband.[28] Harry Baur died on April 8, 1943, after enduring excruciating pain.

As for Joseph Goebbels, he was only worried about his picture. He finally screened it in September 1942.

The new Tobis production *Symphonie eines Lebens* is finished. It's a musical film entirely composed by Norbert Schulze. The male lead is Harry Baur, who is accused of being a Jew in Paris. His acting in this film is flawless. The whole film is a shining testimony to the German art of film directing. Young director Bertram has thus shown his mettle. I will now continue to follow up the Baur case and ensure that one way or another a decision is made. I would much prefer if the film could be saved, because Baur's Jewish ancestry is far from proven. I also do not believe it. Our Parisian division seems to have been more papist than the Pope.[29]

The propaganda minister's wishes were granted. The film was released at the Berlin Marmorhaus theater on April 21, 1943, thirteen days after the actor's death.

In 1947, a judicial inquiry of Édouard Bouchez was opened. Witnesses were heard. Bouchez was charged with "national disgracefulness" by the Seine law court.[30] However, due to Bouchez's ill health, the hearing of the case was postponed several times, and in the end, he never appeared in front of the court. The special court was dissolved in January 1951. His case was then transferred to the Paris military tribunal and the accused was acquitted on May 31, 1951.

CHAPTER 13

Shooting on the French Riviera

As soon as Continental was created, Greven wanted to make movies in the south of France. Although the country was divided in two zones, the zone occupied by the Germans and the so-called free-zone run by the Vichy government, Greven didn't intend to limit his influence to the occupied zone.

In the summer of 1940, virtually all French filmmakers, actors, and directors were gathered on the French Riviera, where several film studios were located, including the Victorine studios in Nice and the Marcel Pagnol studios in Marseille. But in the autumn of 1940, not a single laboratory was open except the one belonging to Marcel Pagnol. Without a laboratory to process film and print copies, it was impossible to make pictures.

Pagnol was truly an extraordinary character within the French film industry. He was an author, a director, and a producer with his own production company. He had built his own studios in Marseille, and he was the only French filmmaker who enjoyed almost complete autonomy. Alfred Greven knew his plays and his films well; they had met in the past in Berlin. Pagnol remembered that "the head of German cinema in France, Mr. Greven, had received me in Berlin in 1932 at the Renaissance Theater for the two hundredth performance of *Marius*."[1] In addition, several Pagnol plays had been huge successes in Germany, particularly *Topaze, Marius, Fanny*, and *Les Marchands de gloire*.

Greven therefore wanted the film director to join, as quickly as possible, the stable of great directors at Continental. In addition to his skills as filmmaker, he would bring with him his own studios in working order. As soon as Continental was established, Greven left for the free zone to meet Pagnol. The Vichy government was closely watching the activities of this German producer, who was too greedy for its taste. A note from the French intelligence services dated November 6, 1940, mentioned that "the German commissioner for the cinema" was in Cannes with Mr. Chemel, French citizen, production manager, as well as Baron Van Till, Dutch citizen.[2]

When he met with Pagnol in Marseille, he proposed that he "take the reins of Franco-German cinema."[3] Unfortunately for him, Pagnol had no intention of accepting. He mentioned health issues: "I cannot work with you because I suffer from severe depression."[4] Pagnol thus put his activities on hold to avoid working for Continental.

Of course, Greven didn't give up that easily and came back to try to change his mind. In the spring of 1941, he took the train with Robert Beunke, in charge of recruiting actors, and stage manager François Carron. In fact, he wished to rent Pagnol studios to make *Le Club des soupirants* (1941), directed by Maurice Gleize and featuring star comedian Fernandel. Henri Decoin happened to be on the same train; he was preparing *Premier Rendez-vous* and was going to meet with Louis Jourdan in the south so he could sign his contract.

Decoin took advantage of the trip to visit the Pagnol studios. He wasn't very enthusiastic about the Marseille technical facilities: "At Continental, we all know that, one day or another, we'll be forced, like Maurice Gleize, to shoot in Marseille studios. I decide to stop for a few hours in Marseille to see the studios. I visit them and in agreement with Maurice Gleize, who is devastated, I give my opinion about shooting films in such a place."[5] In spite of this advice, Gleize's movie would indeed be shot in that studio.

Greven and Beunke had to sign the contract with Pagnol for the studio rental, and they asked Decoin to come with them to meet him in Monte Carlo. "I accompany them, and I am happy to meet Pagnol and Josette Day. We spend the afternoon in Monte Carlo. Marcel Pagnol discusses the studio contracts with Greven and Beunke. I play roulette; I win five thousand francs."[6] This last detail gives an idea of how detached from reality film artists were compared with the general population. As the cherry on the cake, the next day Greven organized a dinner in honor of Pagnol at the Negresco, a luxury hotel. The guests around the table were Pagnol, Jules Berry, Josette Day, Suzy Prim, Beunke, and Decoin.

However, in spite of all the pressures, Pagnol still refused to work for the company, each time citing health or other problems as an excuse. Nevertheless, he couldn't prevent his studios from being rented. Maurice Gleize, who had been hired to make a musical, *Caf' Conc'*, was instead asked to make a film with Fernandel. Continental contacted writer Marcel Aymé for a script. He sold them a story that was later adapted by Jean Manse, Fernandel's brother-in-law, who happened to be his lyricist and manager.

Unlike in the case of Continental productions made in Paris, it was stage manager François Carron who was in charge of recruiting the staff on location in Marseille. He hired the great art director Georges Wakhevitch: "After my discharge, I immediately met François Carron at Saint-Charles station in Marseille, who asked me, 'Would you like to make a film with Fernandel in Marseille?' I said, 'Gladly.' François Carron told me he would be back in eight days and to go to the studio. It was for *Le Club des soupirants*. And so I went to the studio eight days later, and I signed a Continental contract; I didn't know what it was."[7] Abel Gance's great cinematographer Léonce-Henri Burel, who worked in the south, was also hired. As it was for Wakhevitch, this would be Burel's only film at Continental. The staff at Pagnol studios therefore worked for Continental without having chosen to do so, like Pagnol's prop man Charles Auvergne.

Fernandel was offered a contract for one film, *Le Club des soupirants*. He claimed that in 1941 he didn't know that Continental was German.[8] However, it was his own agent, Robert Beunke—who knowingly worked for Continental—who gave him the contract for signature. In addition, Fernandel knew already Alfred Greven before the war as he had worked at UFA, specifically, on *L'Héritier des Mondésir* (1939).

By October 1941, Marcel Pagnol was hopeful that Continental and Alfred Greven had forgotten about him, and so he decided to start work on the production of a trilogy called *La Prière aux étoiles* with Pierre Blanchar and Josette Day. Unfortunately, they hadn't. "I had finished the first two films, and I was starting the third one when a Greven emissary arrived at the studio and congratulated me on my good health. He told me Mr. Greven was going to come to see my films and that he would look after their distribution. I replied immediately that my films were not a success and that I was going to destroy them."[9] The next day he asked a bailiff to come over and in front of him he destroyed the negatives with an axe.[10] It represented a loss of 6.3 million francs for the producer-director. And as he was constantly hassled by Vichy and the Italians for rental or requisition of his studios, in January 1943, he decided to sell them to Gaumont. He would remain inactive for the rest of the occupation. We can only salute his courageous attitude, as he could have easily taken advantage of Continental's distribution arm or even have worked with Italian companies. He preferred silence to compromise.

Greven took his revenge against the recalcitrant filmmaker by making nasty remarks about him in a report sent to the Organizing Committee of the Cinema Industry: "I notice that [*La Fille du puisatier*], like all Pagnol films, has a

Ad for *Le Club des soupirants* (1941) (Fondation Jérôme Seydoux-Pathé)

marvelous script as its basis, but technically it's a model how a film should not be made."[11] It is a great example of Greven's bad faith: he tried everything possible to get this supposedly talentless director under contract.

Even though Continental didn't use film studios in the south of France after that, it nevertheless continued to shoot other films on location there. In September 1941, Jean Dréville began shooting *Annette et la dame blonde* (1942) with Louise Carletti in the vicinity of Cannes. Aimé Chemel had contacted the film director during the summer of 1940 to ask him to join Continental. But, unlike his colleagues, he couldn't use a personal project for his first film. He was then asked to choose one among a selection of three scripts owned by the firm: *La Main enchantée*—which would become later *La Main du diable*— *La Fausse maîtresse*, based on Honoré de Balzac's novel, or *Annette et la dame blonde*, based on Georges Simenon's novel. Dréville selected *La Main enchantée* and signed a contract for the film. He selected Jean-Louis Barrault and Jany Holt for the leads. Then Bauermeister intervened and asked him to take another actor instead of Barrault. Dréville got worked up: "It's not possible! If we are going to make something stupid, count me out!"[12] Then Bauermeister organized a meeting with Greven. The director offered to cancel his contract, but the boss asked him to choose again among the available scripts. The next day, Dréville announced, "There is a modest film I like very much. It's a charming American comedy. It's harmless. It's *Annette et la dame blonde*. The contract will be, I suppose, with Darrieux?"[13] Greven nodded in agreement. "I prepare the film [script] with Michel Duran. I contact Darrieux. And ten days before the shooting, I find a note on my desk. It's not Darrieux anymore; it's her stand-in, [Raymonde] La Fontan, a bit player. I go back to Greven, very angry. . . . We finally agreed on [Louise] Carletti."[14] But the problems were not over for Dréville, because, shortly after, Henri-Georges Clouzot, who was now in charge of the script department, decided he didn't like this one at all. As a result, there was another conference with Greven. It was Henri Decoin who helped him out of this tricky situation. He told him, "Don't worry. I'll fix it. We'll work on the screenplay together, and in eight days, it will be done!"[15] Shortly before the shooting was to begin, around mid-August 1941, Dréville and Decoin worked together on the shooting script to give it less of an American slant; the dialogue had already been written by Michel Duran. Greven was also in the free zone at that time; he was staying in Antibes. He took the opportunity to go visit Fernandel and Raimu. He also visited the set of *Annette et la dame blonde*.

Dreville was delighted when Greven finally left. "I must say that during the shooting of the film, I have never been so peaceful. I didn't hear from Greven

Ad for *Annette et la dame blonde* (1942) (Fondation Jérôme Seydoux-Pathé)

or anyone. I was the undisputed king. I could have asked the actors to walk upside down."[16] However, during the editing phase, Dréville realized he was going to have to fight again. The editor was changed without consultation: "At the screenings, I had my first real fit inside the company. I said, 'If you bother me at each screening, it won't do. Or do the editing yourself, and let's forget about it.' They relented. 'No, do the editing as you want it,' they told me. Then once again, it is absolutely peaceful. I do the editing. Greven screens the film and says, 'I like it very much. It's excellent. We don't need to change anything.'"[17]

Unlike Decoin, Carné, and Christian-Jaque, Dréville wished to go on working with the German firm because it allowed him to avoid Vichy censorship. And he had no qualms about working for the occupying forces: "Working with German money, it makes no difference. I would have agreed if I had been to do meaningful work. I'd rather make a good little unpretentious film at Continental rather than a bad one at Pathé or elsewhere."[18] In spite of his good will, no other project ever came to fruition. According to him, Greven threw a fit and banged his fist on the table during discussions about script or casting. His management system became tyrannical, and Dréville never had another job at the firm.

Even if Continental had no permanent representative in the south of France, there was a man who commuted regularly between Paris and the Riviera. This man was Robert Beunke. He was paid directly by Continental to hire actors, while at the same time he continued working for his former clients such as Fernandel. The Vichy intelligence services discreetly kept an eye on him and intercepted the phone calls he made and telegrams he sent to the firm's headquarters.

According to screenwriter Carlo Rim, Beunke was a shady character. "Before the war, I remember clearly that Beunke admitted frankly he was Jewish, because at that time, it perhaps served him. Then later, he became Aryan and antisemitic."[19] Other suggested he was born in the Netherlands and was a naturalized French citizen, which was incorrect. Robert Beunke was born in Paris on July 9, 1887. His father was a shop assistant and his mother taught dance and gymnastics. But there was no doubt that he was a zealous recruiter for Continental, in particular in seeking to hire recalcitrant screenwriter Carlo Rim.

Jean-Marius Richard, also known as Carlo Rim, was a journalist with a sparkling wit and southern joviality. Born in Nîmes in 1902, he was first a cartoonist before going to work for *Le Petit Provençal*, his father's newspaper. He later took over various newspapers and magazines like *L'Intransigeant*, *Vu*, and *Marianne*. He started working in the film industry during the 1930s as screenwriter. One of his greatest successes was *Justin de Marseille* (1935), directed by Maurice Tourneur, about the underworld of the Mediterranean city.

Discharged on August 15, 1940, he decided to stay in the free zone. Unlike many of his contemporaries, Carlo Rim had no illusions regarding the French political situation. He was not dazzled by elderly Pétain, the so-called savior of France. As early as December 1940, he wrote a savage epitaph, "Here lies Pétain/Born in Verdun, died in Vichy," which was spread by word of mouth very quickly and even mentioned on BBC programs.

Carlo Rim stubbornly refused to contribute to the Parisian collaborationist press or radio. "Absolutely determined to wait until the end of the events without engaging in any journalistic activity, I resolved to stay in the free zone, because, in those days, it looked as if the demarcation line could offer some kind of protection for those who refused to go near the Germans. I must confess that I had another even more compelling reason to stay in the free zone; my wife is Jewish and her political activities in certain Parisian circles made us fear the worst."[20] Alice and Carlo Rim therefore settled in Cassis in Bouches-du-Rhône.

Penniless, Rim survived by doing literary broadcasts on the Marseille radio. Later, he wrote film reviews in the supplement *Dimanche illustré*. He remembered that summer of 1940 and feelings that those who watched friends go back to Paris experienced: "It was still the extraordinary period when we had not forgotten psychology. When you saw a pal crossing the zone, it was exactly like treason. After [Marcel] Achard made his first trip to Paris, I told Alice, 'I won't shake his hand anymore.'"[21]

He nevertheless tried to resume work as a screenwriter. Raimu offered him the opportunity to work on *L'Arlésienne*, which was directed by Marc Allégret. But the project was made without him. A film with Viviane Romance produced by André Paulvé never came to fruition either. "It seemed I would never make another one," he remembered, but then in October 1941, he met with Fernandel, and told him:

"If you want us to make a movie, I just wrote a short story from which I think I can get something amusing." It was *Simplet*. Fernandel replies, "I'd be delighted." I tell him, "I already saw Guy-Maïa. We are going to make this film in Marseille. We'll shoot in honorable conditions with what is available. Guy-Maïa is perfectly solvent." I take Maïa to Fernandel's in Marseille. We agree on the film. This is where a character comes in whose rather dubious activities must be disclosed; Beunke was present during our meeting. . . . One day, [he] comes to see me. The talks with Fernandel and Maïa were already pretty advanced. So, he comes to Cassis and tells me, "Here it is what's happening, Fernandel doesn't want to work at Guy-Maïa's." I reply, "We agreed. They even debated the amount. I think Fernandel agreed on the fee offered by Guy-Maïa." Beunke says, "It's out of the question. Anyway, my dear Carlo Rim, we cannot make films anymore in the free zone. . . . Your prejudices against the occupied zone and Paris are absurd. All this is grotesque. We are entering a new order; we must work normally. We have been through this extremely painful humiliation, but we must, all the same, get over it." I reply, "My pal Beunke, you won't convince me. I do not want to make this film elsewhere, only in the free zone."[22]

Beunke didn't give up, and he phoned Rim a few weeks later. Their phone conversation was intercepted by the Vichy intelligence services. The transcript confirmed what Rim said and revealed an added element in their disagreement. In proposing Rim's script to Continental, Beunke obtained for Fernandel not only starring credit but also the opportunity to direct it. Rim was furious.

As for the moral side of the affair, if I can call it so, I'll add that if the Germans won the war—and it is a pretty sad fact for all of us—they mustn't win the war in all domains. You are the Continental representative and therefore of the Germans. Well, I am happy to tell you that I never received any money from them or anyone else. . . . If you send me a clown as director, I will reject him and my script won't be directed by him. They'll shoot my film with me or not at all. For ten years, I've been working in film; this has never happened to me. I don't give a damn about the script. I'm better off than Mr. Greven, thank God! . . . My film will be directed by Carlo Rim and no one else, with Mr. X or Y as supervisor, and that's it! Fernandel is a brilliant comedian, a pleasant rank-and-file priest who pleases crude people, that's understood. But, for the rest, he is nothing. To hell with him! . . . Whatever the privileged situation of the Germans in France, I'll show them that there are still French people who have backbone and that not everybody is collaborating. Remember this, especially that I am not the kind to be pushed around. If Fernandel is good in *Regain* and *Angèle*, it's because he worked with Mr. Pagnol and because Mr. Pagnol writes the script. After that he shot others that are junk. People like Fernandel who earn six hundred thousand francs per film, I don't want them anymore, especially as director. I therefore will stop [writing] my script until you come to me and say, "Mr. Fernandel is not the director of my film." I don't need that. I am an author. I will revoke my contract and drop you![23]

In spite of this flat refusal, Beunke phoned Rim's wife, Alice, later that evening to reiterate the advantages of working for Continental:

> We have one of the three best technicians in France, [Christian] Gaudin, the best
> French photographer [Roger] Forster, and directors Carlo Rim and Fernandel.
> We'll bring a sound van from the occupied zone. We have unlimited funds; there
> won't be any budget. . . . Greven is the managing director of thirty film theaters
> across France. Ultimately, he is the man authorized by the German government
> to deal with all these affairs in France. . . . Greven is full of goodwill toward him.
> Only, Carlo speaks too much about Franco-German incidents. Now, Greven
> doesn't want to discuss military or political questions. He is oriented toward the
> artistic and industrial. To people who told him, "With your power, you must
> compel so and so to do such and such thing," he replies, "I do not want to live
> in coercion but in collaboration." . . . He is pro-French to boot. That's why,
> because we are lucky to have him around, we must use him. It's good politics.[24]

The Continental agent's eloquence did not alter Rim's opinion. A few days
later, he and his wife met Beunke at the Noailles Hotel in Marseille. Alice
remembered that

> Mr. Beunke explained to my husband that Fernandel's fee was higher at Conti-
> nental Films and that he insisted on making the film for that firm. My husband
> got very angry and was very insulting toward Beunke. He reiterated that he
> would never sign with Continental. Then, he left the Noailles without a word.
> I stayed with Mr. Beunke, excusing my husband's violent temper. "It's pointless
> to keep on trying, he won't change his mind." Then Beunke told me with a look
> of pity, "Carlo Rim is wrong to have such a bad temper. He seems to forget your
> origins. His obstinate refusal could bring you trouble, as these gentlemen want
> to shoot his script. I must add that they are aware of various foolish things your
> husband did in Cassis. And his uncompromising attitude can only be consid-
> ered a gesture of ill will toward them."[25]

Alice went back home to Cassis panic stricken. Carlo Rim indeed had never
hidden his pro-Ally feelings, and he had even gone as far as to toast the British
victory during a Franco-Anglo-American dinner in Marseille on December 31,
1941, provoking the wrath of the Spanish consul. Greven was perfectly aware
of the facts, as Beunke let Rim know. As for Alice, she had another reason for
being scared. She had a thirteen-year-old son from a first marriage who was

still living with his father in Paris. He wore the yellow star, and his father, a Russian Jew, was hiding from the Gestapo. She had tried in vain to get a pass that would have allowed her son to join her in Cassis. In addition, the police had already searched the homes of some of her Jewish friends and some of them had been arrested in the occupied zone. Alice begged her husband to change his mind and to sign a contract with Continental. As Alice stated, "He agreed to do it with great sorrow, giving me an unforgettable proof of his affection for me."[26] His signing of the contract in January 1942 gave them the hope that they would one day be able to obtain a pass for the child.

Simplet got under way in February 1942. Carlo Rim had still not been back to Paris. Fernandel directed the film with the technical help of Christian Gaudin, who acted as both assistant director and editor. As Rim predicted it, Fernandel proved a perfunctory director. Nevertheless, the head of Continental was pleased with the result, as he sent his actor-director a gift as a thank-you gesture. Fernandel responded warmly: "I thank you very sincerely for the present, fit for a king, that you sent me for the production of my film *Simplet*. I hope you won't be disappointed and that it will be a success."[27] Apparently, Greven sometimes offered valuables such as gold cigarette cases to his favorite collaborators.[28] It should be noted that such gifts were strongly reminiscent of those offered by American gangsters to their best friends in the 1930s.

Part of the film was shot on location in Antibes in February 1942. Rim visited the set and met Bauermeister for the first time: "He paid me a thousand compliments. He was extremely affectionate and made no allusion to [what Beunke had said]. But, even so, he told me, 'Mr. Rim, we are very happy you accepted to make *Simplet* with us. We know your opinions. We know you were not always on our side.' I replied, 'I never ever will be!' He retorted, 'Besides, we do not talk politics at Continental.' They never mentioned my wife. It was at the same time tense, cordial, and rather equivocal."[29]

In June 1942, Rim crossed the demarcation line for the first time when he visited the set at the Billancourt studios. He was looking for a way to obtain a letter of transit for Alice's son without arousing suspicion toward the child's father. He knew that through Continental he could get the precious document. But he also had to be very careful with the German managers. Lady Luck was in a good mood; he met a company employee who seemed to him "like a Montparnasse lady, rather interesting." He told her, "I don't know what will happen; you might put me in jail. But you seem sympathetic to me." She replied, "We'll try to sort something out."[30] She was called Mrs. Goertik and was of Russian origin.[31] Rim was then not aware that she had already helped

Pressbook cover for *Simplet* (1942) (Fondation Jérôme Seydoux-Pathé)

several people in a hurry to leave the occupied zone for the free one. She gave him the required visa, and he was able to take the child with him to Cassis, passing him off as his own son. His benefactress was fired from the company shortly afterward. Greven therefore never knew about this service rendered.

Relationships between Rim and Continental became stormy shortly before *Simplet*'s release in September 1942. Rim discovered on the film poster and credits that he had to share the script credit with Jean Manse, Fernandel's brother-in-law, who wrote the lyrics. "Before the war, I could have asked for the posters to be redone or sent some stamped paper. I tell Continental, 'I want the posters to be redone.' They reply, 'You don't think we are going to redo the posters for a small error!' I retort, 'I consider it very serious.' They promised they would apply stickers; they didn't do it."[32] In addition, a number of sequences were cut by order of the management without anyone being able to intervene.

Rim kept speaking his own mind while writing film reviews for the *Dimanche illustré*, published in Marseille during the occupation. He has no qualms about expressing his condemnation of several Continental productions, including *Simplet*. He even went further in refusing the advertising Continental offered to pay for in his newspaper. Greven asked him why, and he replied, "Because I do not accept paid advertising, and in particular not from Continental because I want to be able to say precisely what I think of Continental films although I work with you."[33]

Despite Rim's evident unwillingness, Greven still insisted that he work for the company again. Rim tried to invoke various pretexts like a lack of ideas, the fact he lived in Cassis far away from Paris, and that he wanted to stop working for cinema. But Greven stuck to his guns; he wanted him to sign an exclusive contract with Continental. Rim rushed to Pathé to establish a fictitious contract for the year 1943. Bauermeister smelled the rat and asked Rim to provide two more scripts. The screenwriter then decided to pass on to the company two synopses he had registered years ago at the Society of Authors that had been refused everywhere. The first one was called *Le Val d'enfer* (1943).

Continental decided to put *Le Val d'enfer* into production in October 1942. The firm had just hired Michel Simon, who was back in Paris after having spent three years making films in Italy. The company seized the opportunity to organize a celebration in honor of the great actor in a Parisian hotel with Bauermeister. In the pictures published by the press, we can see a laughing Michel Simon besides Albert Préjean, Noël Roquevert, and film critic Lucien Rebatet. The director of *Le Val d'enfer* was also present. Maurice Tourneur had been working for Continental since its creation. Sitting in front of Carlo Rim, he looked worried, and he was still wearing his overcoat and gloves. In spite of the presence of the laughing Swiss actor, he looked gloomy. As for Rim, he knew the inconvenience he was going to experience would be the same as with the previous film.

Just as the shooting was about to begin in Port Miou in Cassis, one of the calanques close to Marseille, the German army invaded the free zone without warning on November 11, 1942. The shooting was suspended. Carlo Rim decided to leave Cassis as soon as possible to protect his family. They left for Barcelonnette, in the French Alps, which was occupied by the Italian army and therefore seemed less dangerous. Once there, Rim joined the maquis and created a clandestine newspaper titled *Ça ira* (a reference to the Revolutionary song). He would never go back to visit Continental sets in Paris.

The end of the demarcation line marked also the end of shooting in the south of France. Henceforth, most films, including *Le Val d'enfer*, would be shot in studios or on location in the Paris region.

CHAPTER 14

New Directors

Hired as screenwriter-dialogue writer in December 1940, Henri-Georges Clouzot was quickly tempted by film directing after observing the work of Georges Lacombe and Henri Decoin on *Le Dernier des six* and *Les Inconnus dans la maison*. As head of the script department, he already had important responsibilities within the firm, and there was no doubt he enjoyed a privileged relationship with Alfred Greven.

Politically speaking, Clouzot was not a collaborator in the sense that he did not belong to any collaborationist party. But he acknowledged that "in National Socialism, there are things that touch me—I won't deny it—the social aspect. I am above all an anticapitalist. . . . I found something in the social concerns of the Germans that touched me. This is perhaps a solution than can combat capitalism."[1] This statement shows a shameful political blindness. Yet he decided to hire only qualified screenwriters and didn't hesitate to reject proposals steeped in collaborationist propaganda offered by writers such as Jean d'Argrève. He told them, "I am really sorry. Whether you are a collaborator or not, this does not prove that you are able to produce a good movie or a script. I will look at it the same way."[2]

Clouzot hired several people to help him in his department. Ironically, their political views were very different from his and were even more so from those of the Germans. Claude Vermorel became a script reader in September 1941. Clouzot was aware that he embraced communist ideas but was not aware of his activities as Resistance fighter. Vermorel's work at Continental was not that critical, but he did infiltrate the enemy firm, forming Resistance groups among studio technicians. In charge of finding subjects for movies, he pushed aside adaptations of two Honoré de Balzac novels, *Le Père Goriot* and *Le Colonel Chabert*, which according to him had no place in a German company. He worked on an adaptation of the Maurice Yvain operetta *Yes*, which he personally supervised. But, in the end, his adaptation was not used and would instead be produced under the title *Défense d'aimer* (1942), directed by Richard Pottier after Vermorel had left the company. His main contribution was helping Clouzot with a few scenes of *L'Assassin habite au 21* (1942), which happened to be the first film Clouzot directed.

Vermorel offered the following explanation of Greven and Clouzot's close friendship: "It's rather a tendency for Clouzot that fits with his nature. He is always—I think—at the service of the person who he works for. . . . Clouzot's fault is this: he didn't think a German boss was different from other bosses."[3] Clouzet and Greven often dined together with their respective girlfriends.[4] The director's attitude reflected the contradictions of that ambiguous period. He gladly had supper with his German boss while at the same time hiding a friend hounded by the Gestapo in his own apartment.

In a letter to Georges Simenon, Clouzot explained why he didn't manage to convince Greven to adapt *Le Voyageur de la Toussaint*, which could have been his first film as director: Continental liked the atmosphere of the book and its plot, Clouzot noted, but "unfortunately, Mr. Greven judged it would be difficult to get the public to swallow such harsh criticism of middle-class society, after the already brutal stance we took with *Les Inconnus dans la maison*. If *Le Voyageur de la Toussaint* were to be accepted by audiences and censors, we would have had to adapt it to the point of distorting it. And you know that if that's the practice at some firms, neither Mr. Greven nor me wish to establish such policies at Continental, especially when we like the novelist's talent as we like yours."[5] This letter reveals Clouzot's important position inside Continental: he had the boss's ear. But it also exposes striking contradictions. He claimed Simenon's novel was rejected because the company worried about it being censored. And yet Continental Films didn't have to go through Vichy censors. And ultimately, Louis Daquin would direct an adaptation of the novel in 1943 for a French production company that was subject to Vichy censorship. Furthermore, Clouzot would soon shoot an even more violent movie than Simenon's novel: *Le Corbeau* (1943). It is therefore questionable whether Clouzot was really sincere in his explanation to the novelist.

In the end, Clouzot's first film as director was an adaptation of Stanislas-André Steeman's novel starring Suzy Delair and Pierre Fresnay playing Mila Malou and Inspector Wens. Clouzot was given only twenty-one days to make *L'Assassin habite au 21*. He was in the same boat as the other directors regarding the number of takes allowed by the management: only two. If he took a third one, then he would be summoned by Greven for an explanation. The work

Ad for *L'Assassin habite au 21* (1942) (Fondation Jérôme Seydoux-Pathé)

schedule therefore had to be perfectly organized to meet such a tight deadline. The shooting started on May 4, 1942, at the Billancourt studios.

From the start, Clouzot showed incredible professionalism and technical virtuosity. Actor Pierre Fresnay remembered how quickly his director moved from one shot to the other: "As soon as the shot was over, Clouzot said, 'Cut! The scene is over, it's good. Print it. Put the camera here!' He never hesitated. He was ready with his angle. Absolutely ready. Nearly all the people who work well know exactly where they are going, but to such a degree . . . And he was never wrong!"[6] Clouzot also showed his tetchy character in his treatment of his companion Suzy Delair on the set. Pierre Fresnay felt uneasy when he saw him violently slapping the actress.

In *L'Assassin habite au 21*, Clouzot used the cream of French cinema character actors, including Pierre Larquey, Noël Roquevert, Jean Tissier, and André Gabriello. They had all participated in several other Continental productions, but in that film, they found parts that fitted them like a glove, thanks to Clouzot's juicy dialogue.

Among these actors, Gabriello was the only one with an exclusive Continental contract; he participated in twelve films. His career was a distillation of the ambiguities and contradictions in the entertainment world during the occupation. Famous as a cabaret artist in Paris, his name was removed from the playbill in October 1940 when a small group of Nazi sympathizers, the Young Front, threatened to break the windows and throw stink bombs in the music hall where he was playing because he was a Freemason. The Germans, wishing to avoid the scandal, decided to ban him from the stage. Left with no other alternative, Gabriello went to see the Young Front: "I had, aged forty-four, to go to ask some eighteen-year-old hoodlums for permission to feed my family, and I had to give them a pledge stating I would never again be a mason."[7]

In June 1941, he joined a Gaullist Resistance movement lead by one of his friends. At the end of March 1942, he was asked to go on a tour in Germany to entertain French prisoners and workers. When he declined this request, he was told that his work permit would be revoked. Therefore, he agreed under duress to make the trip. On his return, the collaborationist press put pro-German comments into his mouth that made him look like a zealous collaborator in the public eye. After having small roles in six Continental films, the firm offered him an exclusive contract in autumn 1942. He signed a one-year contract with an option for the following year. He then got larger parts.

At the same time he was making movies, Gabriello was also still working as cabaret artist. He was particularly criticized for this activity after the liberation, especially for telling stories in German. He explained that "most of the artists who worked in nightclubs, circuses, or in the provinces in theaters and music halls were told by their directors or tour managers to sing in half French half German" but acknowledged that that was no excuse, adding that "if I told harmless traveling salesman-type stories in front of the Germans, it's because I was without a red cent and because the French had—especially in 1940—to leave at 11 p.m. so they wouldn't miss the last subway train or to avoid being arrested by a patrol. To keep one's job, you had to make the customers laugh."[8] Alfred Greven sometimes came to see him in the cabaret where he played and would bring him home in his car after the show.

In spite of this seemingly pro-German posture, his name was constantly dragged through the mud by the collaborationist press, which criticized his Freemason membership. He was also denounced as a Jew, and the police came to search his home. And yet his colleagues at Continental did not understand his humor. Assistant director Jean Devaivre remembered a funny story he told on the set of *Cécile est morte!* (1944) about how the unknown soldier under the Arc de Triomphe might be German. In the presence of Greven, his Continental colleagues expressed their general disapproval of him. Devaivre probably never suspected that Gabriello was a member of the Resistance like him.

L'Assassin habite au 21 was a resounding success in cinemas when it came out in August 1942, and Clouzot was praised in the press for his excellent direction. "His first work is a perfect success! It's true that, even as a beginner in directing, Georges Clouzot is yet an old hand in filmmaking. He has been, in turn, screenwriter, dialogue writer, adapter; the author of *L'Assassin habite au 21* knows the cinema inside out. This experience allows him to tackle film directing with all the resources needed. And in the difficult genre of the detective film, his first try is a masterstroke!"[9]

You might think that Continental was the only one offering opportunities to young talent. In fact, a number of young filmmakers got their start during the occupation period. French cinema didn't have to compete anymore with American productions, and many great French filmmakers had left France. To escape antisemitic persecutions, Max Ophüls and Léonide Moguy had gone to Hollywood, while Pierre Chenal left for Argentina, where he carried on with his brilliant career. Jean Renoir, René Clair, and Julien Duvivier also had left for Hollywood. Producers were therefore inclined to offer new talent the opportunity to direct feature films. It was in these circumstances that Jacques Becker came to direct *Dernier Atout* (1942), Louis Daquin *Nous, les gosses* (1941),

Robert Bresson *Les Anges du péché* (1943), André Zwobada *Croisières sidérales* (1942), and Gilles Grangier *Adémaï bandit d'honneur* (1943). Claude Autant-Lara also saw his career flourish with a succession of small masterpieces such as *Le Mariage de Chiffon* (1942), *Lettres d'amour* (1942), and *Douce* (1943), with actress Odette Joyeux in the lead.

Some film people enthused about a so-called golden age of cinema during the occupation, but they were overlooking the miserable lot of their colleagues excluded from the film industry by antisemitic laws. Filmmaker Raymond Bernard, writer Tristan Bernard's son, is a case in point. Bernard was at the peak of his career at the end of the 1930s after the incredible success of his version of *Les Misérables* (1934), but he had to try to survive in the south of France before being forced to hide with the maquis to escape certain arrest. He thought about going to America but gave up the idea because he didn't want to leave his elderly parents alone. Numerous screenwriters were also victims of this iniquitous system, like Jacques Companeez. As for screenwriter Léopold Marchand, his Jewish wife, Misz Hertz—a friend of Colette—committed suicide in 1942 shortly before the Vel' d'Hiv' roundup.[10]

At the same time as Clouzot, another young screenwriter became a Continental director. André Cayatte began shooting his first film on May 1, 1942. Titled *La Fausse maîtresse*, it offered Danielle Darrieux the lead in a modern adaptation of a Honoré de Balzac short story. Politically, Cayatte was Clouzot's opposite; he was a fervent patriot and Resistance fighter. But this didn't prevent him from working for a German company, albeit under very specific circumstances. Before the war, when he was a journalist, he had published anti-German books after joining the International Brigades during the Spanish Civil War. At the outbreak of war in 1939, he was mobilized on the Maginot Line.

I fought from the first day until the last on the Maginot Line as soldier, corporal, staff sergeant, sergeant, chief master sergeant, senior officer cadet in the colonial infantry. I have two Croix de Guerre, one from the beginning and one from the end. And I was taken prisoner. At the moment when everybody thought it was over and rejoiced to be a prisoner, at that time, I had only one desire, to get the hell out of here. I tore all my papers, all my identity cards very carefully. Finally, one day, I manage to escape. . . . I ended up in Paris, without any identity card, with eight hundred francs, and a wife who on October 3 [1940] had just given birth to a child. A wife, a child, eight hundred francs, without any form of identification, not even enough to get a ration card . . . It was not fun![11]

His situation was particularly dangerous, and he had very little chance of getting a job with any French employer. Luckily, by accident he happened to meet Aimé Chemel, Continental's first production manager. "On the Champs-Élysées, I met somebody I had worked with before the war, [Charles] Méré with Chemel. Chemel asked me, 'Are you doing anything?' I said nothing." Cayatte subsequently had another conversation with Chemel, who told him:

> "I see you are in trouble; that's clear. You can work in the firm I am involved with right now." And he tells me how Continental works. . . . "The aim is to produce French films using French technicians, without any propaganda intervening, as you'll be spiritually free in the conception of yours works." And he quotes me the names of the people already hired—which constitutes an important reference—Carné, Christian-Jaque, Lacombe, Tourneur, etc., as actors, Harry Baur, and people like that. He saw I was hesitating. I wasn't a good catch because my opinions were obvious, as I had joined the International Brigades in Spain. . . . I had a very clear opinion regarding Germany. After listening to all that, I told Chemel, "That's still worrisome." He replied, "No! Besides, it's one of the conditions of French cinema resuming; there will either be Continental or nothing at all."[12]

Meeting Chemel for a third time, Cayatte confessed to him that he had no identity papers and noted that he wouldn't be able to get a work permit without them. "I must say Chemel was very kind. I didn't know Chemel until then. I have great gratitude for him; he was incredibly classy. He told me: 'I am too happy to help somebody in your situation. . . . Leave it to me; I will arrange to get identity papers so you can get a contract at Continental.'"[13]

Cayatte got all the necessary documents and was finally hired in January 1941. They asked him to work on the script of Fernandel's first film, *Le Club des soupirants*. But the work he ended up doing was rejected, and they decided they would hire Jean Manse, Fernandel's brother-in-law and a lyricist, instead. During these first few months, Cayatte never got to meet either Greven or Bauermeister. But sometime in March or April 1941, he was suddenly called up to Greven's office. He knew what was coming. "On his desk, Greven had several cuttings, papers, and letters." Greven said to him, "It seems you are an escaped prisoner. I received two anonymous letters." They were two possible alternatives: say yes or say no. I said yes, as it would be very easy to check it. It wasn't difficult; you just had to trace the origin of my identity card. It stopped there. He said, 'Well.'"[14]

Cayatte painted a striking portrait of Continental's big boss with all his contradictions and his moodiness. "I must say he was a curious character, a rather extravagant human animal—he had been trepanned—deceptive, kicking the table with his foot while at the same time having a big laugh, and always on edge, always on the verge of threatening."[15] In his situation, Cayatte had no option but to lay low and work without being noticed. Greven called him again a few months later and was even more threatening than the first time. But nothing happened afterward.

Cayatte worked as Dréville's assistant director on *Annette et la dame blonde* (1941), which demonstrated his versatility. He also allowed himself to be credited as screenwriter for *Caprices* (1942), directed by Léo Joannon, as a service to a Jewish colleague, without being aware of the way the director had acquired the script from Jacques Companeez and Raymond Bernard.

He got the opportunity to become a director in May 1942 with *La Fausse maîtresse* (1942), a modern adaptation of a Balzac short story in which he directed Danielle Darrieux. The film was shot on location in Perpignan and completed at the Billancourt studios. Nevertheless, Cayatte wanted to leave Continental. He encountered other producers in Paris who offered him projects, such as Édouard Harispuru, which made him want to get out.

> I had only one desire, to leave and get the hell out of here. . . . At that point, my contract had expired, and Greven was not in France. He was, I don't know where, in Portugal or elsewhere. When he wasn't there, the firm drifted. With him, it was dictatorship on a grand scale. Greven away, nobody took any initiative. We could take the opportunity to do whatever we wanted. I took opportunity to leave. At that time, I was going to make *Farandoles* for Harispuru. We put the film together; we hire technicians; I choose the script myself, the actors, and exactly eleven or twelve days before the start of the shooting, Greven comes back, learns about it, and calls me. A dreadful session during which he tells me, "It's quite simple: you cannot get the hell out of here like that! You cannot go. I'll have you sent to a camp!" A terrifying session, . . . so bad that I said, 'Well, I stay.'"[16]

Although he had to stay at Continental under duress, Cayatte nevertheless made two of his best films for the company with *Pierre et Jean* (1943), a superb adaptation of a Guy de Maupassant short story, and *Le Dernier sou* (1944), a crooks' story with a shady atmosphere close to the film noir genre.

If Continental allowed young directors to get a start, it was also the scene of shady maneuvers from an established filmmaker.

Ad for *La Fausse maîtresse* (1942) (Fondation Jérôme Seydoux-Pathé)

CHAPTER 15

The *Caprices* Affair

When he joined Continental in October 1940, Léo Joannon had the reputation of a successful comedy director with such films as *Quelle drôle de gosse!* (1935) starring Albert Préjean and Danielle Darrieux. Unlike his other colleagues, he had no script to propose to the firm management. However, he knew of an interesting project the Majestic Film company—with which he had worked just before the occupation—has been planning.

Screenwriter Jacques Companeez had sold the company an original script titled *Princesse de Réveillon* in 1939. Joannon thought at one time he was going to direct it. But the Majestic managers had decided to give it to Raymond Bernard, following Joannon's decision to volunteer in the navy.[1] Raymond Bernard, a respected director known for his talent and kindness, had done the shooting script with Companeez, while his brother Jean-Jacques Bernard took care of the dialogue for the project, now retitled *Caprices*. Majestic Film hired Belgian actor Fernand Gravey and French actress Edwige Feuillère for the two lead roles. The sets had already been erected in the studio when, on May 14, 1940, the company decided to postpone the shooting following the sudden German offensive in the north of France. Because several studios went on working until the beginning of June, including Neuilly, where Jean Grémillon finished the shooting of *Remorques* (1941) on May 28 and the editing on June 3, and Billancourt, until its studios were bombed on June 3, Majestic Film's decision not to start the film production appears deliberate.[2]

Of course, Joannon thought immediately of that ready-to-shoot script and suggested Continental Films acquire it from Majestic. He was aware that Raymond Bernard, his brother, and Companeez could no longer work following the passage of new antisemitic laws. However, he had to sort out the problem of the film rights. On October 8, 1940, Joannon, who was the lucky owner of a pass allowing him to go to the free zone, went to Juan-les-Pins, where Companeez

Ad for *Caprices* (1942) (Fondation Jérôme Seydoux-Pathé)

was living. Joannon explained to Companeez that it would be impossible to list his name in the film credits; Companeez was in a weak position, and he agreed to sign a letter transferring the rights of the original subject. Joannon therefore became the author. Joannon didn't hesitate to illegally use blank sheets of paper signed by Companeez for Majestic Film before the exodus in order to validate Companeez's ceding of the rights. Majestic Film seemed to want to get rid of this project that could not be filmed by its authors, as they were not allowed to work as Jews. The company used Joannon as its middleman, which was possible thanks to his pass, a rare commodity in those days.

However, the letter ceding the rights signed by Companeez had a provision that would render the agreement null and void in the case that Majestic couldn't produce the film or sell the rights to a new firm before December 31, 1940. And yet Majestic sold the project to Continental Films on January 8, 1941, eight days after the expiration date of the agreement.

On January 28, 1941, Joannon again visited Companeez in Juan-les-Pins and confessed that Majestic had sold the rights of *Caprices* after the expiration date of the agreement. Joannon begged him for help: "He was insistent that I agree to extending the October 8 agreement, telling me that if Continental Films (a German company) knew the offense he committed—the fraudulent blank endorsement—he would be immediately imprisoned."[3] Companeez gave him an extension until March 1, 1941, on a piece of paper backdated to December 23, 1940, to allow him to escape being prosecuted by Continental. The option expired again, however, as Continental still hadn't put *Caprices* into production by March 1941, and moreover, Companeez had not received payment for the purchase.

Joannon made a serious mistake in forgetting that Raymond Bernard still owned rights in the film, as he had deposited the screenplay and shooting script written with Jacques Companeez and Jean-Jacques Bernard at the Society of Authors. And Bernard didn't hesitate to call Aimé Chemel, the production manager of Continental Films, to tell him that his company had acquired the rights of a film from a firm that didn't own them. The fact the script had been deposited meant that Raymond Bernard and his coauthors owned a portion of the film rights. Léo Joannon was terrified when he learned about that phone call.

He made another visit to Cannes to meet with Raymond Bernard and Companeez. He started to cry: "I have a child. I have a wife. You mustn't . . ."[4] Companeez recalled how they both agreed to help him, recounting that Bernard "was touched" and so they "gave up again." Bernard gave "Joannon a letter freeing him, meaning he gave him a chance with Continental."[5] Joannon's attitude changed suddenly after he got the required document. He pulled himself together and said, "Now, from a completely impartial standpoint, I'll see what I can do," by which he was referring to what he could do to ensure Companeez and Bernard got paid.[6]

During the last meeting between Companeez and Joannon in Nice on March 11, 1941, the discussion turned sour. Companeez had sold his share of the rights to Bernard on March 4. Joannon became threatening when Companeez refused to help him. Companeez wrote to Bernard that it was then that Joannon "stopped begging me to save him from prison" and told him that he had to rescind the sale of the rights to Bernard and "sign papers prepared in Paris to clear him of the multiple and serious frauds he had committed." Companeez noted that Joannon said that "despite the friendship he had showed me so far, he would not hesitate at all to use all the means that his special situation with the occupying authorities put at his disposal to protect himself. He reminded me insistently that I as well as my family was Jewish, which, in this instance, certainly made us vulnerable."[7] In order to protect his wife and two young daughters, Companeez signed the documents. What's more, Joannon promised him a payment he would never receive. Just before Joannon left, Companeez told him, "I think, Léo, you took the wrong path." Joannon replied, self-confident, "Not at all! You know, I have always been an antisemite. Now we are not doing anything. But wait a bit! Once the Germans have gone, then, we will make a clean sweep of all the Jews."[8]

On March 14, Joannon went back to see Raymond Bernard; he threatened him just as he had threatened Companeez. "Using the influence that you'll see I have with the Germans, I will get your two brothers arrested, Jean-Jacques Bernard, who was vice president of the Society for Authors, and Professor Étienne Bernard, head of the department at Tenon hospital." Raymond replied that his brothers were not in hiding and their situation was in perfect order. Joannon retorted that that was "not important. They'll find at their homes Gaullist pamphlets. These pamphlets are ready."[9] He even added that he wanted to burn the "pernicious works" of his father, Tristan Bernard. However, despite these threats, Bernard did not back down. He decided not to give up. He knew the law was on his side.

On April 30, 1941, he sued Majestic Film for illegally selling a film it didn't own. It showed real courage for a Jewish filmmaker to bring a lawsuit during the occupation. It was only on May 15, 1944, that the Paris Industrial Tribunal would render a judgment in favor of Raymond Bernard, who at that time was hiding with the Vercors maquis. He was right to refuse to compromise, as he won his lawsuit. Majestic Film was required to restore the rights in the film to him and to pay him a salary still owed as well as damages.

Joannon considered himself the first director selected to make *Caprices* before Majestic decided to give it to Raymond Bernard. He thought he was legitimately the owner of the film bought by Continental. He didn't recognize Raymond Bernard's rights in it. In October 1940, following the promulgation of the first antisemitic laws, Joannon had proposed a motion in favor of his colleagues who had been forbidden to work, in particular Raymond Bernard and Jean-Benoît Lévy, so that they could get an exception to allow them to work. Following this motion, he met Bernard in Cannes, who took him in his arms to thank him. He told him he had no intention of accepting an exception to work as a director. Joannon took this statement to be a renunciation of the *Caprices* project. Having learned about the illegal transactions regarding the film, Bernard called Aimé Chemel to warn him. Joannon was furious and terrified of the consequences. He admitted he had a fiery conversation with his colleague but denied making threats.

Joannon's fears were for nothing, as it turned out, for Continental Films simply ended up disregarding the rights problem and putting *Caprices* into production in June 1941. Joannon asked André Cayatte to help him prepare a new shooting script and new dialogue without telling him the full story. Cayatte thought he was acting as a front man, helping a colleague who could not work, and Joannon never told him about Raymond Bernard. Unfortunately, Greven hated this new version of the script. Joannon remembered that "after reading the German translation of the new manuscript, Alfred Greven got into a rage and told me that manuscript was worthless and he wanted me to go back to the original manuscript. I refused. After much discussion, I went back to it in part."[10] In the end, the film directed by Joannon used much of Raymond Bernard's work.

The purchase of *Caprices* by Continental had also serious consequences for the two actors originally selected for the leads. Edwige Feuillère learned when she returned to Paris in November 1940 that Continental had acquired the contract she had signed in April 1940 with Majestic Film. Because of the exceptional circumstances, she had agreed to a salary that was substantially lower (50 percent less) than what she was used to. Continental was therefore getting a very good deal in fetching a screen star at bargain prices. During the winter of 1940–41, the firm kept asking her to fulfill her contract. She managed to play for time, using as an excuse the fact that she was performing in *La Dame aux camélias*. Unfortunately, the show closed on April 15, 1941. On April 30, she was summoned by Alfred Greven. He told her the shooting of *Caprices* was scheduled to start in eight days. Feuillère told him she would not make the film because she disliked the script. Greven replied that if she already agreed to make the film for a partially Jewish firm, she could now very well do it for a German company. Feuillère continued to demur. The manager of Continental moved on to threats: "He used the well-known arguments: a prohibition against working, arrest, and ends up predicting a career for me among prisoners in a camp."[11] In the end, a few days later, she learned that the company had decided to give the part she refused to Danielle Darrieux. However, her problems were not over; she would still have to make a film for Continental, *Mam'zelle Bonaparte* (1942), under the direction of Maurice Tourneur.

As for Fernand Gravey, the male lead, he clashed with Joannon from the start. The director came to meet him in his dressing room at the Ambassadeurs Theater in November 1940 and told him he would like to put a different actor in the lead role. Gravey flew off the handle and replied he didn't see why he should have to withdraw from a project with Majestic Film. Joannon told him to think about it and came back a few days later, telling him that if the Germans produced the film, he would have to bow to them. "Might is right." One of the Majestic managers, Roger de Van Loo, also phoned Gravey several times to ask him to withdraw. Realizing he was fighting a losing battle, Gravey agreed to terminate his contract, forfeiting 50,000 francs as a result. Joannon had won.

In May 1941, with Danielle Darrieux now in the lead role, Joannon wanted to hire Claude Dauphin in order to re-create the starring couple of *Battement de cœur* (1940). He met him in Nice and tried to convince him to join Continental. Dauphin was reluctant, but as at that time he was trying to help his brother, the playwright Jean Franc-Nohain, get authorization to stage his play *Bonjour la France*. He stated he would work for Continental for free if he could get the authorization. At first, Greven agreed. But when he was given a German translation of Dauphin's letter, he blew a fuse, thinking the actor was going over the top with his demands, and told Joannon to find somebody else.

In the end, Continental hired Albert Préjean without even consulting Joannon, who thought he wasn't good enough for the part. It was, however, a wise choice, as he had made six films with Darrieux between 1934 and 1935; they had been a sparkling couple in such comedies as Robert Siodmak's *La Crise est finie* (1934).

The shooting started at the Billancourt studios on June 30, 1941. As soon as the film was finished in August 1941, Continental took over the editing. A new editor was appointed to modify the original edit, and the music was recorded without the director's knowledge. Joannon realized he had lost control of his film. Though he had signed a contract for four films, he left Continental after the first one. He even bought back the rights of *Le Camion blanc* (1943), which would have been his next film and which would end up being made by a different film company.

This sad affair shows how a man, one whom Jacques Companeez had considered a friend, could suddenly become disreputable. This metamorphosis happened, of course, during a troubled period when Vichy's antisemitic laws had left many vulnerable to all kinds of pressure. The collaborationist press contributed to the general moral decay, causing many people to lose their moorings with respect to right and wrong. In the end, Joannon's compromises at Continental didn't bring him much profit, jut a single film over which he lost control.

After the war, Raymond Bernard started proceedings against Léo Joannon, but the matter was closed owing to lack of sufficient charges in January 1946. However, the director's reputation was now tarnished. Journalist Henri Jeanson—under the pseudonym Huguette Ex-Micro—used vitriolic humor to castigate him in a column for *Le Canard Enchaîné* in October 1944: "Mr. Joannon makes a caprice or the Hun's fly."[12] Yet he was too hasty in suggesting that Joannon was directly responsible for the arrest of Jean-Jacques Bernard, Raymond's brother. Even Jean-Jacques Bernard himself thought his arrest, several months later, was unrelated to this miserable *Caprices* affair. Joannon received a severe sanction from the purge committee: he was forbidden to occupy a managerial post in the profession and he was not allowed to join a board of directors. This sanction was extended until October 20, 1948.

It was about time that the true authors of the scripts were credited in the film titles. Jacques Companeez remembered the suffering he and his family endured during the occupation. "I was in a terrible situation during those last years in Nice. I was hiding, I had no money at all. My family was scattered all around France."[13] One of his two small daughters, hidden by farmers, would become a filmmaker. Nina Companeez wrote and directed *Voici venir l'orage* . . . (2008) for French television, in which she tells the story of her Russian family who first took refuge in Germany and later in France.

Ironically, *Caprices* was the French film that Goebbels appreciated the most among Continental Films productions. After he watched it on May 12, 1942, he wrote, "It's one of the rare French films that meets our criteria for quality. It's amusing to observe that the Germans had to go to Paris to give a face to French cinema."[14] One wonders what his reaction would have been if he had known that the script and dialogue were the work of a Jewish screenwriter and a Jewish filmmaker. In any case, it's one of the few Continental films that was released in Germany, opening on August 7, 1942, under the title *Einmal im Jahr*.

CHAPTER 16

Richard Pottier

Richard Deutsch, known as Pottier, was born in Graz, Austria, on June 6, 1906. He was certainly one most of the most engaging personalities among the men and women working at Continental. Pottier left his native country in 1934, as he was against the Nazis from the start, and he obtained French citizenship in 1937. Because French producers thought his surname was too German, he gallicized it, adopting his wife's maiden name. He recalled his time in the French Army during the war as a private: "I was mobilized in 1939 at the 280th Infantry Regiment in Auxerre. I fought like everybody else. And I was taken prisoner with my company on June 21, 1940, in Tours. I was injured. Part of my jaw was blown away, and my hand was injured. I was freed by the Franco-German health service at Villemin hospital in February 7, 1941. My discharge took place in front of two majors, one French and one German."[1]

Back in Paris, he took the necessary steps to obtain a work permit in the French film industry. After he had gathered up the necessary paperwork, however, Raoul Ploquin, head Organizing Committee of the Cinema Industry, refused to give him the permit. Eventually, he was able to procure one from Dr. Paulheinz Diedrich of the Propaganda Office. Diedrich had

summoned me and I spent three quarters of an hour being questioned, standing in his office, asked to answer the following questions. Why did you get naturalized? Why did you change your name? (Because I'm called Deutsch) When did you get naturalized? When did you leave Austria? (or rather, as I had said Austria, he said Germany). I gave him all the information and finally, he asked, "Are you Jewish? Come back in three weeks." Indeed, three weeks later, I was summoned again. He said, "Your information has been verified, and I have a proposal to make. You are a former Austrian; your father and mother are in Austria. You now have the best chance of being reinstated in your former nationality."

I answered, "Mr. Doctor, it's not what I'm asking for, but a work permit." "Why?" "I have my reasons. First of all, I married a French woman; I have a French child. I owe my career as director to France. I was mobilized and I fought for France. I was a French prisoner of war." "Is that all you have to say?" Then, he threw my card, which landed at the other of end of his large office. I picked it up. "However, before you sign any contract for a film," he told me, "I'd like to be warned." "Why?" I answered. "Do you understand?" "Yes."[2]

The unfortunate Pottier's troubles were not over. The Nazi authorities were furious with him and considered him a traitor to his former country, while the French, for their part, did not show the kind of gratitude one might expect toward a man who had risked his life to protect his new country. After getting his work permit, he went to see producers. The first one he spoke with was Raymond Borderie, whom he had made a film for that the Germans banned.[3] Pottier recalled that

> he was very nice and told me, "I'm going to give you a film; you need to work." Then, the second time he called me, he said, "When I mentioned your name to Ploquin"—then, all producers had to go through Ploquin—"he remarked it's better to give work to a Frenchman." I don't know if you understand what that can do to a man who became French by choice and was wounded for France. I had tears in my eyes, and I said, "It's not possible he told you such a thing!" And I understood that Mr. Borderie was afraid to hire me, of inviting trouble. I suppose Ploquin mentioned the problems I had with Diedrich and told producers, "Beware, you could have problems."[4]

Through Charles Robert-Dumas, the author whose novel he adapted in his film *Le Monde tremblera* (1939), Pottier was introduced to Oberleutnant Kögl, who was also of Austrian origin.[5] Kögl reassured Pottier and told him that he might be able to sort things out with Diedrich: "Don't worry. The fuss with Diedrich is going to die down, he is arrogant, etc."[6] In addition, he gave Pottier a letter of recommendation for Continental addressed to Greven.[7] But this letter would be of no use. Pottier would learn later that Greven was on very bad terms with Kögl.

After an eight-month struggle, he finally managed to make a musical, *Mademoiselle Swing* (1942), for a French production company, the Société Universelle de Films. But the fact that the title made reference to an American style of music was not well received by Dr. Diedrich, and he banned the film, although he had approved the script before the shooting. Thanks to Kögl, though, Pottier managed to get the film released.

In the summer of 1942, a new law was promulgated regarding liberated prisoners. Pottier had to have a second medical examination to ascertain his fitness to work. He went to the Continental Hotel, where the prisoners' office was. He was told, "Your injury doesn't prevent you from talking; you can lift weights with your hand. What else do you need? You are fit."[8] Pottier knew what it meant. "From this moment, here is what I had to expect: either go back to a prisoner of war camp, or work in Germany, or work for the Todt Organization," building the Atlantic Wall.[9]

It just so happened that Jean-Paul Dreyfus, known as Le Chanois, who worked at Continental as screenwriter, mentioned Pottier's name to the company managers. Pottier was summoned to 104 Champs-Élysées and offered the opportunity to direct an adaptation of Georges Simenon's novel *Signé Picpus*, one in his Inspector Maigret series. He knew he had a choice between working as a prisoner or making films. Pottier chose Continental to stay close to his wife and child.

However, the firm had a little surprise for him. His contract didn't mention the title of the film, and in the end, he was told to take over the direction of a musical, *Défense d'aimer* (1942), with Paul Meurisse and Suzy Delair. The film had been started by Pierre Colombier, but he was sacked eight days into the shooting. He had just spent eight months recovering from a femur fracture, and though he managed to stand up with the help of camphor injections, he had many problems with the temperamental Suzy Delair, who refused to do what he asked her and threatened to call Greven on the phone. So the management decided he was not the right person for the job.

Pottier, unlike Colombier, immediately made the recalcitrant new star understand she had to behave, and he did so in Clouzot's presence.

> Before lunchtime, she made remarks to the continuity girl. I told myself: that's the right moment to tell her off. Then, turning to her, I said, "The continuity girl is here to make suggestions, and I forbid you to criticize her." Then she said, "I'm going to call Greven." I answered her, "Then, let's go together." But she chickened out. Then, I called Greven, asking him, "Who is this little woman? Kick her out." And it's what I did. I told her, "Go to the phone, Greven will answer you." The matter ended there. But Clouzot had told me, "I'll be calling Continental myself." "It has nothing to do with [you]," I answered. "These are personal matters. She must learn her trade first."[10]

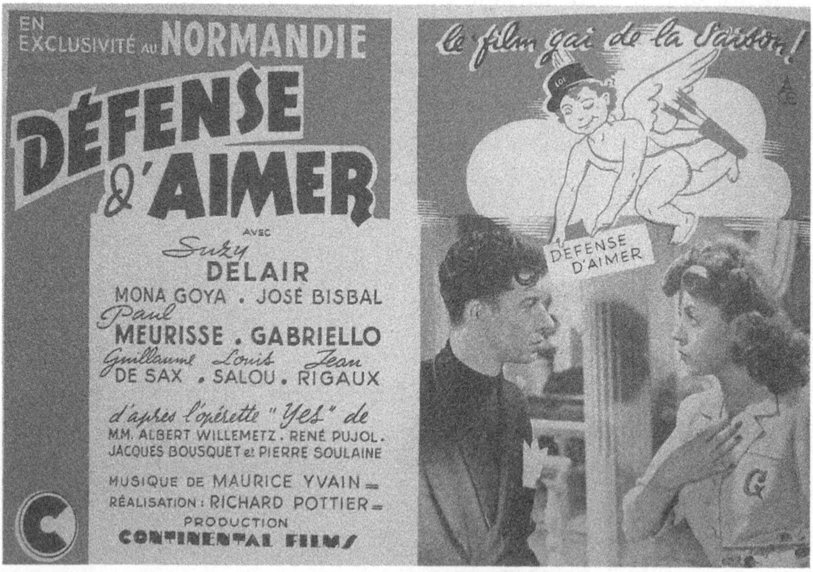

Ad for *Défense d'aimer* (1942) (Fondation Jérôme Seydoux-Pathé)

After this spat, Clouzot left him alone, and Suzy kept a low profile.

Défense d'aimer was an adaptation of *Yes*, an operetta by Albert Willemetz and Maurice Yvain that also starred Paul Meurisse, a young actor who had already appeared in two other Continental films.[11] Meurisse made his debut as crooner in cabarets and then was lucky enough to be hired by the Marigny Theater to perform in *Trois jeunes filles nues*, an Albert Willemetz and Yves Mirande operetta that opened in April 1941. After a successful run, he was summoned by Continental Films. After being showered with compliments, he was told straight out he had been selected to play an important part in *Ne bougez plus* (1941), a comedy directed by Pierre Caron. He tried to play for time, claiming he had a planned a recital tour around France. But that was a wasted effort, as eight days later, he was summoned again, and as if by magic, Greven showed him a file stating that his entire repertoire of songs had been censored by the German Propaganda Office. Meurisse concluded that "in this firm, they didn't use half measures!"[12] *Ne bougez plus* would turn out to be the worst turkey in the entire history of filmmaking, according to Meurisse. He then appeared in Decoin's last film at Continental, *Mariage d'amour*, which was botched by Greven. Meurisse hoped *Défense d'aimer* would be his last film with Continental.

On the set at the Neuilly studios, Pottier was under constant surveillance by the management. His stage manager, Jean Rossi, remembered how one morning, following the filmmaker's decision to retake a scene, he received a phone call. "I leave the set to go to the control room. Just as I was setting foot on the control room, I am told, 'Mr. Rossi, Mr. Bauermeister is calling you on the phone.' I said, 'Ah! Ah! What's the matter?' So [Bauermeister] said to me, 'You shot that yesterday evening. Why are you doing a retake this morning?' Pardon my French, but I said shit. I said, 'Do you have a television set in your office? I have just finished!'"[13] In this situation, Pottier managed to stay calm, while Rossi turned pale when he realized Bauermeister had arrived on the set, hot on his heels.

Pottier's second film was *Picpus*, which Pierre Colombier had hoped to direct at Continental before being fired. Colombier had sent several letters to Bauermeister to try to cajole the powerful production manager. In the end, bowing and scraping were no use at Continental. Those looking for a job were often unsuccessful. The pool of professional technicians was large enough that they did not need to hire the sycophants.

The novel was adapted by Jean-Paul Le Chanois, who had the difficult task of making Maigret look tailor made for Albert Préjean when nobody expected

Ad for *Picpus* (1943) (Fondation Jérôme Seydoux-Pathé)

the actor in the part. Georges Simenon was very pleased with Le Chanois's work and even wrote him a letter to thank him. Le Chanois was a Resistance fighter, and right from the very beginning, he had fun writing dialogue with double meaning. "I stuffed the dialogue with as many things as possible against the police without overstepping the permitted limits, but enough to mark the occasion. I had fun doing this: having a cat called Déa so that at one point I could say, 'Déa croaked.'" Marcel Déat was a notorious collaborator who was sentenced to the death penalty in absentia after the liberation. On the other hand, censors removed a scene in which a waiter brought a bottle of wine to a table and said, "1918 . . . A great vintage!"

Pottier lost control of *Picpus*, just as Decoin and Joannon lost control of their films during the editing stage. And yet he used his own money, 10,000 francs, to retake some scenes. The filmmaker lamented how the film had been "completely ruined by cuts made without my consent. I tried to leave because I thought, it's impossible to work like that. But there was another factor: when you left this firm, you were automatically declared available to the labor organization to work in Germany, whether you left it on good terms or bad terms. But you risked the worst if you left on bad terms."[14]

Pottier therefore stayed with the German firm until it stopped producing films in the spring of 1944. He made five films in total, just like Maurice Tourneur, who, like him, was in an uncomfortable position in relation to the German authorities because of his naturalization.

CHAPTER 17

Maurice Tourneur

Maurice Thomas, known as Tourneur, was born in Paris in 1876. But he migrated to the United States in May 1914 and became an American citizen in 1921.[1] The French authorities issued an expulsion order against him in 1924 for being a draft dodger in time of war. He came back to France in 1926, managing provisionally to escape expulsion. Violently attacked in the French press in 1928 for having made a film about World War I aviators titled *L'Équipage* (1928), Tourneur had to leave the country by order of the French authorities. He left for Germany for eighteen months before being authorized to return to France at the end of 1929. However, his personal situation remained precarious.

He was considered a foreigner at risk of being deported, and every year he had to renew his residence permit. The occupation didn't change his status. He was no longer a French citizen, and at the same time, his American passport had expired after he had spent more than two years in his native country. If the French authorities still considered him an American, he was in fact stateless, having lost his French citizenship. He belonged to the first group of filmmakers hired by Continental, and like his colleagues, he agreed to sign a contract in the knowledge he wouldn't be required to make propaganda films and that the French authorities had recommended that those in the film industry accept the work to allow the French film industry to get going again.

Tourneur explained, "When Continental asked me if I wanted to work with them, there were two things that were understood. The first is that we wouldn't make any kind of propaganda of any sort. The second is that all the collaborators, whether directors, screenwriters, and up to the last grip or prop man, would be French citizens. And likewise the laboratories had to be French laboratories. In addition, the processing and printing had to be done by French workers. These clauses were respected on both sides."[2] Of course, neither Tourneur nor any of his colleagues were aware of Greven's control over the Cinéma Tirage L. Maurice laboratory.

For his first film, Tourneur wanted to select the subject himself, like his colleagues did. In October 1940, during a meeting of the Organizing Committee of the Cinema Industry at 92 avenue des Champs-Élysées, he met screenwriter Albert Valentin and asked him to come to see him at his home on Boulevard Suchet. Valentin brought two or three scripts, and among those, Tourneur selected *Noces de cendres* and told him he wanted to buy it. The film was put into production on May 12, 1941, at the Neuilly studios under the title *Péchés de jeunesse*, with Harry Baur in the lead. The script was developed by Charles Spaak while Michel Duran worked on the dialogue. It became a portmanteau film made up of four stories, using the same structure as one of the great successes of the past decade, *Un Carnet de bal* (1937), directed by Julien Duvivier. The subject was as far as it could be from Vichy morality: Harry Baur was looking for his four illegitimate sons. Continental could produce a film about such a topic as it was not subjected to French censorship; however, the Vichy regime hastened to restrict the film to spectators sixteen and older.

René Le Hénaff, who had started editing *Péchés de jeunesse*, discovered on this occasion the constant interference of Greven, who was often accompanied by Clouzot. After screening several sequences, the producer declared the film to be badly edited. "When I arrived in the production room, Mr. Clouzot was there. Mr. Greven told me, 'You're this, you're that.' He was very unpleasant. Mr. Clouzot didn't say anything to me, but he supported [what Greven said]. In any case, he didn't insult me, because Mr. Greven nearly insulted me."[3] He was then removed from the film and the editing work was given to Jacques Desagneaux. Le Hénaff was aware that Tourneur, unlike Clouzot, had hardly any power inside the company. "Mr. Tourneur behaved very correctly. He didn't support me or anything. He stayed neutral about this."[4]

Tourneur, like his colleagues, had to attend parties organized by Greven when famous German screen actors were visiting Paris. When Swedish-born star Zarah Leander came on May 20, 1941, the head of Continental invited the upper crust of French cinema to Ledoyen-Impératrice. The press of the period demonstrated its usual accuracy by reporting the presence of Maurice's son, Jacques Tourneur, when he was in fact working in Hollywood!

Tourneur went to some of these parties with his partner, actress Louise Lagrange. Although he was not divorced from his first wife, he presented Lagrange as Mrs. Tourneur, in order, no doubt, to avoid embarrassing questions.

During one of these evenings, Louise met Greven. The head of Continental seemed to fall under the spell of this lovely girlish-looking brunette. She recalled:

> Alfred Greven was charming. You really had to hate Germany not to be polite to him. One day, our home was invaded with flowers. He even sent a tree. Luckily, we were living on Boulevard Suchet and so we could put it on the terrace! He did all he could to be invited for lunch at our home. We never agreed to. He wanted me to work for Continental. Maurice said it was out of the question. He insisted. He did everything to get me to agree. He offered me a big part. I still refused.[5]

Like Maurice, Louise was born in France. But she was at that time the widow of an American producer and therefore an American citizen. They became even more vulnerable when the United States declared war on Germany in December 1941.[6]

In September 1941, Tourneur started his second feature for the firm, *Mam'zelle Bonaparte*, a biopic of Cora Pearl, one of the most famous demi-mondaine of the Second Empire. Edwige Feuillère was selected for the part after she had refused to make *Caprices*, following the purchase of her contract by Continental. In the face of threats from Greven, she couldn't refuse a second time. But she had conditions:

> I agree to play the lead female part (Cora Pearl) in your film *Mam'zelle Bonaparte*, which will be directed by Maurice Tourneur, in accordance with the script you sent me. I have reservations regarding the scene of the duel, which I will make only if I am decently clothed. It looks to me that certain scenes in which the dialogue is overdone could be improved. . . . Mr. Dewalde told me you had cinematographers [Robert] Le Febvre, [Jules] Kruger, and [Armand] Thirard under contract. I want to signal my preference for Le Febvre and Kruger, who have already photographed me.[7]

In the end, Jules Kruger was selected.

Mam'zelle Bonaparte was a sumptuous production in terms of sets and costumes. It also used a massive number of film extras for the Opera ball sequence at the Billancourt studios. Tourneur tried in vain to get them to scream when they stormed the orchestra. In spite of his efforts to make them shout louder, he didn't get a convincing result. Then at noon, he decided to call a recess. He asked, "Who is hungry?" and clapping their hands, the extras cry, "Me! Me!" He knew now how to get the required effect.

Ad for *Mam'zelle Bonaparte* (1942) (Fondation Jérôme Seydoux-Pathé)

It's not surprising that the simple mention of food elicited such a reaction from the film extras, who were probably starving, like the rest of the Parisian population, who could not afford to buy food on the black market. Tourneur mentioned that Continental employees had access to a cooperative where they could buy coal and coffee, two rare commodities in those days, as rare as gold.[8] He said that personally he had never wanted to get supplies from them. He was relatively well paid by the company; he earned 200,000 francs per film. However, just before the war, he had received 25 percent more to direct *Volpone* (1941). Continental's salaries were therefore, relatively speaking, not very high. For example, Henri Decoin received only 150,000 francs for *Premier Rendez-vous* (1941), while he would be paid 250,000 by the Regina company for *Le Bienfaiteur* (1942).

Tourneur remembered that the working conditions deteriorated quickly inside Continental. "At the beginning, everything was fine; we made films that were not bad. Little by little, it went wrong! We had to work in dreadful conditions. They were extremely unpleasant people in the firm, apart from Greven, whom we hardly ever saw! We had to make films in twenty or thirty days. We had endless discussions. It became impossible. I thought about quitting when America joined the war."[9] Tourneur immediately felt the effects when Germany declared war on the United States on December 12, 1941. His bank account was frozen; he could not get money out or even sign a check. He had also to sign a register at the nearest police station every week and knew he could be sent to an internment camp as a foreigner from an enemy country. He made a decision. "I thought then it was better to stay quietly put and to take advantage of this kind of protection the firm offered me."[10] Indeed, as of August 10, 1942, he was no longer subject to the police measures.[11]

However, the protection he received was limited. For example, the Germans had stolen his car. When he tried to recover it, providing the new German registration number and his vehicle registration papers, he got nothing for his pains. They even confiscated his registration papers!

The theft of his car, however, was nothing compared with the ordeal awaiting him. Louise Lagrange, his partner, was arrested by the occupying authorities on September 24, 1942, as an American citizen. She was sent to an internment camp in Vittel, a spa town where the Germans were gathering British, Canadian, and American women they aimed to use as bargaining chips to get back German prisoners in Allied camps. If she had agreed to sign a Continental contract, she certainly would have avoided this imprisonment. Tourneur was distraught. They were not married, and therefore he couldn't help her get out of her camp, nor were any visitors allowed at Vittel. Asking Greven for help would prove difficult given Louise's refusal to participate in the German firm's production. All he could do was wait and see. She would manage to get freed after two and a half months owing to the recovery of her French nationality, without any intervention from Tourneur.

It just so happened that he had started to make his third feature for Continental in August 1942, *La Main du diable*, based on a script by Jean-Paul Le Chanois.

CHAPTER 18

La Main du diable

Maurice Tourneur did not originally have a hand in the subject for *La Main du diable*. In February 1941, the trade press mentioned that an adaptation of Gérard de Nerval's short story by Jean Aurenche was about to be put into production under the title *La Main enchantée*.[1] In 1941, Jean Dréville gave up the direction of the film following a violent discussion with Greven regarding the casting.

Jean Aurenche explained that Greven wanted to make *La Main enchantée* with Fernandel. And because the screenwriter didn't agree, he stopped working on the project. He even added, "If Greven had been a good producer, there was no reason why I shouldn't make a film for him. Greven didn't know how to do his job properly. He always called me back after each film we made together. We had a straight-up brawl; I left but kept receiving phone calls from him."[2]

In the end, it was Jean-Paul Le Chanois who got the story, which he decided he would write an updated adaptation of. The arrival of Le Chanois inside Continental had always surprised people. How could a Jewish communist screenwriter whose real name was Dreyfus work in a German company? In fact, his situation starkly exposed the idiocy of the new Vichy antisemitic laws and their blind implementation by Organizing Committee of the Cinema Industry services. Le Chanois remembered that "in 1940, when the Germans arrive, I am in the following situation":

> I have a Jewish name, which is Dreyfus, a name that is hard to have in an oppressive German regime. On the other hand, I am not affected by these racial laws; I have three Aryan grandparents, and I am baptized. However, in 1940, no film-making. I start working as delivery cyclist for several months. Later, they realize I can do more, and I become sales rep for batteries and radiators. . . . When

Ad for *La Main du diable* (1943) (Fondation Jérôme Seydoux-Pathé)

Continental was being established, we thought it would be a Nazi propaganda organization. I remember meeting some comrades at that time, in October 1940, and discussing Continental, saying, "Here is a company that is going to be the [German film] company in France. Let's do everything to avoid it." . . . Regarding my own personal case, during the whole year 1941, I worked as an electricity sales rep. And then, I saw gradually filmmaking starting again, and for a man who loves his job, it was very sad to see it from afar and to see my friends starting to work again and to tell myself that I will never do it again. I tried to work again. I applied for a card as assistant director and editor. Mr. Ploquin's kind services answered me: "But, sir, you are called Dreyfus." I said, "Yes, but I am still allowed to work!" I changed my name; I took my mother's maiden name. They replied, "It's going to cause you trouble. The Germans are very strict; we are not willing to give you the authorization." "How come you cannot give it to me?" "Your reasons are not sufficient."[3]

Without a trade card, Le Chanois was reduced to working as ghostwriter for another screenwriter, in this case Jean Aurenche. But then he learned that screenwriters, unlike assistants and editors, did not need a card from the Organizing Committee of the Cinema Industry to work. So he began writing a script for *Le Moussaillon* (1942) that was being produced by Georges Sénamaud and directed by Jean Gourguet. Although his name had not been mentioned anywhere in the press, the Organizing Committee of the Cinema Industry and the production company received an anonymous letter: "How is it possible? There is a Jew working. It's appalling. We'll get him arrested; you're going to be in trouble."[4] The antisemitic collaborationist press, in particular *Au Pilori*, took up these accusations. The company decided to make the film anyway. "The first day in the studio, they ask me to come over to rearrange a scene, and it starts again. I had been seen, and they had decided I shouldn't work."[5]

Le Chanois realized he had to get hold of an essential piece of paper to stop these denunciations. He went to the Commissariat-General for Jewish Affairs to get a document certifying he was not Jewish. While the management was at first reluctant to give it to him, he got the document without having to exert any pressure because he was considered Aryan according to the laws of the time. He thought that now everything would be fine. But he was wrong. When *Le Moussaillon* was about to be released, the producer refused to list his name in the film credits, as he was afraid of the reactions from anti-Semites.

To silence once and for all the poison pen letter writers, Le Chanois tried once again to get a card, even though he didn't really need it, as well as a work

permit from the Propaganda Office. For that purpose, his friend Claude Vermorel, who worked at Continental under the supervision of Clouzot in the
script department, told him, "I'm going to write you the following letter:
'Mr. Le Chanois, we would be very happy to hire you for our firm. You write
scripts, certainly interesting ones, and we would be glad to have you as an
associate.'"[6] Clouzot signed the letter, which had been typed on Continental
letterhead. Armed with that document, he went to the Propaganda Office. "I
was received by big, fat Hirsch. I explained him my case, drawing a diagram
because he spoke very bad French. I showed him my certificate and the Continental letter. He said, 'Very good.' And he asked a secretary to prepare and
stamp a card for me. With my card, I went to the Organizing Committee of
the Cinema Industry. I saw a guy named Guyonnet, Ploquin's secretary, the
one who had refused to give me my card. Mr. Baldet was very nice and told
me, 'I'm very happy things could be sorted out for you this way.'"[7]

Now that his papers were perfectly in order according to Vichy laws, Le
Chanois thought he was going to be able to work in peace. The Sirius company hired him to write the script and dialogue for *Huit hommes dans un
château* (1942), to be directed by Richard Pottier. Jean Aurenche had been
considered for the job, but he had to pass owing to lack of time, as he had
already signed a contract for Claude Autant-Lara's *Lettres d'amour* (1942). On
the first day of shooting, the company received phone calls and anonymous
letters: stating that Le Chanois's real name was Dreyfus. The producers pan-
icked; the film could be banned. Fortunately for him, Pottier took his side
against them. He understood perfectly his situation after being told he was
not "French enough." However, producers refused to mention his name in the
film advertising and they only barely agreed to allow him to be listed on the
film credits.

Le Chanois told Vermorel about this endless hassle. Vermorel replied, "Listen, you won't manage. And the best way to shup up those bastards, now that
you have a letter from Continental, is to work there."[8] This time, Le Chanois
thought about the proposition: "Continental in 1942 is not at all the Continental in 1940. In 1942, it looks like a normal commercial company, managed by
three Germans, but whose staff and direction are French, whose productions
were *L'Assassinat du Père Noël, Le Dernier des six, La Symphonie fantastique*, a film
glorifying composer Berlioz, all productions having no trace of propaganda as
we feared they could at the beginning. Relatively speaking, Continental was like
some kind of a German Paramount. Nobody seemed to contribute to German
or Nazi propaganda, or in any case, show pro-German sympathy."[9]

Le Chanois was a Resistance fighter from the very start of the occupation, operating under the nickname Marceau. As soon as he had returned to Paris in August 1940, he had contacted Resistance organizations, in particular the General Federation of Labor, a communist trade union. In September 1941, he started to organize a network through the creation of the Committee for the Liberation of French cinema. He produced type-written pamphlets, in the absence of a mimeograph machine, which he discreetly distributed, and he infiltrated two studios and one laboratory. For him, joining Continental was would allow him to kill two birds with one stone: he could work without being constantly denounced as a Jew, and he could also infiltrate the German company. He requested the authorization from his leaders and received the following answer, "As soon as you don't do anything wrong, you can do it. And as long as you are doing Resistance work, you have to do it."[10]

So Le Chanois became screenwriter for Continental Films, where he would write four scripts while at the same time being active in the Resistance. He created a Resistance branch inside the two studios belonging to the company, Billancourt and Neuilly. He distributed pamphlets. For November 11 and July 14, he created posters, framed in the tricolors, which he put up in the locker room, the lavatories, and the corridors of Billancourt studios. The management launched an inquiry into those illegal posters. Later, he managed to get hold of the contract signed between Léopold Maurice and Greven to sell Greven the Cinéma Tirage L. Maurice processing and printing company. He copied it page by page using the same typewriter the original had been typed on, which allowed him to then steal the original. It would be used as evidence after the liberation. Le Chanois also stole cameras as well as film negatives and positives that he would use to film the Vercors Resistance fighters in his documentary *Au cœur de l'orage* (1948) as well as a documentary of the Paris liberation.

Le Chanois was a conscientious screenwriter to boot, and he wrote a superb updated adaptation of Gérard de Nerval's short story, bringing it closer to the Faust legend. Clouzot gave him the work after Aurenche backed out. The script was very well received, and he went on to work on the dialogue.

Tourneur was selected to direct the film. He had more room for maneuver than Dréville in selecting his actors and decided to hire Pierre Fresnay for the part of painter Roland Brissot. Fresnay had already made two films for Continental playing the deadpan Inspector Wens. Fresnay, Le Chanois, and Tourneur had also all worked together in 1935 on *Kœnigsmark*. They liked each other. Le Chanois recommended a new assistant director to Tourneur: Jean Devaivre, who happened to be a member of the Resistance as well.[11]

La Main du diable was put into production on August 21, 1942. Tourneur had a top-notch technical crew that featured art director André Andrejew, cinematographer Armand Thirard, cameraman Louis Née, and assistant cameraman Jean Dicop, who both shot all his films. It was no accident that Greven had hired Thirard right when the company was created. He had inquired about French cinematographers and quickly learned that this one was first rate: a lighting genius as well as a technician who worked quickly and efficiently. He could be compared to the wonderful American cinematographer John Alton, who managed to make certain B movies memorable thanks to his chiaroscuros he achieved in no time at all. If there was a Continental style, it was certainly due to Armand Thirard, who made eleven films there altogether. Nevertheless, he did try to leave the company on several occasions.

His relationships with Greven were tense. He found the orders that came from the management to be oppressive, and his dismay in reaction to menacing letters he received was understandable, like one he received from Greven during *La Symphonie fantastique* that requested he let Greven know if he could take "shots at Cirque d'Hiver with four Mole-Richardson lights at 120 amperes" and that threatened that if Thirard told him it was not possible, then he'd "be forced to give your job to another cinematographer."[12] He also had arguments with Rudolf Hans Bauermeister, who always supervised shootings. Hired with a yearly contract in August 1940, Thirard couldn't leave the company the following year, as he was in the middle of the production of *La Symphonie fantastique* and couldn't leave the director Christian-Jaque in the lurch. He tried again the following year, but Bauermeister threatened him, telling him that if he left Continental, he would automatically be declared available to be sent to Germany to work. He decided to stay with the firm until the autumn of 1943, at which time the threat was carried out. He managed to escape his fate thanks to Aimé Chemel's intervention on his behalf. Chemel happened to know people at the Ministry of Employment, and was able to get Thirard hired by his firm, Les Compagnons du Film.

The management gave the team a meager twenty-eight days to produce *La Main du diable*. Jean Devaivre managed to work out a precise schedule by eliminating the dialogue written by Clouzot and going back to Le Chanois's original script. Tourneur was a quick and efficient director. However, Pierre Fresnay remembered it took him two hours to decide how to begin his first scene, but the reason for that was that Louise Lagrange had been arrested on September 24. Devaivre stated he directed during the first week because Maurice, deeply depressed, was unable to. However, this statement was not confirmed by any other testimony. Even though he was anxious and upset, Tourneur stayed on the set for the whole production. Fresnay was the first to celebrate his director's talent, even as he noted his struggle with the first scene:

> He was aging, but not elderly. And everything subsequently proved there was no deterioration in his abilities. The film was very well made, but I was struck by this paralysis [at the start], which I conclude was a merit. Apparently, he had not prepared anything, or, at least, he had not managed to convince himself he was properly prepared. It's absolutely certain Maurice Tourneur was, on that day, in the estimable position of a person who wasn't sure he had prepared his scene well . . . and of a man who was starting a production, and gave himself the freedom to wonder about it. I have never seen that in cinema, where the law of time is an essential law! It made a deep impression on me.[13]

In spite of these difficulties, *La Main du diable* was an unquestionable success and is today considered a timeless classic. Yet, when it first came out on April 21, 1943, it received mixed reviews: "A serious mistake, according to me, is the transposition of the story to contemporary life. It doesn't fit with a story of spells, severed hands, magical power, and intervention from the Devil. . . . Director Maurice Tourneur, the author of a few solid films, didn't manage to give his story the right film tone."[14]

Film composer Roland-Manuel was fired before he could finish the score, which was then given to Roger Dumas. Roland-Manuel was sacked because the firm discovered he was Jewish. Yet although he was born Roland Lévy, he had only two Jewish grandparents and his spouse was Aryan, which should have allowed him to get a work permit. And he had already composed the score for *Les Inconnus dans la maison* without any problems. It's possible he was the victim of a denunciation. He had composed that previous score with Manuel Rosenthal's clandestine participation, and Rosenthal was indeed a banned composer.[15]

CHAPTER 19

Maneuvers in the Unoccupied Zone

If Continental Films was the leading French film firm, particularly in the occupied zone, the Vichy government still wanted to control the industry. Until November 1942, the French intelligence services in the unoccupied zone were at work listening, watching, and reporting the activities of not just Continental employees but others in the film industry. Such monitoring might seem as though it were illusory, given the strength of the occupying power. But the reports offered a picture of professionals in the French film industry that sharply distinguished them from collaborators and their pathological antisemitism and collusion with the occupying forces.

The Vichy authorities kept a close watch on all fronts, including the comings and goings of the Continental managers in Paris, Cannes, and Nice. If Greven hardly ever went to the French Riviera himself, his representative Robert Beunke spent a lot of time there meeting with actors and screenwriters. His phone calls were taped and the telegrams he sent to the firm headquarters in Paris were intercepted.

Although he tried to deny it, Beunke was much more than a simple agent working for Continental. In addition to getting contracts with actors or screenwriters, he also kept Greven informed about film productions in the unoccupied zone. In August 1942, he sent a telegram to Greven from Nice that proves Greven wanted to know what was going on in the industry: "Agreement Franco-Italian Film Consortium signed and will take effect in December—stop—Production French-speaking films in Italy would be intensified and large appeal to French artists—stop—Jewish artists effectively excluded from entertainment in unoccupied zone since August 6—stop—Three productions in Nice at the moment."[1]

During the summer of 1942, the firm was trying to launch a new production that would be shot on locations around Cassis, close to screenwriter Carlo

Rim's house. Rim prepared a script for Maurice Tourneur titled *Le Val d'enfer*, whose actors had to be recruited mainly from southerners living in the unoccupied zone. Beunke sent a telegram to Bauermeister relaying the latest developments: "Informed Carlo Rim of urgency of going to Paris. He promised to be in Paris tomorrow Tuesday or Wednesday—stop—All unoccupied zone artists approached for VAL D'ENFER still free except DENNSY, who signed contract for a theater tour three months ago but says might be able to get herself free."[2] The project would fall apart following the invasion of the unoccupied zone in November 1942. And to Rim's great sorrow, the cast would end up consisting of a mixture of Parisians and southerners and being shot in Moret-sur-Loing, near Paris.

It was also during the autumn of 1942 that one of Continental's greatest stars would desert the German firm's sets. Danielle Darrieux joined her fiancé, Porfirio Rubirosa, in Vichy. He was free at last after an exchange for German diplomats in Lisbon, after months of internment in Bad Nauheim. Darrieux was still under contract with the German firm. She still had two films to make and was looking for a way out, and she found it thanks to Rubirosa in Vichy, where the French police were keeping a close eye on her:

> The press announced the imminent marriage of artist Danielle Darrieux to the representative of the Dominican Republic in France, Mr. Rubirosa on numerous occasions. This union had been delayed because of certain formalities Mr. Rubirosa had to go through with his government. We learned today that the fiancés decided some time ago to speed things up and that the wedding will thus take place tomorrow morning at the Vichy town hall in the strictest privacy. This sudden decision, the reasons for which the future couple did not disclose, was made to stymy a lawsuit that the German firm Continental Films proposed to bring against this artist. Danielle Darrieux, who had signed a contract last year with the famous German firm and should have been making a film in Paris for this company right now, refused to do so, in spite of several requests to go back to the occupied zone. Faced with a threat of a lawsuit, she decided to hasten her marriage, which will allow her to argue she cannot go back to Paris because she is the spouse of a diplomat representing a country at war with Germany.[3]

Indeed, as the wife of a diplomate from an enemy country, she was automatically sent to Megève with her husband, where they were put under house arrest. Yet Greven could not come to terms with the idea of losing the company's brightest star. He sent André Cayatte and Henri-Georges Clouzot to

Pressbook cover for *Le Val d'enfer* (1943) (Fondation Jérôme Seydoux-Pathé)

urge her to come back to Paris. But as she refused flatly, they had to give up. However, a consequence of her decision was she could not work anymore and would not make a single film until the end of the war.[4]

Vichy also kept a close watch on the French filmmakers and actors who had left for the United States. Jean Gabin, Michèle Morgan, René Clair, and Julien Duvivier preferred exile to compromise and so took advantage of their contracts with American film production companies to escape. Jean Renoir joined them later. These artists were openly attacked in the collaborationist press. Maurice Bessy wrote, "In 1936, René Clair had accepted the Legion of Honor in accord with the Republican code of conduct. Four years later, still faithful to that same code of conduct, he leaves for the United States: freedom for us."[5]

Yet the French government wanted them to return back to France. They were contacted about this by the French ambassador in the United States. Julien Duvivier wrote to his brother Pierre, who had stayed in France, to tell him why this approach looked dubious to him. "Five of us (Clair, Renoir, Morgan, Gabin, and me) received an official letter from the ambassador stating that the French government was anxious to see us come home. I found myself in a serious situation. And after thinking it through very carefully, I wrote the answer you'll find enclosed."[6] Besides the contract that kept him busy with his producer Alexander Korda, Duvivier had good reasons to be dubious about this proposition. His last film produced in France had disappeared completely, banned by Vichy. He asked the French consul, "What happened to my film, *Untel Père et fils* shot during the winter of 1939, with the support of the French government, that exposed the life of three generations of middle-class Frenchmen, three times violated and tormented? This film had cost the American company Columbia seven million, which held me responsible for its disappearance."[7] He also had no confidence in the new French government and told his brother, "I advise caution in your relationships with officials. Be careful not to put me in the spotlight. I do not believe at all in the collaboration you are telling me about. I cannot under any circumstances go back to Paris. Think of my last work in France, and remember that once certain people get me, they won't release me. You understand me, I hope."[8] He was perfectly right to fear retaliations, as his letters were intercepted by Vichy intelligence.

All the attacks and compromises of this confused period are reflected in the behavior of a French filmmaker active in the unoccupied zone. Abel Gance had been considered one of the greatest French film directors of the 1920s but had lost most of his prestige in 1940. He was often ridiculed in the press for his lyrical flights of fancy and his expensive productions. Maurice Bessy was one such journalist who poked fun at the filmmaker: "We must, says [Gance], console ourselves in these bitter moments we are living in with poetry. We must, like the great Greek tragedians, turn to poignant, strong, lyrical subjects that lift the soul. Our world lacks a purpose, a why. We must restore it. The cinema must take the message of France abroad, the message of the spirit that cannot be vanquished."[9] He applied this theory in making *Vénus aveugle* (1941), starring Viviane Romance and produced at the Victorine studios. It was one of the first films made after the armistice in the unoccupied zone. Even though it was dedicated to Maréchal Pétain, Gance was violently attacked in the press. He as well as his lead actress and producers were labeled Jews. "By the way, Viviane Romance's name is Hortmans. She was born of a Jewish mother with an unknown father. She just made a film with the Jew Meccati, *La Vénus aveugle* under the direction of the Jew Abel Gance, at the Victorine studios in Nice, managed by the Jews Schwob and Schlosberg. Either you are in the family, or not."[10]

Abel Gance, like Viviane Romance, was born out of wedlock. He gained a legitimate father when his mother married Adolphe Gance in 1897, when he was eight. In these conditions, it was virtually impossible for him to provide the necessary proof of ancestry the new Vichy laws demanded, that is, the birth certificate of his four biological grandparents. He decided nevertheless to go on working at all costs while trying to obtain the documents required to prove he was not Jewish.

For Abel Gance, cinema was more important than politics. He was ready to do anything to be able to produce the film of his dreams. The transcription of a telephone conversation in March 1942 confirmed this: the great filmmaker tried to obtain the direct support of the German authorities. At that time, he was working on *Le Capitaine Fracasse* (1943) in the occupied zone. Because he was staying at the time in the unoccupied zone, he had trouble getting letters of transit for his wife and his secretary. The Organizing Committee of the Cinema Industry's big boss, Raoul Ploquin, refused them because he went through two different channels at the same time to ask for them. As Gance said with his usual wit, Ploquin "behaved like an offended dope." Therefore, he contacted the German vice consul in Marseille to ask him if he would help sort out his affairs and told him about his latest attempts: "Céline went to Berlin. He saw a very important figure in the regime; they talked about film. My name was mentioned with a lot of sympathy and they thought of me for the great film in favor of the rapprochement."[11] This conversation suggests that as far as Abel Gance was concerned in the spring of 1942, the Germans would remain victorious for a long time to come. Moreover, when his inter-locutor mentioned his imminent departure to the front, Gance reassured him, "I think your stay within the army will be short. At the end of summer, you'll be back."[12] He was willing to compromise to make a big film, with, in addi-tion, the help of the antisemite writer Céline, who happened to be one of his friends.

In spite of all his collaboration attempts and compromises, Gance would have to flee to Spain in Summer 1943, unable to prove he was not Jewish. He was all at once a victim of the state antisemitism, a supporter of Maréchal Pétain, and a filmmaker ready to collaborate directly with Germany. He illus-trates perfectly the gray areas of this confused period when the boundaries between right and wrong blurred in a most frightening way.

CHAPTER 20

Documentaries

Continental Films is best known for the thirty feature-length fiction films it produced. But it also produced eighteen documentary shorts. The reason it produced these had to do with the modification of the rules regarding film exhibition in France. At the start of the occupation, the familiar prewar double feature program was banished and replaced by a feature film preceded by a documentary short. To meet these requirements, the company offered two of its greatest cinematographers, Armand Thirard and Robert Le Febvre, the opportunity to make shorts as early as 1941.

Many documentaries made during the occupation were propaganda, such as *Français vous avez la mémoire courte* (1943), directed by Jean Morel and Jacques Chavanne, an anti-Bolshevik pamphlet, and *Les Corrupteurs* (1941), directed by Pierre Ramelot, which was screened on the occasion of the anti-Jewish propaganda exhibition *Les Juifs et la France* (1941) at the Palais Berlitz in December 1941. *Les Corrupteurs* was produced by Nova-Films, a company run by Robert Muzard, a close friend of Dr. Diedrich, who received his funds directly from Germany. This firm specialized in documentaries against Jews, Freemasons, and communists as well as in ones that promoted the compulsory work service.

Muzard produced a notorious fiction film titled *Forces occultes* (1943), directed by Jean Mamy, which violently attacked the parliamentary regime of the Third Republic while denouncing the usual "Judaeo-masonic plot." Muzard pretended the project was forced on him by Dr. Diedrich, and he claimed he cut some of the most shocking sequences, reducing the film's length from 1,600 to 750 meters. He nevertheless received 1.2 million francs from the Germans to produce it.[1]

The distribution of such works was not simple. Theater operators were not clamoring to integrate them to their programs. Therefore, the regional branches of the German Propaganda Office had to order them to screen *Forces occultes* for a given period, accompanied by two short documentaries.[2] People were not exactly lining up to watch them either. As one operator in Épernay explained in a letter to the distributor complaining about this compulsory program:

> I confirm my telephone communication to you today pointing out the disastrous box office receipts for the program *Forces occultes*, which you sent us on the order of the Organizing Committee of the Cinema Industry. The audience's discontent manifested itself right from the first screening on Friday, August 13, which took care of the publicity for the next day. The result is that the gross takings were eleven thousand and sixty-one francs instead of the forty-five thousand francs the year before on the same date. For this reason, I contacted the Reims Propaganda Office—phone number 47-12—to tell them about the loss we incurred following the screening of this program. I therefore asked to be authorized to withdraw the first two shorts and to replace them with a feature film. This afternoon, I received a phone call from the Reims Propaganda Office informing me that Dijon agreed to withdraw the two shorts and to allow them to be replaced by *Ces Dames aux chapeaux verts*.[3]

Newsreels were also shown along with documentaries. The audience didn't seem to appreciate the propaganda in the newsreels either, according to French intelligence: "During the screening of newsreels at the Marbeuf theater in Paris, showing the bombings of London, murmurs of protest were heard in the auditorium. On the other hand, there was applause when they screened the results of the RAF raids over Berlin."[4] These reactions did not thrill the occupiers, who decided they were going to make it plainly clear what was forbidden: "At the exit from the theater, spectators' names were taken down by German police officers, and the theater was closed by the occupying authorities."[5]

In such conditions, it was understandable why Continental Films never produced documentaries with a political message. The company did not want the audience to run away because of propaganda that could compromise the box office takings of its feature films. However, Continental served as go-between for Alliance Cinématographique Européenne, the French UFA subsidiary company in charge of the distribution of *Force occultes*, buying the film for 200,000 francs and then selling it back to the company.[6] While Greven always claimed he avoided propaganda, he nevertheless played a hidden role in the distribution and hiring of technicians for this type of documentary.

The year 1942 was a turning point in the war. In September, the Vichy government ratified the requisition of French citizens old enough to work for the compulsory work service. The noncompulsory "relief" system having proved inefficient, the Germans embraced true conscription. This new imposition would push more and more young people to go underground and to become Resistance fighters. The film industry was also hit by the requisition of parts of its staff. Inside each French film production company, lists of essential staff were drawn up in order to preserve the smooth running of the firm. Continental was spared. One could escape compulsory work if one had a contract with the German company, but if one left the company, one could be requisitioned immediately.

At the end of 1942, Continental hired people to produce a propaganda documentary promoting working in Germany. The film had a working title, *La Relève*. The company had to find German-speaking operators and directors, and so it called Joseph-Louis Mundviller, a great cinematographer who had worked with Abel Gance on *Napoléon* (1927). He was born in Alsace on April 10, 1886, in Mulhouse, when the city was called Mülhausen and was registered under the name Joseph-Ludwig Mundwiller. During World War I, he had volunteered in the French army. His brother was killed wearing the French uniform and his parents never recovered from his death. Like many Alsatians, he had no sympathy for Germany.

Continental offered him a job as cinematographer for this documentary:

> I was summoned by Continental, and they told me, "You speak German, it would good if you went to make films in Germany for us." Then, naturally, they made me understand I didn't have a choice, that my work permit could be rescinded. I agreed to make a film (because I must add I had been in the Resistance for five years). It was a film about the French working in Germany. I thought it was better if was made by a Resistance fighter rather than by a collaborator. When I agreed to go there for four weeks, Bauermeister called me in and told me, "You must stay there for several films." I said, "I won't stay in Germany. I agreed to do one film. If you want, I'll go for one film."[7]

His contract, dated November 16, 1942, was signed by Bauermeister and Greven, as in the case of all contracts for artists hired by Continental, although the firm was only a front for a German company, Deutsche Filmherstellungs und Verwertungs.

Yet Mundviller would shoot only about three scenes in Paris for that film and would never go to Germany. He was perfectly aware of the propagandistic nature of the subject. He was given a two-page synopsis: "It was certainly a film made to show the good sides of working in Germany."[8] He decided to put in the strict minimum amount of work: "I started the film in bad weather because my intention was to botch it. Mind you, everybody has to eat. In four years, I made one film. They offered me fifteen thousand francs a week and all expenses paid to go to Berlin. My intention was to sabotage the film as much as possible."[9] He knew the light was bad, but he told his bosses it was excellent. He filmed a scene on rue Saint-Antoine in front of a recruitment office as well as took shots of the Porte Dauphine subway station and the Arc de Triomphe. He then waited for the trip to Berlin, which never happened. He sent several letters to Bauermeister, who didn't reply. And finally, on March 1, 1943, he asked for his contract to be terminated: "For three and a half months, I have been at the disposal of the aforementioned company. Today, March 1, I cannot possibly stick any longer to the proposal mentioned in my letter from January 29 and I am obliged to ask for full payment from today of the weeks or fraction of weeks that could elapse until the termination of the contract in question."[10] However, Continental daily shooting reports showed that Mundviller worked with Serge Griboff at the Billancourt studios and on location in Paris for a few days from November 26 until December 13, 1942, for *La Relève*. According to Griboff, the project was abandoned following the death of Pierre Ramelot, the director of *Les Corrupteurs*, who had been approached to direct it.[11]

Yet a documentary would be made under the title *Travailleurs de France* (1943), directed by Serge Griboff and with Albert Militon as cameraman. Militon had been hired for *La Relève* at Mundviller's suggestion to be his assistant, for 3,000 francs a week in November 1942. Even if the script had been modified, the film was a genuine piece of propaganda showing the supposedly marvelous working conditions of French citizens in Germany. The film was subcontracted to Robert Muzard's Nova-Films, yet there was no doubt that Continental played a major role in the recruitment of technicians for it. Militon's contract was typed on a standard Continental application form. The film was shot in Germany (Berlin, Palatinate, Leipzig) and in Austria (Salzburg).

Travailleurs de France was a documentary designed for the parents of young people called by the compulsory work service to convince them they were lucky their children would have the chance to work in Germany. The film begins with a couple receiving a letter from their son who was working over there. The reading of the letter takes us to Germany, showing the son arriving at the camp, receiving a thorough medical examination, and being given training as a precision mechanic in a factory. Apparently, everything was done to make the stay as pleasant as possible: there was a library with French books, the dormitories were spotless, there was an excellent industrial kitchen managed by French workers, and so on. This idyllic version of work in Germany bore little resemblance to the genuine working conditions of the unfortunate young men who had been sent there by force. Writer François Cavanna, who was one such young man, describes the terrifying working conditions, the meager fare, the bugs in the dormitories, and the constant surveillance they had to endure as workmen who could be accused of sabotage in his book *Les Russkoffs*. It was, he notes, a life that was not worth living that pushed more than one man to mutilate himself to get out of such a hell, without being necessarily successful, as in his case.

Griboff, the director of the documentary, was born Russian and had become a naturalized French citizen. He had been himself a prisoner of war in Germany. He managed to escape thanks to his knowledge of the German tongue and to forged identity papers identifying him as a male nurse. He had worked before the war for Universal as head of the technical department. Back in France in March 1941, he got a job at Tobis, where his job was sync editing documentaries. When he agreed to make *Travailleurs de France*, he thought that, unlike *La Relève*, it would not be propaganda: "It had been understood that this film, which I was only directing, would not be propaganda but news."[12] Griboff pretended he could film whatever he wanted in Germany, avoiding the model internment camps he was shown. But the Germans didn't like the film because of its sad tone. Some footage of hard work was cut, and the recorded commentary was obviously perfectly in line with the collaborationist feelings of the time, celebrating the German army on the Russian front: "Germany is making a superhuman effort—a living symbol of sacrifice."[13]

In the end, this documentary was never released in cinemas. It was only shown during private screenings at the giant Gaumont Palace theater in Paris, for a special audience, the families of French deported workmen. It was, however, mentioned in the trade press in July 1944 as being screened for a lecture tour by the Bruneton organization. The documentary was praised as "made with a visible concern for objectivity and truth, showing the working conditions of thousands of men gathered in camps and working areas."[14]

Other directors were approached to direct documentaries. Richard Pottier, as an Austrian- born French citizen, was also asked to make a propaganda film about French workers in Germany:

In January 1944, Mr. X made me come to his office and gave me four pages of typewritten text, telling me, "Mr. Greven told me you had nothing to do for the moment. So here it is, that's three-day work. He offers you two hundred thousand." I said, "What is it?" "It's a small thing, you'll see the actors and what we can do." . . . Now, it was a propaganda film to encourage French workers to go to work in Germany. . . . When I saw that, I said, "Sir, excuse me, but you are mistaken, I do not do this kind of work." "Why?" "For the simple reason that I have been a prisoner, and I'm not going to encourage others to go to Germany." "It's not about prisoners but about working." "No, I won't do it." "You must be well off." "No, but I don't do this kind of work."[15]

The documentaries officially made by Continental Films did not contain anything reprehensible. They could have been made during peacetime because no reference was ever made to the occupation. Robert Le Febvre made thirteen of those short films, which ran between ten and twenty minutes. He told the story of the nineteen bridges in Paris in *Paris sur Seine* (1941) and of Collioure in *Collioure* (1943) and took viewers for a visit in a fruit canning factory near Perpignan for *Abricots en boîte* (1943). In *Les enfants s'amusent* (1942), he showed viewers young kids having fun on a beach in Cannes, Montmartre, and the Tuileries garden in Paris. Le Febvre had to do the filming, directing, and editing all by himself. The company gave him little recognition for his work. When he needed to have an operation for a hernia, Continental refused to pay for his hospital expenses, insisting it was not a work-related accident. He also had to fight the management to obtain his salary while he was convalescing.

In the same vein as his colleague, Armand Thirard documented the history and recipes of Champagne in *Champagne* (1945) and of sugar with *Le Sucre* (1944). *Le Sucre* was released only in October 1945 as a supplement to *Les Caves du Majestic* (1945). A reviewer mentioned the irony, given that the audience had not seen any sugar for a long time: "This documentary shows us a unique and well-established method for making beautiful white sugar, then a little less white, then finally brown. We are told what must be done and must not be done to make the sugar hard and ready for consumption. Everybody laughs quietly, thinking it's really useless, as sugar—it's a secret, do not repeat it—is rather hard to come by for the average consumer. So because we see an enormous amount of it on the screen, we don't understand. Here is the sole and genuine enigma offered to us this evening, dedicated to a whodunit."[16]

CHAPTER 21

Le Corbeau

If there is a single emblematic Continental film, it's *Le Corbeau* (1943), certainly the most important work and the most famous ever produced by the German firm and even more, one of the greatest masterpieces of French cinema. Its production history is fascinating, showing how Henri-Georges Clouzot managed to overcome all obstacles to conceive this scathing movie that remains today as disturbing as when it was released in 1943.

While the film denounces poison-pen letter writers, its script was not nevertheless contemporaneous with the occupation. Indeed, screenwriter Louis Chavance had registered the subject at the Film Authors' Association on November 27, 1937, under the title *L'Œil du serpent*. The six-page synopsis he registered was described as a "romantic story." Chavance's original version contains the main outline of the story: in a small provincial city, Dr. Monatte is the victim of a poison-pen letter writer who accuses him of carrying out abortions. A married woman named Laura whose husband disappeared in the colonies and who is secretly in love with Monatte is the author. She accuses her sister-in-law, a spinster nurse, of being the author of the letters before being discovered by Monatte and committing suicide.

Clouzot modified the plot quite a bit. Originally, Dr. Germain Monatte (Pierre Fresnay) was married to a young woman named Denise. In the final script, he is a widower working under the pseudonym Rémy Germain and Denise (Ginette Leclerc) is merely his mistress. And more importantly, the real culprit is not Laura (Micheline Francey) anymore but her husband, Dr. Vorzet (Pierre Larquey). The husband is not missing either but a pivotal character in this detective story. The culprit doesn't commit suicide but is murdered by a patient's mother who was one of the victims of the anonymous letters.

Chavance had started working on the subject in 1932. In 1933, he had contacted Dr. Edmond Locard, the director of the laboratory of scientific police

Pressbook cover for *Le Corbeau* (1943) (Fondation Jérôme Seydoux-Pathé)

in Lyon and a specialist in anonymous letters seeking information about poison-pen cases. Locard then sent Chavance documents relating to an extremely famous case that happened in Tulle in 1917. A woman, Angèle Laval, had written a flood of poison-pen letters signed "the snake's eye" that encouraged emulators and caused tragedies in the town. Thanks to a group dictation to check people's handwriting, the culprit was unmasked by Locard.

The script had been accepted by director Claude Heymann for the Photosonor company in 1938. But the project did not come off. Chavance then presented the subject to Continental in 1943. Clouzot was immediately interested, though the German managers looked at it suspiciously. "Bauermeister found the subject too violent and too harsh," according to Clouzot. "I fought with Greven, who told me, 'It's an extremely dangerous film.' But I wanted to do it; I liked it. It was a revolutionary film. He told me, 'Well, you take all the responsibility. Do it!'"[1]

The fact that Clouzot was able to get an authorization to make such a film from Greven was in itself a feat. It shows the special relationship between the two men. Clouzot has been often called "the man of the firm" because of this almost friendly relationship he had with Greven. He had the boss's ear, and Greven had enough confidence in him to allow him to tackle such a subject.

Although Greven was under the authority of Max Winkler and of propaganda minister Joseph Goebbels, the producer often made decisions without consulting them. Goebbels had already summoned him to Berlin in May 1942 to tell him off. The screening of *La Symphonie fantastique* had made Goebbels realize that French people were able to produce a film glorifying their country, but in his view, the French film industry should not compete with the German one. Propaganda was the job of Germany; France should only produce pure entertainment that brought in a healthy commercial profit.

On May 19, Greven found himself face to face with Joseph Goebbels and his second-in-command, Fritz Hippler. Goebbels noted in his diary what he said during the meeting.

> Greven is entirely wrong in thinking he had to raise the standard of French films. It's a mistake. It's not our job to provide the French with good movies, and it's certainly not our task to give them movies that are beyond reproach in terms of their nationalistic tendency. If French people in general are satisfied with light corny stuff, we should endeavor to produce this kind of cheap rubbish. It would be folly for us to promote competition against ourselves. We must proceed in our movie policies as the Americans do vis-à-vis the North and South American

continents. We must become the dominating movie power on the European continent. If pictures are to be produced in other countries, they must only be of a local limited character. It must be our aim to prevent as much as possible the founding of any new national industry, and if necessary to hire for Berlin, Vienna, or Munich such stars and technicians as might be in a position to help in this. After I talked to him for a long time, Greven realized the wisdom of this course and will pursue it in the future.[2]

The perfect illustration of what French cinema should be in Goebbels's view were comedies such as *Caprices* or *Annette et la dame blonde*. Yet, if we are to believe what he wrote in his diary where he recorded his day-to-day activities, he saw only a tiny portion of the films produced by Continental.[3]

Greven's visit to Berlin seemed to appease the propaganda minister. In June 1942, Goebbels discussed the Paris situation again with Fritz Hippler, who had just come back from a visit there. In the end, he was happy to learn that Greven was the master of French cinema. On the other hand, he cursed the German managers of UFA who were unable to produce films of such quality, according to him.[4] A year later, in July 1943, Goebbels still thought that the films produced by Greven were too good and that it would be better to export the best talents in French cinema to Germany and to send Greven to Prague to encourage the local production of films.[5] His prime obsession remained the predominance of German cinema over its European competitors.

It was in this context that Greven made the decision to produce Clouzot's movie. He didn't contravene Goebbels's orders in doing so, as unlike *La Symphonie fantastique*, *Le Corbeau* could hardly be understood as nationalist propaganda. If the script offered a dark view of a small provincial town, the plot was that of a thriller for which the audience had to wait until the last frame to discover the name of the culprit.

On May 10, 1943, Clouzot started shooting his film in Monfort-l'Amaury under the working title *Laura*. Pierre Fresnay spoke of exhausting days working in that small town fifty kilometers west of Paris: "The atmosphere on the set of *Le Corbeau* was extremely unpleasant for me, and the work was overwhelming. I had to get up early in the morning, go to work at Montfort-l'Amaury on trains that were very slow. And it was tough and we worked very long days."[6] The director did nothing to improve the atmosphere, as if he was consciously trying to make his lead actor uncomfortable. Fresnay recognized the effectiveness of that method: "It's probably what helped me, what allowed me to be a character less open than what I am in general. I felt strained. My scenes with Ginette Leclerc disturbed me."[7] In the part of Dr. Germain, he achieved one of his best performances on the screen: a taciturn misanthropic doctor who is the focus of a poison-pen letter writer. He becomes Denise's lover (Ginette Leclerc), a crippled nymphomaniac, while searching for the identity of the person who accuses him of being an abortionist. The character mirrored the personality of the director, and Fresnay was conscious of it: Clouzot had a personality that matched "his morbid condition." He was, as Fresnay noted, "a sick man," suffering from a collapsed lung, and "had to go back regularly in hospital for treatment. It's important to know to understand his character."[8]

The filmmaker's harshness was confirmed by assistant director Jean Sacha. After six weeks, he suddenly left the production, while they were shooting in Montfort-l'Amaury, on account of the way Clouzot treated him:

> Clouzot is a pretty special guy in terms of health, in terms of psychology. He spent five years in a sanatorium. And I had become his bête noire, the scapegoat assistant. Each time something went wrong, he said, "It's Sacha's fault." And really, I felt it was wrong. . . . I walked out in the middle of the production because I didn't like Continental's methods and the people it employed. And I also couldn't take Clouzot's personality anymore; I was fed up to the back teeth. At the beginning, we got on well; then on the set, he became impossible. I told him, "I cannot work with you anymore. You treat me like a dog." He said, "Well, all right. I'll sort this out." He's a bastard, an extraordinary guy, but a bastard.[9]

Sacha confirmed that Clouzot intentionally gave the script a dark tone, a tone he had not perceived when he first read it. "There is a cut sequence that wasn't even shot. It's a sequence that gave a comic turn to the thing. It's a sequence that included, for example, a peasant who sat down at his table with a letter. He just received an anonymous letter. . . . He looked at his wife suspiciously, then he read it and left. Then, there was dead time. One felt the letter denounced the wife for having slept with X. He came back, he ate his soup, and went out again. . . . Clouzot wanted to shoot that sequence, he never managed to do it."[10]

Clouzot selected as director of photography Nicolas Hayer, who had just been hired by Continental. This great cinematographer had already worked with Jacques Becker on *Dernier Atout* (1942) and with Abel Gance on *Le Capitaine Fracasse* (1943), and Clouzot was clever to hire this master of chiaroscuro. Ironically, without his knowledge, he had taken into his crew an eminent member of the Resistance who joined Continental on the approval of his net-work leader, Jean-Paul Le Chanois. "In September 1942," Hayer recalled, "I was called up by the Continental company, by Mr. Bauermeister, who offered me a year-long contract on the basis of eighteen thousand francs a week. I also asked for a month's vacation and the ability to hire my camera crew. Every-thing was agreed to."[11] However, he had to delay the effective date of his contract by several months because he had already signed contracts to work on several other movies. In March 1943, he was called up again and agreed to sign for a single movie that would serve as a trial before signing for a year. Le Chanois told him to accept, as he would then be able to help him recruit studio workers for the Resistance. In addition, members of his camera crew had been called up by the compulsory work service and their hiring by Con-tinental would allow them to avoid provisionally having to go to Germany.[12] Hayer was not the only Resistance fighter inside the crew. The sound engineer William-Robert Sivel was also a member of a clandestine group of 1939–40 war veterans.

After he signed his contract, Hayer was given a copy of the *Corbeau* script. He found nothing particularly shocking in reading it: "When I read the script, I didn't at all think it was an anti-French propaganda film. Reading the script highlighted for me a satirical and morbid conception of the medical envi-ronment in a provincial town. And Clouzot, to whom I made my remarks, explained to me that it was also a criticism of certain French people who had been exploiting the use of anonymous letters for the past two years."[13]

The shooting ended on July 3, 1943, at the Billancourt studios. Shortly before the end of the shooting, Hayer had a violent argument with Bauermeis-ter about unpaid overtime. The result was that his second assistant, Étienne Laroche, was immediately fired without his knowledge. Of course, his twelve-month contract was rescinded. He made only one film at Continental, and donated a large part of his salary to the Resistance and participated actively in the shooting of the film about the liberation of Paris.

Le Corbeau was released in theaters on September 28, 1943. The opening titles didn't credit any editor. It had been edited by Marguerite Beaugé, who probably took over the work begun by another editor. She acknowledged that she had edited the film and that she had had a row with Bauermeister about her work.[14] Shortly after the fight, she wrote to him to try to get back in his good graces:

> First, I must apologize for not having paid you a little visit before I left for my
> vacation, but I know you are so busy, and I didn't want to waste your time. I will

return as you requested on Wednesday, September 8. I hope that later you'll give me a few days to pick up my son from Pacy-sur-Eure. Now, I want to ask you if you are angry with me, because, for a while, I have had the feeling things are not as they used to be between us. If I have done something that upsets you, do not be afraid to tell me; whatever it was it was unintentional. As for me, I think I always do my work with as much passion as pleasure. And if I have done something wrong, it was quite unintentional. . . . I hope everything is fine for our film *Le Corbeau* and that it will be very successful.[15]

The tone of this letter shows that Marguerite Beaugé seemed to value her job at Continental above all else. The reason for her attitude was to be found in her personal life.

Born in Blois in 1892, she was the daughter of a cobbler. Her professional ascent was impressive. At twenty, she was working in Paris as a laundress and gave birth to a daughter, Yvonne, out of wedlock. Unmarried mothers in those days were social outcasts. Yet Beaugé must have been a very strong-willed woman. She said she started working in film at Vitagraph, and by 1918, she was working for Abel Gance as editor of *La Xème symphonie*. She became his regular editor, taking part in the mammoth editing of *Napoléon* in 1927. After the arrival of talkies, her career didn't falter; she worked with Henri Decoin, Julien Duvivier, and Robert Siodmak. She trained her daughter in the craft, and the girl started editing in 1934. She had to have had a very strong personality to be able to climb the ladder of her profession, especially given that she gave birth to a second child in 1932, a son, whose education she had to provide for all by herself. She presented herself as a widow to avoid gossip. Her daughter married a documentary director named Marcel Martin in 1937. Martin directed documentary shorts promoting sports, including *L'Appel du stade* (1941), according to the guidelines set by the Vichy government. Beaugé lived in Neuilly with her daughter and her son-in-law.

Beaugé was perfectly frank regarding her work at Continental and her relationship with the German managers. "From a work standpoint, I had a good relationship. I think I was doing my job well."[16] As for the letter she wrote to Bauermeister, she explained that "I had quit my job after numerous discussions regarding the last film I edited, and I was afraid those discussions might lead to my son-in-law being called up to go to Germany."[17] She was hated by other editors at the company, such as Charlotte Guilbert, whose work she took over. She was too close to her bosses for her colleagues' liking, and she didn't mind saying that "some methods of the organization were good from a strictly technical point of view."[18] Her position in this regard was reported after the liberation. She received a severe sanction: suspension without pay.

Le Corbeau became the mechanism of a particularly original publicity campaign in the press denouncing poison-pen letters. Marcel Colin-Reval, the publicity manager at the Alliance Cinématographique Européenne, remembered the effect of this campaign:

> The articles and information published by us had such titles as "The Shame of the Century: Anonymous Letters," "The Crime of Our Time," and "Is the Law Strong Enough to Punish the Authors of Anonymous Letters?" Etc. This campaign actually got me into personal trouble with the Gestapo, which "asked" me to put an end to it. It should be noted that in spite of this, all the newspapers published our press releases against anonymous letters for eight days and that this campaign was carried out around France as well as in Switzerland, which prompted rather serious reports from the provincial headquarters and Propaganda Office.[19]

It should be noted that Colin-Reval was a very active member of the Resistance.

The press was in general full of praise for *Le Corbeau*: "This film is truly and above all sensational. Its nonconformism, its quiet violence, its bitterness, its diabolical intelligence in every detail, its ferocious irony, and its iridescent cruelty are going to stun or delight, and sometimes both."[20] Film critic Jacques Audiberti even called the film "a rather fantastic masterpiece."[21] But some reviewers were also alarmed by the darkness of the subject. They were frightened by the tone and the film's moral: "We are transported to the prewar years, when directors like Marcel Carné and Jean Renoir were making the masterpieces *Quai des brumes* and *La Bête humaine* and became the visual poets of a confused area, feeding the most sordid pathological problems to a jaded public. We thought this period was over and that we would never see again such a striking example of a reprehensible state of mind. *Le Corbeau* sets us straight, and the fact that the film is popular with the public proves us wrong."[22] Others lambasted right-minded people who didn't appreciate Clouzot's unflattering picture:

> This film's adversaries will have a field day. It is dark, even morbid; it's not comforting to those who cling tenaciously to the illusion of a perfect humanity. So what? If in the name of national revolution, a few self-centered morons are shocked by this film, it was inevitable. . . . The purity we want to ascribe to our

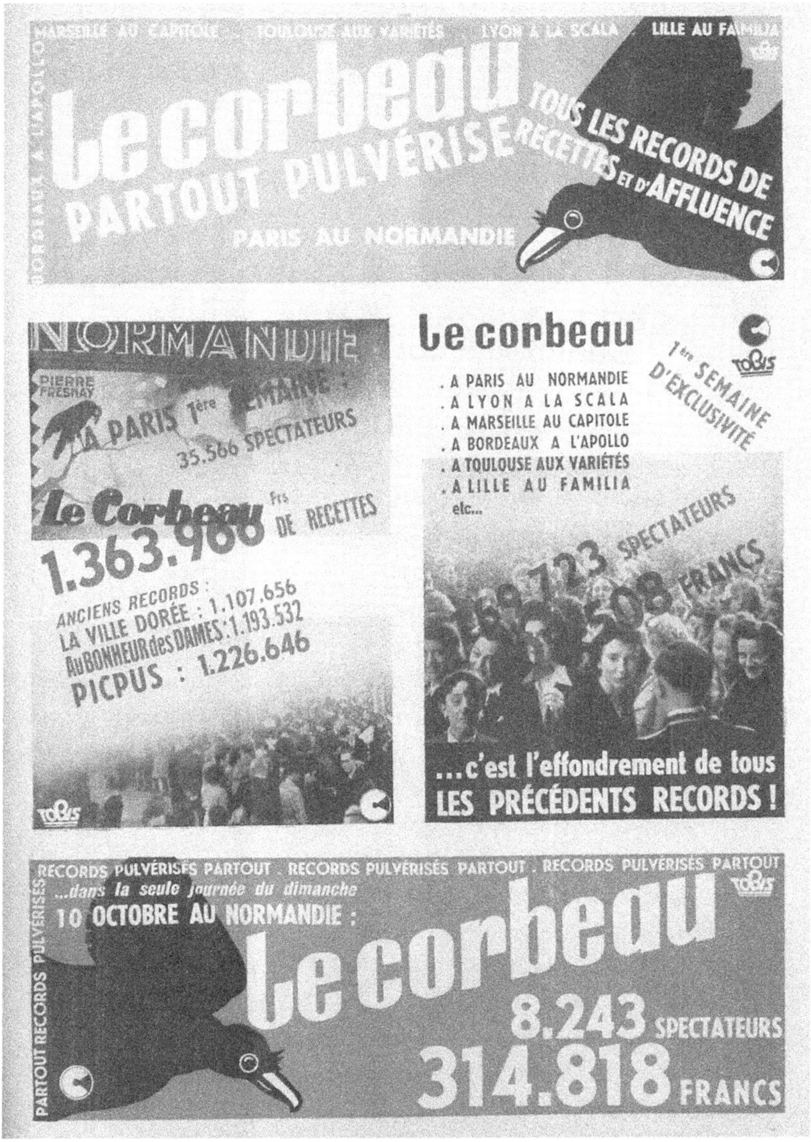

Ad for *Le Corbeau* (1943) (Fondation Jérôme Seydoux-Pathé)

institutions and to the people of this country must not lead us to cover over existing defects. . . . Neither do we want to make beautiful films with good feelings. Spread the word to Vichy and to the Organizing Committee of the Cinema Industry![23]

If the collaborationist press was uncomfortable with Clouzot's scathing masterpiece, the clandestine press felt the same. In December 1943, a small journal—duplicated by mimeograph—titled *L'Écran français* started to circulate. Anonymous editors of this journal violently attacked the film: *Le Corbeau* is

> exclusively about France. . . . 'A small town here or elsewhere,' we read, but, in any case, in France. This small town contains only vile French people, including the lead character, collaborator Fresnay. As there isn't any censorship at Continental—and the suppression of censorship makes a film more attractive than millions—an ease of expression that makes people believe in freedom of thought pervades *Le Corbeau*: a crude trap, a truly Nazi one to boot. In the middle of a pile of filth, gratuitous, by the way, as there isn't a reason for it, the only justification provided being the madness of the main culprit, the obsession with sacrilege is front and center: the film starts with the cemetery; the church is the location of rendezvous; a man who committed suicide is blessed there; an anonymous letter is dropped [from a gallery] inside the church; another letter falls off the [back of the] hearse; the funeral marches through a fair; the medical field is dragged through the mud; the abortion theme becomes a leitmotif; everything is ugly, scathing, up to the little girl listening through the doors and taking part in the corruption that pervades the city. [The film is] an apology for anonymous letters that goes as far as showing us how they can be safely done: a recipe that can, that must, serve the Gestapo. But what makes the danger even greater is that the film is very well made technically. Mr. Clouzot, director, hired hand, and his teammate Chavance, a pseudorevolutionary who refuses, he said, to put on a backpack for the Allies but consents to sell his pen to the enemy—it's easier—served Mr. Goebbels well. In short, a film that fails to show a single image other than a grimacing one—the normal expression of Ginette Leclerc—is not a human film: it's the definition of a pure Nazi movie. And at France's expense![24]

If *Le Corbeau* had been a piece of Nazi propaganda, as this anonymous author maintained, it would have been distributed in Germany. But it never managed to make it past the German censors, although there were rumors

Ad for *Le Corbeau* (1943) and *Mon amour est près de toi* (1943) (Fondation Jérôme Seydoux-Pathé) that the film had been released across the Rhine under the infamous title *A Small French Town*. Colin-Reval, however, was adamant that was not the case:

> This film was never released in Germany, under any title, the distribution of this film having been refused by UFA, the only distribution firm in Europe (except in France, Belgium, Switzerland, and Spain). The UFA management let Continental know by letter that *Le Corbeau* didn't suit the German mindset. . . . Following this incident, UFA even decided to completely suspend the distribution of new Continental films, a decision that "did upset a lot" Continental's manager. For months, German authorities had been looking for pretexts to suppress the release of French films in European countries, emphasizing the "danger" for German cinema represented by French film releases.[25]

So, far from pleasing the occupying authorities, the film was disturbing enough to be censored. This was also confirmed by Nicolas Katkoff, in charge of dubbing Continental films in German: "It was refused by German censors."[26]

Clouzot never said why he fell out with Greven shortly after the release of *Le Corbeau*. He even had a project ready to shoot: *La Chatte* written by Jean Anouilh, to star Michel Simon.[27] But if *Le Corbeau* managed to block the distribution in Germany of all future Continental productions, it's reasonable to assume that the big boss must have been livid. In any case, Clouzot left the firm and remained out of work for the rest of the occupation. As for his girlfriend, Suzy Delair, she claimed she was sacked from Continental after being fresh with Greven.[28]

However, the hysteria generated by *Le Corbeau* persisted, rearing its head with a vengeance during the film industry's purge. Clouzot denied that he ever wanted to make an antinational propaganda film:

> I cannot understand why people think *Le Corbeau* in particular highlights a corrupt humanity. I feel, for example, that *Le Voyageur de la Toussaint* emphasizes precisely the same characteristics. It has given rise to madness. In *Les Lettres françaises*, which was published underground, a number of articles claimed that *Le Corbeau* was being screened in Germany under the title *French Province*. Everyone jumped on that. It ended up creating a frenzy. . . . The Organizing Committee of the Cinema Industry, which felt differently, said, "It's bloody annoying that Continental can make films that French firms cannot make because of censorship reasons."[29]

In his defense, he invoked the testimonies of irreproachable screenwriters and authors who presented their views of *Le Corbeau*.

Journalist and screenwriter Henri Jeanson noted that

> after watching this film three times, it never came to my mind that it was an anti-national work. I believe, on the contrary, that *Le Corbeau*, written, played, directed, lit, and photographed by French technicians, proves that we are not so incapable and that we have in our country what it takes to win the battle of film. To pretend that the story we are told in *Le Corbeau*, that the characters in it, are a reflection of a whole country is absurd. Otherwise we must say that *Pension Mimosas* represents the French middle-class, *Pépé le Moko* the French colonial empire, *La Bête humaine* the French railways, *Quai des brumes* the life in our ports, *Goupi mains rouges* our small farmers, and Capitaine Hurluret the French army! Warning: if we judge and condemn *Le Corbeau* from that point of view, it would create a deadly precedent for our cinema and provide our future censors with new and probably decisive arguments.[30]

Screenwriter Jacques Prévert agreed with Jeanson: "I already told you the personal reason I didn't like much *Le Corbeau*. But because this unfortunate bird has become the bête noire and scapegoat of the corporation, I want to specify that, in fairness, it's absolutely impossible for me to condemn this film as anti-French propaganda."[31]

Clouzot also received the support of Jean-Paul Sartre, although he worked for the clandestine *L'Écran français*. He garnered the support of various art and entertainment personalities: "The persons, whose names follow, while formally disapproving of the fact that Mr. Clouzot made films inside Continental, testify that they were present at the screening of *Le Corbeau* and that they found no trace of anti-French propaganda: Mrs. Tania Balachova, Pierre Bost, Simone de Beauvoir, Michel Leiris, André Roussin, Jean-Paul Sartre, Michel Vitold, Claude Vermorel."[32]

Simone de Beauvoir described her feelings regarding the film in her memoirs: "Clouzot had made *Le Corbeau*, based on a script by Chavance. Some members of the Resistance accused him of contributing to enemy propaganda: screened in Germany, the film would present a repulsive picture of France society. In fact, it never crossed the border. Clouzot's friends made the point that the film attacked anonymous letter sending, while the occupying forces urged French people to denounce their neighbors on the sly. We did not think that *Le Corbeau* had any moral message nor that there was any reason for it to arouse patriotic indignations: we thought Clouzot had talent."[33]

In the end, it was Jean-Paul Le Chanois who most accurately summed up the matter. After rewatching the film in January 1947, he stated, "I think this film is amoral, but not a propaganda piece."[34] The impact of *Le Corbeau* can still be felt today. A poison-pen letter writer is called "Corbeau" in the press and in everyday speech. Having a word connected with a movie enter the common language is certainly the greatest recognition it can receive.

CHAPTER 22

The Difficult Years

In the summer of 1943, Continental had only three directors left under contract: Maurice Tourneur, André Cayatte, and Richard Pottier. These three filmmakers would direct high-quality works under increasingly difficult conditions until production ceased completely in the spring of 1944.

Two other directors joined the firm and left it quickly during that period: René Jayet and Albert Valentin. Jayet stayed only for a short period, just a few months—from January until March 1943—during which time he produced a small comedy titled *Vingt-cinq ans de bonheur* (1943) that featured one of the greatest character actors of French cinema, Jean Tissier.[1] Jayet found the atmosphere within the firm to be oppressive: "In the office where I worked, in the lock itself, in the middle, there was a magnifying glass. It sounds like a joke, but it's true. And from the outside, one could see what was going on, and so you could be watched at all times of the day."[2] If the surveillance was constant in offices, it was not any better on the set: "And when you said something or did something on the set, at any time, if you made a personal decision, five minutes later, Mr. Bauermeister was told. We never knew who was the spy in the firm who did that, but certainly on the set, there was somebody. It was an extremely tense atmosphere of pressure."[3] According to the assistant director Georges Metchikian, Richard Pottier was called in to finish the film.

Vingt-cinq ans de bonheur was adapted by Jean-Paul Le Chanois, and he wrote the dialogue in collaboration with Germaine Lefrancq, the author of the original successful play staged in 1941 at the Théâtre Michel. He stated that the work he put into this adaptation was minimal. He also concluded that "it was a very bad movie."[4] This comedy is certainly not memorable. However, the plot concerns a double adultery deeply at odds with Vichy moral standards. The unfortunate Mr. Castille, played wittily by Jean Tissier, learns on the same day that he is the father of a young girl whose mother is not his wife

Pressbook cover for *Vingt-cinq ans de bonheur* (1943) (Fondation Jérôme Seydoux-Pathé)

and that the boy he thought his son was the result of an affair his wife had with another man. The subject was, for sure, incompatible with the principles of the "national regeneration."

Actor Jean Tissier appeared in nine productions at Continental Films. Jean-Paul Le Chanois gladly came to his defense, as he particularly appreciated him: "I know you too well not to be aware that you have your head in the clouds. You don't really know what you are doing, the gala evenings you participate in, not even the contracts you are signing, and it creates problems for you with producers. But it is that Jean Tissier we love, the one who doesn't take himself seriously, who always look as if he wants to sell you a piece of paradise, a kind of poet or dreamer."[5]

If *Vingt-cinq ans de bonheur* was just an ordinary comedy without any depth, another filmmaker, André Cayatte, had the opportunity to adapt two great French works, Émile Zola's *Au Bonheur des dames* (1943) and Guy de Maupassant's *Pierre et Jean* (1943). Cayatte wished to cast Danielle Darrieux in the part of Denise for *Au Bonheur des dames*. But she had already left Continental at that time. He undertook a trip to Megève together with Clouzot to try to change her mind, but she was determined never to work for the German firm again. In the end, Blanchette Brunoy was selected to play the lead opposite Michel Simon. Simon had been recruited originally for *Le Val d'enfer* (1943), which should have been made in November 1942. Because of the invasion of the free zone, the production had been postponed, and Simon was replaced by Gabriel Gabrio.

Film critics were not convinced by Cayatte's adaptation, in spite of an excellent cast. Reviewer Didier Daix summed up the film's defects: "Cayatte installed Zola on a cardboard set. He knows how to use the camera skillfully, but his action is badly defined; his set has no reference point; his images are only images. All that remains in an honest middle-class average that never seems to want to reach any height. The film, all in all, is too short for the novel. Only the skeleton remains and the necessity to summarize constrained the adapters, preventing them from exploring the emotion where it is, with the poets."[6]

However, Cayatte managed to produce his best film at Continental with his adaptation of *Pierre et Jean*. After screening Albert Valentin's *Marie-Martine* (1943), the director and producer both decided that Renée Saint-Cyr would be perfect for the female lead, the part of Alice Rolland. While they considered casting Gaby Morlay, they realized she couldn't be convincing in the first part of the film, where she was supposed to be twenty. When Saint-Cyr read the

Pressbook cover for *Au Bonheur des dames* (1943) (Fondation Jérôme Seydoux-Pathé)

script, she was immediately persuaded she had the part of her life, "I read, I reread, André-Paul Antoine's excellent story based on Guy de Maupassant's short story, and when Continental summons me—all the administrative staff, impressive, behind a long table, Greven at the center—I feel more like an accused in my chair in front of them."[7] The actress was not unknown to the company, as she had appeared in *La Symphonie fantastique* (1941), directed by Christian-Jaque. With her usual confidence, she discussed various modifications she wished for her part with Greven. She thought she would be thrown out and be told to get lost. But, quite the contrary, Greven agreed with her about modifying the script to give it a lighter touch and to add comedy in order to give more depth to the drama.

Saint-Cyr signed her contract on August 17, 1943.[8] She would be paid a fee of 550,000 francs, with income tax deducted at the source. The payment would be made in four installments: 100,000 at the signature of the agreement, 50,000 on the first day of production, 200,000 at the twentieth day of shooting, and 200,000 two days after completion of the production. She would not receive any extra payment in the case of retakes. And of course, she confirmed she had trade card as well as a work permit authorized by the German authorities. In addition, she declared on her honor that she was Aryan. The contract was signed jointly by Greven and Bauermeister.

Production started on August 30, 1943, and took place under extremely difficult conditions. The Billancourt studios were close to the Renault car factory, which was one of the main targets of allied bombings. The film crew was in a less-than-ideal position during air raids. Saint-Cyr admitted she was not fully aware of the danger: "We had daily alerts and nearly every morning, as soon as we started the first shot of the day, sirens interrupted work. These interruptions were infuriating. Makeup girls, editors were hysterical, and we watched, powerless, frozen, in front of the doors, on the sidewalk. I remember one bomb fell on the bridge facing the studio and hit water and gas pipes, and we saw gigantic columns of flames and water shooting up toward the sky."[9] Those Allied bombings created a mixture of fear and hope. They sometimes had unexpected effects. When a bomb exploded in the Seine, hundreds of dead fish rose to the surface. This gigantic power-driven fishery attracted masses of starving Parisians. Equipped with shrimp nets, shovels, and even broom handles, people tried to catch a meager pittance to improve their everyday meals.

One day as the alarm was ringing, Saint-Cyr's colleague Noël Roquevert reproached her for taking everything so lightly and told her to go to an air raid shelter, because as the lead actress in the film, she had to protect the

Ad for *Pierre et Jean* (1943) (Fondation Jérôme Seydoux-Pathé)

production. It turned out to be a bad idea. She left in her car with actor Bernard Lancret and her dresser, to go to the nearest shelter, Porte de Saint-Cloud subway station. All three ended up under a deluge of bombs that destroyed the whole area.

If studio life was no picnic for the actors, it was even worse for minor employees. Saint-Cyr's dresser, who had been faithful to her for years, was sixty-four years old. Marie Bourland, called Pollos after her husband, who had made a career as film extra and stuntman under that nickname, lived in Belleville, on the other side of Paris. And every morning, she had to wake up at 4 a.m. to walk to the Billancourt studios. In the evening, she had to take care of her blind husband and did not get into bed until midnight. And yet every morning, she arrived at the studio, smart and cheerful. Continental paid her a miserable salary she had to accept, 900 francs a week.

Stage managers did not have much fun either. Gabriel Bleinat, nicknamed Géo Sandry, worked as location manager.[10] He had to organize the rental of cars, various props, and furniture necessary for the shooting. "It was a tough job," he noted, "because the truck was reserved for furniture. I had to go on errands using the subway or on foot during air raids. My only advantage was job security."[11]

For Resistance fighters inside the studio, life became increasingly dangerous. The German army was bogged down on the Russian front, and the Vichy government became harsher. The "terrorists" chase became more aggressive. Jean-Paul Le Chanois realized he had to go underground: "I had to leave Continental when my contract expired in August 1943, and I left it also because the police were hot on my heels in Paris, not because of my work at Continental but because I had been denounced for my underground work, my terrorist work for other people."[12] While in hiding in Normandy, he still came back to the capital to pursue his activities for the Resistance: "I found a small house near Dreux where I lived. I went on leading the Resistance work I had been doing; I went on typing texts there, coming three days a week to Paris, taking the train in Houdan and changing in Versailles and Issy-les-Moulineaux to avoid roundups, which were frequent."[13] During one of these visits, he met Jean Tissier, who greeted him and asked him politely if he needed anything; the actor was perfectly aware that Le Chanois was wanted by the Gestapo.

His comrade Jean Devaivre was assistant on *Pierre et Jean*, taking care of the timing of the shooting script. He stayed at Continental and worked on the production of *Cécile est morte!* and *Les Caves du Majestic*. In March 1944, he hurriedly left the company to join the maquis in Saône-et-Loire, as he feared being arrested.[14]

In spite of all the hazards, Renée Saint-Cyr had fond memories of the production and the direction of André Cayatte, whose sensitivity she appreciated: "He demanded a lot. He obtained even more. Cayatte was a leader of men. We believed in him. He repeated to me what I knew already, that one mustn't underestimate melodrama, that one must give it all, shamelessly. Then one can realize what a precious springboard it can become."[15] Indeed, Renée Saint-Cyr plays an unhappy married woman with remarkable talent. She is married to an uncouth selfish man, played with subtlety by Noël Roquevert. After a short-lived affair with Jacques Dumesnil, she gives birth to a second son; her husband is kept in the dark regarding the biological father. Twenty years later, older and resigned to her fate, she observes with horror the rivalry developing between her two sons (Gilbert Gil and Bernard Lancret) after the second receives a big inheritance. Carefully avoiding any pathos, Cayatte directed his actors very closely and produced a subtle melodrama that remains as powerful as it was when it first came out in December 1943.

It was also thanks to the work of two great technicians, whose names were not even mentioned in the credits, that Saint-Cyr delivered one of the most memorable performances in her career. Makeup artist Chakhatouny was a wizard with his fingers and managed to make the actress look twenty years older.[16] "He created a genuine sculptural work in accentuating the muscles, in adding mauve and brown colors to the curved parts, in accentuating the flat parts. The eyes were softened by the tinting of the eyelids with a nearly white mauve. Of course, neither the mouth nor the eyes were made up."[17] As for the costume designer Rosine Delamare, she allowed her to move seamlessly from the elegant Belle Epoque young lady to the distressed mother in giving her a washed-out mauve flannelette dressing gown to wear that made her look older. This famous costume designer came to work for Continental in 1942, even as she was a member of the Resistance in the Commandant Vaillant network.[18]

When the film came out at the Biarritz cinema on December 29, 1943, Delamare confessed she cried like a romantic schoolgirl, even though she was a very tough woman. The critical reception was indeed extremely enthusiastic for Saint-Cyr.

> She has a human and charming face, a slightly throaty and touching voice. She is pretty to see, a little aloof, smiling and unhappy under her little 1913 hats and in her beautiful striped dresses. And then, when she plays the mother, ill-treated

by her son, she has sincerity in her voice, her attitude is dignified, and she has a beautiful, secretive, and hardened face. We often have beautiful young ladies and elderly artists full of intelligence and intensity. It's very rare to discover a "real woman." Two or three times, in this picture, and precisely in its less good parts, Renée Saint-Cyr gives the impression we are watching one.[19]

On November 30, 1943, shortly before Cayatte's picture premiered, another Maupassant adaptation directed by the talented German director Helmut Käutner was released on French screens. *Romanze in Moll* (1943) was a superb achievement showcasing the talent of actress Marianne Hoppe. The German filmmaker unofficially used a Maupassant short story, *Les Bijoux*, which is not mentioned in the credits, and French reviewers picked up on that. In comparing the two pictures, film critic Roger Régent noted:

We must make a special place for Miss Renée Saint-Cyr who plays Alice. We had the opportunity recently to be severe with her. . . . This time, her performance is absolutely remarkable, and this character of the sacrificial lover and tortured mother owes a lot to her sensitivity. This Alice, so close to the Madeleine from *Les Bijoux* (*Romanze in Moll*, played by Marianne Hoppe), touches us more than any of the heroines played by Renée Saint-Cyr, who, this time, knew how to age, which is what we reproach her so justly for not having done in *La Symphonie fantastique*.[20]

The German Parisian newspaper *Pariser Zeitung* also published a raving review of this Maupassant adaptation:

André Cayatte's picture faithfully follows Maupassant's short story. *Pierre et Jean* belongs to the lesser-known works of the author, probably because it's far more sober and because there is hardly any erotic element. From that point of view, the work is ideal for a picture adaptation. Cayatte tastefully and tactfully reveals the psychological aspects without neglecting or overdoing the visual aspects. A typical Maupassant atmosphere is re-created with a delicate and sarcastic humor that imbues the images but that is sufficiently contained to avoid becoming farce. . . . The actors deserve the greatest praises. In the part of the young woman and even more as the older mother of two, Renée Saint-Cyr appears wonderfully true and human in one of the best performances of these last years. Another magnificent characterization is offered by Noël Roquevert in the part of her husband hesitating between the obstinate brute and the benevolent father. . . .

There is no doubt *Pierre et Jean* belongs to the best adaptations of Maupassant's short stories.[21]

As for Richard Pottier, he was directing a script written by Carlo Rim, *La Ferme aux loups* (1943), a comedy-mystery that provided young actors with a great opportunity to show their talents. If neither François Périer nor Paul Meurisse were newcomers to the camera, one young actress was making her debut after having been an extra in other Continental films. Under the name Martine Carole, Marie-Louise Mourer, then twenty-three years old, got the female lead.[22] According to Jean Devaivre, she got this promotion thanks to Alfred Greven, who wasn't insensitive to her charms.[23] If this promotion via the producer's office cannot be confirmed, on the other hand, there was no doubt that another young actress, Annie France, was the girlfriend of the production manager, Bauermeister. Indeed, stage manager Paul Olive alluded directly to their relationship in one letter to him: "I hope you had good restful holiday and that Miss Annie and you are in excellent health."[24] This relationship allowed her to make five pictures at Continental, although her career completely ended after the liberation.[25]

Carlo Rim's script had been registered at the Society for Authors before the war. Nobody had wanted to purchase it. Yet Richard Pottier managed to make *La Ferme aux loups* a nice mixture of mystery and comedy. A reporter (François Périer) and a photographer (Paul Meurisse) end up investigating the mysterious death of two Russian émigrés who happened to be twins. Their boss's pretty secretary (Martine Carole) helps them, accompanying the young men to the mysterious "wolf farm" where one of the bodies was discovered.

Rim never came to the set during the shooting at the Billancourt and Neuilly studios, which took place between August and the end of September 1943. He also never corresponded with the director Richard Pottier. Rim was furious about the way his script had been treated by Continental, complaining that one of the Russians at the firm had modified it. "There is a Mr. Andrejew, who was an art director, when we were shooting *La Ferme aux loups*. It seems he is a White Russian; he cut everything in my film that constituted a satire of White Russians. He cut two scenes. I tried to remove my name; there was nothing I could do, like for *Simplet*. At Continental, they would not budge on this."[26]

Paul Meurisse was likewise unhappy but was also under a lot of pressure and so agreed to make a fourth picture for Continental. Having made his debut in *Ne bougez plus* (1941) under the inept direction of Pierre Caron—during which

Pressbook cover for *La Ferme aux loups* (1943) (Fondation Jérôme Seydoux-Pathé)

his character tirelessly repeated, "Pathetic! Pathetic!" under his breath, as if it were a commentary on his director's lack of talent—he then made *Mariage d'amour* (1942) and *Défense d'aimer* (1942). After these three pictures, the firm wanted him to appear in Cayatte's *Au Bonheur des dames*.[27] Meurisse didn't want to and asked the director to remove him from the cast, but Cayatte told him he was powerless regarding decisions made by the management.

Meurisse dared to refuse the part, confronting Greven and Bauermeister. He thought the law was on his side and brought an action against Continental for undue pressure that constituted a prejudice to his artistic career. The lawyer he contacted warned him not to initiate such proceedings against a German firm. But he was adamant. "I was pumped up. I believed that taking a firm line always paid off. We very quickly received confirmation of this; the picture was made without me. I had won."[28] But his success revealed itself to be a Pyrrhic victory. A few weeks later, a policeman arrived at his door and told him he was about to receive a summons for the compulsory work service.

Meurisse realized he had no choice. He made an appointment to see Bauermeister. When he showed him his summons for the Todt Organization in La Rochelle, Bauermeister burst out laughing and phoned Greven in the neighboring office.[29] The big boss made an entrance. The upset actor observed, "They really had a good laugh! They were doubled up with laughter; they slapped their thighs with their fists. These two morons took the piss out of me with a complete lack of good manners."[30] He went home, defeated. The next day at noon, the phone rang; he was summoned by Greven. When he arrived at his office, Greven made him sign a contract. He was hired for *La Ferme aux loups*, whose shooting was scheduled to start at the Billancourt studios in August. It proved as eventful as the one for *Pierre et Jean*. They frequently had to stop shooting because of the bombings. The still cameraman was killed during one of the air raids.

In the end, *La Ferme aux Loups* proved to be an unpretentious picture but one that had a certain charm thanks to the interaction between Périer and Meurisse, who managed to re-create the sparkle of American comedies. Martine Carole was rather more ornamental than really convincing as the juvenile lead. The reviews were mixed. According to one, *La Ferme aux loups* is "a rather hybrid picture. We are deprived of certain elements necessary for a real detective film without their being replaced with enough fantasy. . . . François Périer is excellent. He needed all the skills he possesses to play such an insignificant character."[31] Meurisse's talent was also praised: "There is something ironic, nonchalant, deadpan, and, let us use the adjective, Keatonian about his

Ad for *Ne bougez plus* (1941) (Fondation Jérôme Seydoux-Pathé)

acting, which promises, in the hands of a clever authoritarian director, to make him a surprising juvenile lead comedian."[32]

Meurisse never heard from Continental during the rest of the war. He was nevertheless scared the compulsory work service would call him up as some point. Yet it was Continental Films that launched his career as a film actor. He made four films for that firm and was very surprised he was never summoned by any purge committee after the liberation. He was probably not famous enough for that privilege.

CHAPTER 23

La Vie de plaisir

La Vie de plaisir, directed by Belgian filmmaker Albert Valentin, received as much commentary as *Les Inconnus dans la maison* and *Le Corbeau* because of its acerbic social criticism, which was considered antinational after the war.

Albert Valentin, like many of his colleagues, had worked for UFA before the war, including *L'Entraîneuse* in Berlin in 1938 with Michèle Morgan and François Périer. He recalled an incident during the shooting of the film that revealed how German technicians regarded the French people who came to make films in Berlin studios: "The German grips invited us to the canteen, [Raoul] Ploquin, Michèle Morgan, and François Périer. The grips told us, 'Perhaps we'll be at war tomorrow. We wanted to shake your hand. We are not enemies; we do not bear a grudge against France.' They were strictly grips, lighting technicians. It was in the cafeteria, and we had closed the cafeteria door. Michèle Morgan can testify. She started to cry."[1] This demonstration of sympathy at the time of the Munich Agreement contrasts with the way German technicians were treated at the same time during the shooting of Maurice Gleize's *Le Récif de corail* (1939). Valentin remembered, "In Cannes, even in the lobby of Hotel Miramar, people threw stones at German technicians in charge of shooting *Le Récif de corail*. If I say they were stoned; I mean it literally."[2]

At the start of the occupation, Valentin sold a story to Continental titled "Noces de cendres," which Maurice Tourneur directed under the title *Péchés de jeunesse*. Later, he directed three films for a number of French film production firms. In 1942, he met German actress Jenny Jugo and her producer during a visit to Paris. They offered him the opportunity to come to Berlin to make romantic comedies for a much higher salary than the one he received from the French. He refused.

It was in 1941 during a stay at the home of producer Pierre O'Connell that the project was born in Valentin's mind:

Ad for *La Vie de plaisir* (1944) (Fondation Jérôme Seydoux-Pathé)

I read in his library a series of volumes relating very interesting lawsuits, particularly about a divorce suit that I found enormously exciting, because the point of view of the two lawyers was absolutely defensible and contradictory. I was with [Charles] Spaak. I had an idea of a script based on that theme that I wrote, and I offer it to O'Connell, who tells me, "No." I had written it for Jean Murat. He tells me, "No, I am not interested," after consulting Arys [Nissoti]. . . . Spaak was rather excited by the history. I told Murat about it, who drove me to [André] Paulvé.

This last step led nowhere, and so he gave up the project provisionally. However, Spaak took the step of offering *La Vie de plaisir* to Greven without telling Valentin beforehand.

Spaak had worked for Continental in 1941 on two pictures, *L'Assassinat du Père Noël* and *Péchés de jeunesse*. Later, he opted to work only for French production firms. In 1942, he came into contact with André Cayatte. He had already refused several offers from Continental. "I had refused three proposals from Clouzot." The first was for *Caprices*: "I knew Raymond Bernard's story; I didn't want to do it." He then had lunch with Clouzot on another occasion during which Clouzot again tried to hire him: "I said I didn't want to join his company, as I already had signed contracts with French firms." The third time was when "Clouzot asked me to make a film called *Marché noir*."[3]

By September 1942, a number of his projects had fallen through, and so, through Cayatte, he entered into talks with Continental. The company offered him three films with an exclusive contract. He explained he would be free in six months. His contract, which started on January 15, 1943, required that he provide three scripts to the firm. "During six months, I did absolutely nothing but chat with these gentlemen, and I was doing it reluctantly. . . . So, I play the fool. They offered me scripts, and I refused them. I offer to cancel my contract by giving back to Greven the advance I had received. Mr. Greven never answered. I tell him several times that the scripts disgust me. In the end, Greven continues not to answer. But I notified him that he was in breach of contract, as he was not paying me anymore. That was in May 1943."[4] At that time, Christian-Jaque offered him the opportunity to work on a film produced by Roger Richebé. But Greven—who had heard about it—phoned the producer to tell him that "in case Mr. Spaak signed with you, although we are legally in breach with him, Mr. Spaak will run into serious trouble."[5] Cornered, Spaak decided to offer *La Vie de Plaisir*. Bauermeister and Greven immediately saw a good project for Albert Préjean.

That same evening, Spaak called Valentin and told him, "My friend, I am in an embarrassing situation. To get out of trouble, I described the story, and I didn't say it was yours."[6] Valentin replied, "If it gets you out of trouble and ends your legal problems, go on. I am not very excited to work with these people."[7] Greven was initially not very enthusiastic at the idea of hiring Valentin, whom he found unpleasant, but in the end, he asked Bauermeister to call him up. He signed a contract for *La Vie de Plaisir* in June 1943.

Shooting started in September 1943 at the Neuilly studios, which were less exposed to air raids than Billancourt. The filming lasted only five weeks, because of budget restrictions. The company hired a thirty-year-old blonde young actress named Claude Génia for the female lead. Her presence in the cast of a Continental production still raises many questions. Born Claude Aranovitch in Russia in 1913, she was the daughter of Samuel Aranovitch and Esther Kaplan. She should have been banned from working on account of the Vichy antisemitic laws and she should not have been able to get a work permit. And yet she made pictures during the occupation like *Monsieur des Lourdines* (1943), directed by Maréchal Pétain's stepson, Pierre de Hérain. If in that picture her part was small, she played the lead in the Continental picture. We can only speculate regarding her case. Was she receiving help from important people, or did she have forged identity papers that allowed her to get a work permit? Whatever the case, Greven must have known about her origins. Perhaps he hired her in order to have an alibi if Germany lost the war. Various testimonies reveal that the Continental big boss had very early on mentioned the possibility of defeat and was exploring ways he could stay in charge of the company after the arrival of the Americans.

The script for *La Vie de plaisir* is a takedown of a hypocritical and greedy aristocracy. The series of flashbacks that structures the film gives the divorce story a Pirandellian tone. Spaak explained:

> The idea we had was to tell the story of a divorce through which the man and the woman would learn of things about each other's private life that they had kept hidden from each other, so that by the time the court granted the divorce, they would know they in fact love each other and could live together. For the story to work properly, the characters had to be from opposite backgrounds. We invented an aristocrat belonging to the gentry. We called him Mr. de Lormel. We didn't want to make a duke out of him; it's not a well-known title in France. We have been accused of being biased and nasty. I'd like to tell you that France is like my own country. We never thought that in telling a story in which an aristocrat wished to marry his daughter for money, we were attacking France and its prestige.[8]

Valentin also defended his script:

> I have been criticized for showing the French middle class in a disagreeable way. I was sensitive to it. Several friends told me so. I must admit I proceeded in all innocence, because the picture in no way attacks the French middle class. It is never said "We, the French middle class, think like that." If it was happening in Russia, they would be boyars or else an orthodox priest. In England, they would be lords and the bishop of Canterbury. It's international; it's not about the French middle class. In no way are they the embodiment of France or of religion. Similarly, in a film about bad guys set in Belleville, people would think it normal if they misbehaved. If we move the setting to Faubourg Saint-Germain, everybody thinks they should behave like gods.[9]

If the picture has stood the test of time, it is mostly due to Spaak's incisive dialogue as well as to Valentin's elegant direction. Contrasting the proletarian phlegm of Albert Maulette (Albert Préjean), the owner of the nightclub called La Vie de plaisir, with the arrogance of Mr. de Lormel (Aimé Clariond), the patriarch of a ruined aristocratic family threatened with a lawsuit, *La Vie de plaisir* is perfectly successful in capturing opposing social environments. The character parts were played by talented actors, some of whom were members of the prestigious Comédie-Française theater company, like Maurice Escande, whose moniker in the picture was Boëldieu, a sarcastic allusion to the character played by Pierre Fresnay in *La Grande illusion* (1937), also scripted by Spaak. In *Vie de plaisir*, Renoir's noble character becomes an amoral aristocrat.

The picture was released at the Normandie on the Champs-Élysées on May 16, 1944. It was the last Continental production released before the liberation of Paris.[10] The collaborationist press launched a bitter attack on the picture. It didn't appreciate the criticism of the aristocracy. "A friend told me, 'It's a communist picture.' I understood afterward what he meant, because it's also indisputably a revolutionary film with a zest of anarchy."[11] Extreme-right film critic Lucien Rebatet was a bit less scathing, but he regretted that the hero was a nightclub owner: "The portrayal of polite society, with its frivolousness, its elegance often hiding so much ugliness, is the best aspect of the picture. But I imagine I won't be the only spectator puzzled by the Maulette character, the owner of a gambling joint, whom the author made, strangely and paradoxically, the embodiment of honesty, frankness, hard work and the moralist of the story!"[12] Other reviewers were furious at the attack on French moral values. The "tendentious ideas" in the film are, one reviewer argues, likely to incite "social hatred and class struggle" in "weak minds": "The director paints the defects of the upper world by blackening them, by making them ugly on purpose. Of those aristocrats he made corrupt, vile and unpleasant characters; he exaggerated their wild behavior and their vices."[13] Others were even more violent and attacked Continental productions straight out: "After *Les Inconnus dans la maison*, *Le Corbeau*, *Cécile est morte!*, here is *La Vie de plaisir* . . . [Continental] is not a film production firm, it's a demolition contractor attacking French family and society."[14]

And, finally, the two Belgian authors were directly targeted. They dared to criticize France:

> We are familiar with two Belgiums: a nationalistic Francophile and pro-European Belgium passionate about French questions, which could give lessons to the most fervent French patriot, and a Francophobic anti-European and internationalist Belgium, the one that violently sided with Red Spain and despairs today to see a possible French recovery on the horizon. Generally, we ignore the first one, thinking there is no need to tend to our friends who already support us, but the second one, France not only smiled at it but also made some indecent advances. It opened wide its gates, at least its studios.[15]

Ironically, French Resistance fighters in *Les Lettres françaises* also harshly criticized Valentin and Spaak: "For those who still doubt it, for those who refused to see in *Les Inconnus dans la maison*, *Le Corbeau*, and other Continental productions a deliberate intention to tarnish and sap France, *La Vie de plaisir* offers us striking proof."[16]

And yet Valentin and Spaak cowrote *Le Ciel est à vous* (1943), directed by Jean Grémillon, which was praised in the clandestine paper *L'Écran français* for its moral qualities: unlike *Le Corbeau*, which features "cripples and the corrupts who dishonor one of our provincial towns," *Le Ciel est à vous* offers "characters full of French sap, authentic courage, healthy morality, where we find again a national truth that doesn't want to and cannot die."[17]

All these reviews show the futility of the accusations on both sides. But the context of the end of the occupation made it impossible for anyone to offer a balanced judgment of the picture. The views of the one side were the polar opposite of that of the other. Collaborators felt the Nazis and the Vichy regime were running out of steam, while the Resistance vehemently attacked the last supporters of a dying regime. It was in this toxic atmosphere that Continental was about to put into production its last pictures.

CHAPTER 24

Game Over

In the spring of 1944, shootings were severely handicapped, as there were not only air raids and bombings but also numerous power cuts and a rationing of all the materials necessary for filmmaking.

Yet three more films would be made before April 1944. André Cayatte started making *Le Dernier sou* with Ginette Leclerc and Noël Roquevert on December 20, 1943, at the Neuilly studios. But Leclerc fell ill, and shooting was suspended and only restarted in February 1944. Numerous sequences were shot on location, in particular at the Bois de Boulogne and at the Vel' d'Hiv' (Vélodrome d'hiver), no doubt to avoid the power cuts in studios, where sometimes they had to shoot at night.

This neglected picture was written by André Cayatte with Louis Chavance, the author of *Le Corbeau*, and its subject was just as dark as the Clouzot film. Yet *Le Dernier sou* was never criticized because it was released on January 23, 1946, well after the liberation of Paris. It tells the story of a gang of crooks who steal money from unemployed people desperate for a job. Their leader is Stéfani (Noël Roquevert), who promises them well-paid jobs before asking them for a tidy sum to acquire radios that they are then supposed to peddle. He is helped by his secretary (Ginette Leclerc), who is increasingly disgusted by their scam. When she tries to protect a childhood friend (Gilbert Gil) from her crooked boss, he murders her. The picture highlights a dark and corrupt humanity, much as *Le Corbeau* does. Admittedly, the heroine was on her way to redemption, but the film is otherwise bathed in an atmosphere of blatant corruption that is close to that of *Quai des brumes*, one of the pictures most hated by collaborators.

Noël Roquevert as Stéfani rips off suckers and runs his gang with an iron hand. Before this film, Roquevert had been cast in supporting parts and was one of the main character players at Continental; he made no less than eleven pictures, performing in the most representative productions of the firm: *Les Inconnus dans la maison, Le Corbeau, La Main du diable*, and *La Vie de plaisir*. Asked about his political opinions after the liberation, he noted that he "lik[ed] discipline, order, and work and [had] followed Maréchal Pétain's doctrine. He wondered if Maréchal did not agree with England and America."[1] His attitude reflected the mixture of a wait-and-see attitude and blindness among some people in France. While he agreed to work for Radio-Paris, he also gladly helped friends, Jewish or not, who were hiding from the Gestapo. He had a yearly contract with Continental Films and was unapologetic regarding his participation to *Le Corbeau*: "It wasn't a propaganda picture. In that firm, everybody was French; everybody was even Gaullist (I'm not talking about myself)."[2] His statement brings to mind the old supporter of Maréchal Pétain played by Maurice Schutz in Henri-Georges Clouzot's excellent sketch in *Retour à la vie* (1949) who points to a picture of General de Gaulle by mistake while thinking of Pétain. Sometimes reality was close to fiction.

His colleague Ginette Leclerc made some of her best pictures at Continental. When her stance was discussed after the war, it was not in relation to her films but in relation to the company she kept during the occupation. She was involved with actor Lucien Gallas, who played her lover in *Le Val d'enfer* (1943), directed by Maurice Tourneur. At Gallas's suggestion, she opened a nightclub called Baccara at 70 rue de Ponthieu, close to the Champs-Élysées, in December 1943.[3] To get the authorization to open the place, she went to Greven, who put her in touch with the Propaganda Office. This private club quickly proved to be a favorite meeting place for French Gestapo members. She said that once she realized this, she tried to close the club. Unfortunately, Leclerc made other mistakes by mixing with unsavory characters, which did not go unnoticed. In May 1944, she met Pierre Loutrel (aka Pierrot le Fou), a notorious French Gestapo member, in a bar, when she was looking for a car to go to Lille. He offered to drive her there, and she accepted, and she subsequently met up with him several times in Paris, sometimes with French comedian Milly Mathis. She didn't seem to realize how serious her actions were: "I suspected Pierrot Le Fou was a member of the German police because he carried a gun and drove a car. But I never knew he was a member of the Avenue Foch services [French Gestapo]."[4] Her carefree attitude cost her dearly at the liberation.

Continental's last two productions were adaptations of Georges Simenon novels with Albert Préjean playing Inspector Maigret, accompanied by Gabriello as the mumbling Inspector Lucas. They had already made *Picpus* (1943), directed by Richard Pottier, with a script written by Jean-Paul Le Chanois. For *Cécile est morte!*, Le Chanois was not available to write the dialogue, as he had gone underground, and Michel Duran took over. The film was shot in only twenty-four days. Maurice Tourneur managed to make the film fast paced, like the best American B films. Albert Préjean's portrayal of Maigret has often been criticized; he was considered too young, too dynamic, and too talkative. Yet Simenon approved Le Chanois's characterization in the script and even wrote him a letter to thank him.

Alfred Greven had asked Charles Spaak to write the dialogue for *Cécile est morte!*, but he didn't want to do it. He explained himself in a letter to the boss: "And, so Continental persists in making me adapt *Cécile est morte!*, whose story is bad, disgusting in thousand ways, and to do so for an actor unsuitable for the lead. It's an unreasonable position."[5] Admittedly, at that time, Spaak was looking for any means possible to cancel his contract with the firm. However, a few months later, he accepted an offer to adapt and to write the dialogue for *Les Caves du Majestic* with that same actor playing Maigret.

Cécile est morte! was released on March 8, 1944. The criminal stories and the shady characters created by Simenon annoyed the kind souls among the collaborators. According to two contemporary accounts:

> Numerous characters give the whole a very unpleasant tone. When in *Le Corbeau* we were shown a young girl already marked by all vices, we were the first not to protest because Clouzot and Chavance's picture was a genuine work of art. The spectacle of a certain amount of violence, of mental or physical defects, was justified in that case; the scope and exceptional quality of the work authorized such excesses. In *Cécile est morte!*, an insignificant picture lacking any social or artistic ambition, nothing allows such boldness. It is purely gratuitous and visibly looking to attract lovers of indecent shows.[6]

> Spectators rush to this kind of show, comment, admire, deduce, conclude, and as soon as the picture is over, look among the initiates for the one person able to give them the date of the next Simenon or the next Maigret. Exactly like the man on the street who rushes to the newsstand so as not to miss one line of the nth episode of the Petiot affair. It is the crowd's liking for everything ugly, low and villainous, that taste for blood, naked corpses, its own sadistic taste for the others' sadism that are found in the film references.[7]

In the end, in the fall of 1943 Charles Spaak agreed to adapt *Les Caves du Majestic*. He had already written the shooting script when he was arrested by

Pressbook cover for *Cécile est morte!* (1944) (Fondation Jérôme Seydoux-Pathé) the Gestapo on October 22. The reason for his arrest had to do with his relatives. Charles was the brother of statesman Paul-Henri Spaak, who was one of the members of the Belgian government in exile in London. In addition, his brother Claude—also a screenwriter—was married to Suzanne, who was the head of a Resistance group. And it just so happened that Suzanne and Claude had both been arrested by the Gestapo at the same time as Charles. Suzanne would be shot in Fresnes prison on August 12, 1944.

Spaak was transferred to that same prison. His young pregnant wife, expecting their first child, received the same treatment.[8] After a month in jail, the screenwriter received a visit from a German commissioner sent by Continental. He was asked to finish the script and in exchange, his wife would be transferred to a penitentiary managed by the Red Cross and he would be allowed to receive parcels. Spaak was also contacted by Princess Elisabeth Soutzo, a Romanian film producer for whom he had to write a script.[9] "After six weeks, [Continental] and Mrs. Soutzo managed to communicate with me via the Gestapo, because they were German and because Mrs. Soutzo was Romanian, and because they asked their embassy to serve as mediator."[10] According to him, it was Mrs. Soutzo who managed to provide him with paper and ink, enabling him to go back to work on *Les Caves du Majestic*. "I was told, 'It's astonishing, when you know you were in jail, how it turned out.'" There were many details, he added, that came "from my own story."[11] Once the dialogue and adaptation of the Simenon picture were finished, and as he was bored in prison, he wrote *Le Collier de la reine* (1946) for Elisabeth Soutzo.[12] After 143 days in jail, he was finally released from Fresnes on March 10, 1944.

The shooting of *Les Caves du Majestic* started on February 16 at the Neuilly studios under the direction of Richard Pottier. Assistant Jean Devaivre managed to get Spaak on the set, through Bauermeister, in order to rewrite some dialogue. The screenwriter arrived accompanied by two warders and Devaivre offered him a lobster claw—a prop for the shooting—to improve his daily ration. As reported by Albert Préjean, the shooting was often suspended.

The moment the first wails of the siren were heard you could see Maigret, his superintendents, inspectors and sergeants capering along at full gallop, elbows well tucked in, towards the nearest shelter. We dived several yards below ground, murderers, detectives, informers and false witnesses, corpses and pathologists, and stood squashed one against the other while the bombs burst over our heads. The all-clear sounded and we would gingerly pop our noses out of doors. Back we would go to our former positions on the set. Back to the cameras and Maigret's wise deductions. Another wail of the siren: a second stampede, a further flight of pseudo-corpses who didn't want to become real ones![13]

Cinematographer Pierre Montazel stated that, of course, they never shot any sequence in front of the real Majestic Hotel on avenue Kléber, as the hotel was occupied by the military government in France under the command of General Stülpnagel. The production used the facade of the Palais d'Iéna to represent that of the Majestic. Montazel had been hired for *Cécile est morte!* to replace Armand Thirard. At first, he signed a contract for a single picture. But Continental insisted he signed a yearly contract in February 1944 before the start of *Les Caves du Majestic*. When he agreed to sign the contract, Montazel was convinced that the firm wouldn't last more than a year. He was right, as the Simenon adaptation whose shooting ended in April was his last picture. But while the shooting ended in April 1944, *Les Caves du Majestic* was not released until October 1945.

While Continental still had many projects available, ready to shoot, no other picture was put into production before the liberation of Paris on August 25, 1944. Among the most advanced projects was a version of *L'Affaire des poisons*, adapted from Victorien Sardou's play, which should have been directed by Maurice Tourneur with Raimu and Arletty in the leads.[14] But the great actor faked an illness, with the help of his doctor, to delay the start of the shooting.[15] In the end it never got underway. Cinematographer Pierre Montazel had already been scheduled to work on the film, and he remembered a sequence in the script that shocked him: "There were scenes in there I didn't like, such as a story of black mass with details that might have shocked people with certain religious conceptions. I knew the assistant, who told me he didn't want to make that film. He told me, 'I won't be on the set when they shoot that scene. We can assert our rights.'"[16] Montazel never had to confront the management, however, because, in June 1944, eight days after D-day, Continental abruptly stopped paying his salary.

While the German situation looked hopeless on all fronts, Max Winkler nevertheless ordered Greven to start producing films in German. Greven initially refused to comply, telling his superior that

it is almost impossible for me to produce films in two languages at the same time, as I do not have any first-class German nor French dramatic adviser to support me. When you replied that I would simply have to cease production of French films I reminded you that it is not exactly a joy to produce films in an enemy country in wartime. I also informed you, as was my duty, that we would

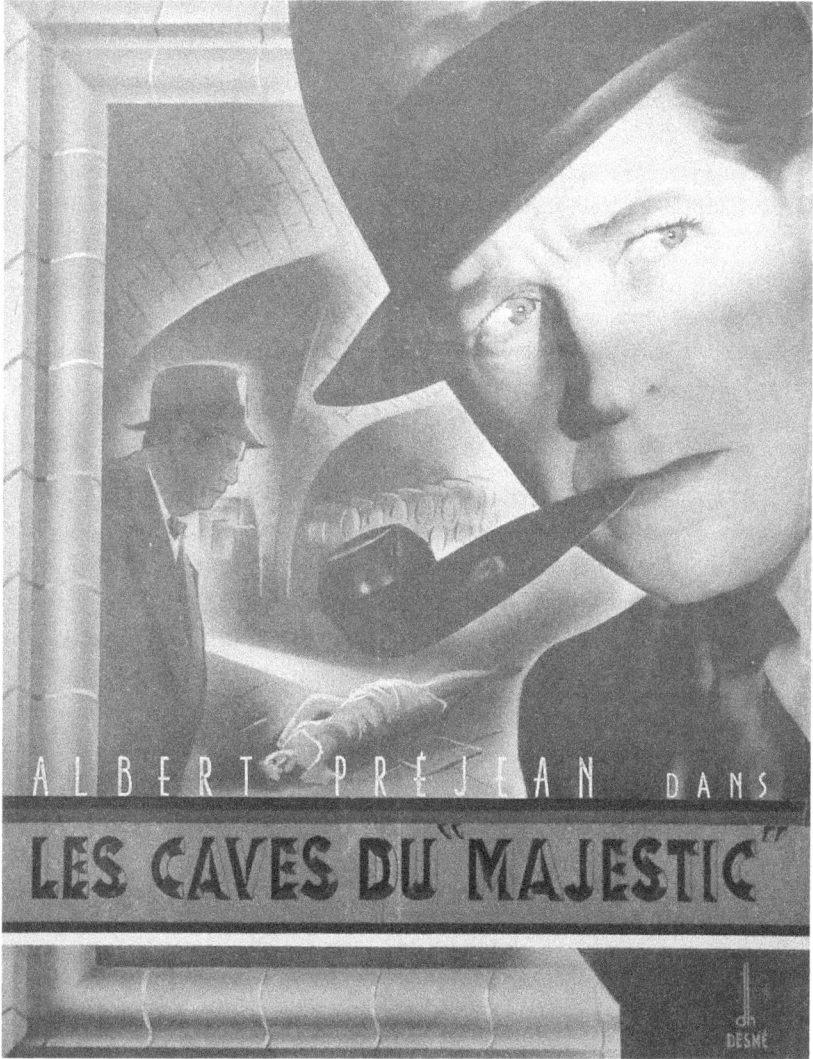

Pressbook cover for *Les Caves du Majestic* (1945) (Fondation Jérôme Seydoux-Pathé)

only be able to hold on to all our foreign cinemas with the help of the French film production. I also advised you that in view of our European ambitions that we have made good use of French films in neutral countries.[17]

At the beginning of 1943, Greven had sent a selection of seven subjects to Fritz Hippler. The head dramatic advisor at the Reich film department gave his instructions, which were relayed to Winkler.

> Greven's production of German films will mainly have to concentrate on light fare like operettas, farces, and comedies that suit the French taste. It is not likely to be in the interest of German cultural politics to produce more serious subjects by French authors, as the choice of subjects presented by Greven already demonstrates. We would undoubtedly end up producing subjects from the genre of late French naturalism (like *La Bête humaine*), which would reveal the negative attitudes toward life and the world of a sick and politically dead people. These are subjects we do not want to expose the European public to.[18]

By the end of December 1943, they had agreed on two subjects. One was the adaptation of André Messager's operetta *Les P'tites Michu*. Greven acquired the rights in January 1944. He had decided to direct the film himself because he didn't have any French director who could do it. He tried to hire—in vain—two Italian actresses who spoke German, Alida Valli and Vivi Gioi, for the parts of the two sisters. In May 1944, he hired Oscar Simm, Wolf Albach-Retty, and Inge Egger for the picture.[19] Of course, the film was never made. Yet the preproduction was advanced enough that Paul Olive had already been selected as stage manager. But Olive did what he could to avoid having to work under Greven: "I was finishing *Les Caves du Majestic*, and *L'Affaire des poisons* was about to start. I had been selected for *Les P'tites Michu* with Greven. I called Mr. Tourneur, who came to see Greven and Bauermeister, and it is thanks to Mr. Tourneur who insisted, at my request, that I was working with him on *L'Affaire des poisons*."[20]

At the same time, Greven was preparing an adaptation of *La Femme au collier de velours*, a novel by Alexandre Dumas inspired by E. T. A. Hoffmann, with screenwriter Jean Aurenche. Yet Aurenche was in an awkward position, as he had never gotten along with Greven, and in the end, he never put his name on any Continental script. Hired to make *La Main enchantée*, he was replaced by Le Chanois, who transformed it into *La Main du diable*. He also wrote an adaptation of *Adrien* (1943), a play by Jean de Letraz, for Fernandel, who was

Ad for *Adrien* (1943) (Fondation Jérôme Seydoux-Pathé)

slated to act in it and direct it. His script had been modified by Letraz; he refused to sign it.[21] It was understandable, as *Adrien* deserves a medal as one of Continental's worst pictures with its labored humor and inept direction.

This activity during the last few months of the occupation implies that Greven thought he still had a future as head of Continental. In fact, he told Jean Aurenche he thought he would be able to stay after the arrival of the Americans: "'The people who won't work with me now, won't work with the Americans.' He implied he had an agreement with the Americans. When he went to Portugal, he said he had met Americans and that his pictures would be released by the Americans after the war. We spoke about Russia. He said the Russians would win the war; he referred to that b****y stupid Hitler."[22] Even if there was certainly a lot of bravado in his comments, Greven showed by his activities he thought he could still produce pictures in spite of the air raids, power cuts, and D-day. He perhaps felt reassured by Goebbels's glowing report, which he noted in his diary in May 1944: "Despite all the criticism, Greven has done a remarkable job here; he is especially excellent in a political sense, which I would not have given him credit for."[23]

At the end of 1943, Greven bought some land in Mesnil-le-Roi, west of Paris, near Saint-Germain-en-Laye. He had a studio built with a vault to preserve prints. He thought he would be able to go on making pictures even as the Neuilly and Billancourt studios were dogged by air raids. In the end, not one inch of film was ever shot there. Shortly after June 6, 1944, Greven moved Continental and the Society for Management and Operation of Cinemas headquarters to Nancy, in the east of France. His secretary Gertrud Aschbrenner went there with the accountants. He also had Continental film prints shipped to him. But this strategic retreat would be the last one. On August 25, 1944, Paris was liberated. Shortly before the arrival of the Allies, Greven fled to Germany, taking with him illegal film prints and Continental funds. Between February 1941 and April 1944, the German firm produced 30 feature films out of a total of 220 pictures produced during that period. It was the dominant film firm of the occupation.

꩜

CHAPTER 25

A Professional Purge

The liberation of Paris was the occasion of an incomparable jubilation among the inhabitants of the City of Lights, who emerged from four dark years of occupation. However, the celebration was short lived for several film actors who were considered—rightly or wrongly—notorious collaborators. Among those, actors who worked at Continental were prime targets.

The Inspector Maigret at Continental, Albert Préjean, was arrested at his home in La Varenne Saint-Hilaire. He remembered the fantastical circumstances of his arrest.

> Five members of the French Forces of the Interior arrived with pointed machine guns and revolvers and took me immediately to Saint-Maur Prison without providing any explanation. I was subjected on the first evening to a simple interrogation regarding my identity. Two days later, I was questioned again by people whose names I did not know, who didn't in fact have any file on me. That main charge against me was, according to them, that I was an influential member of the French Popular Party. I have never been a member of the French Popular Party or any other group of that sort. I stayed in Saint-Maur for ten days, and then I was called by Military Security to give information about Mr. Bauermeister and Mr. Greven, the Continental Films managers. I was jailed at 18 Boulevard Suchet, my file having arrived. I was this time questioned very seriously . . . by Captain Marin. . . . Nothing could be proved against me. I was released on September 23, 1944. I was also questioned about the trip to Berlin by the Sûreté Nationale, rue des Saussaies, which decided not to follow up this case."[1]

The committee in charge of the professional purge of actors sanctioned him; he was suspended for six months from engaging in any professional activity.

Pierre Fresnay, who had been called a collaborator for his involvement in *Le Corbeau* by the underground magazine *L'Écran français*, received a similar treatment on September 5, 1944, at his Neuilly house. The reason for his arrest? "His name was no. 17 on a list of suspects."[2] He was taken to the Palais de Justice jail, where he spent six weeks before being liberated on October 11. Then, he was placed under house arrest at his home on rue Saint-James in Neuilly. He had to go to sign a register every week at the local police station. The police made the usual inquiry among his neighbors, especially among the concierges of rue Saint-James. It revealed nothing reprehensible; quite the contrary, they learned he never received any Germans at his home.

As soon as he was arrested, the playwright and theater director Édouard Bourdet came to his defense and did all he could to set him free. He was not only a good friend of Fresnay but an exemplary figure of the Resistance.[3] In his memoir, he refutes all the charges against the actor. They reproached him for having made four films at Continental and mostly for participating in *Le Corbeau*, which was allegedly screened in Germany. Neither Bourdet nor Fresnay were aware that this last charge was in fact untrue. Bourdet nevertheless specified that if Fresnay had had any suspicion there was going to be such a screening, he wouldn't have participated in the picture. In addition, the actor always refused the exclusive contracts offered by Continental. He made eight films for French production companies but only four for the German firm. It was also rumored he had Germanophile opinions. Bourdet replied:

> Pierre Fresnay is not a Germanophile, but, having served during the two wars as reserve officer, he came out of the second one convinced of the necessity for an authoritarian regime that could impose order. And he thought the Vichy regime, under the aegis of Maréchal Pétain, would meet this need. His sympathies never went beyond this particular point of view. He always refused to collaborate with enemy propaganda organizations, such as Radio-Paris, and never had any relationship with the Germans. I am able to provide, in this respect, a personal testimony. When I asked him last March if he could help me in the steps I was taking for my son, Claude Bourdet, who had been arrested by the Gestapo, he didn't spare his help, and, among other things, he wrote to a certain Dr. Knochen, head of the Paris Gestapo, a letter that was to be given to him by a French industrialist who had been a high school friend of his. In this occasion, Pierre Fresnay stated to me, "It's the first and, I really hope, the last exception I will make to the rule I had set myself not to have any relationship with a German. I am happy it is to help your son."[4]

Fresnay's file was simply closed. He never received any sanction. On the other hand, when he returned to the stage at the Théâtre de la Michodière in May 1945, the first performances of *Vient de paraître*, a Édouard Bourdet play, were disrupted by various protests. On May 15, two people whistled and shouted, "Pierre Fresnay, the collaborator in Berlin!" Evacuated by the police, they announced they would be back another day in force. Indeed, on May 18, the police reported the actor "was greeted by screams of 'fascist, collaborator,' all that accompanied by whistles and disapproving 'boo, boo.' Speaking to the crowd, Fresnay asked what they had against him. The reply was, 'You are a fascist!' Then he asked the following question: 'Am I judged on facts or on my opinion?' The audience, at this point, took up his cause and sustained applause was heard in the theater."[5] On May 19, a group of former concentration camp prisoners back from Germany climbed on stage in their prisoner uniforms, preventing the actor from coming on. The performance resumed forty-five minutes later, after evacuation by the police. And finally, on May 21, seven protesters did the same again. Shortly before the performance, the police saw these seven people together with Pierre Blanchar, who seemed to be giving them instructions.[6]

It is hard to say if Blanchar was intervening to harm Fresnay at that point. On the contrary, he might have been trying to discourage the protestors, an idea that is plausible, given that the disruption stopped after May 21. In any case, Blanchar didn't intervene regarding his professional purge. At the liberation, Blanchar was president of the Committee for the Liberation of French Cinema, the organization in charge of the purge inside the film industry. This committee handled directors, technicians, and producers under the aegis of the Seine prefecture. Actors were taken care off by a completely different committee, the National Committee for the Purification of Dramatic, Lyric Artists and Music Performance Professionals under the aegis of the rue de Valois, the ancestor of the Ministry of Culture. If the work done by Committee for the Liberation of French Cinema proved extremely professional and made use of complete transcripts of interrogations, held witness hearings, carried out examinations with all parties present, and so forth, the second one verged on amateurism. During the hearings, only a vague synopsis of the case was recorded, and sometimes the charges relied on only handwritten notes and denunciations, and no examination in which everyone participated was held. As an actor, Fresnay was supposed to be heard only by the second one, where his case was closed. And Pierre Blanchar deserved better than the sarcasms of a Jean Cocteau, who described him as having the eye of an eagle in the head of a birdbrain. Blanchar had joined the Resistance in 1943; nobody could deny his integrity and his courage, and those who mocked him often had committed actions to be ashamed of. Blanchar systematically refused Greven's offers, and during the occupation, he even gave his brother-in-law Maurice Tourneur a talking-to because he worked at Continental, although that didn't stop him from accepting a job as an actor for Tourneur's first picture after the war.[7]

Among all the actresses who were arrested arbitrarily after the liberation, the only one from Continental was Ginette Leclerc, who had appeared in three pictures. Yet the reasons of her arrest were linked to her relationship with Lucien Gallas and to her unfortunate association with Pierrot le Fou. She spent nine months in jail before being freed without any charges being filed against her. She was suspended from working for six months by the film purge committee, but that was subsequently reduced to three months.[8]

Arletty's and Mireille Balin's cases were related to what was called "horizontal collaboration" rather than any artistic collaboration. Arletty stated loudly and clearly that she always refused to sign with Continental. She even gave the list of the pictures she refused to make: "During the occupation, I refused to make numerous Continental pictures (*Le Dernier des six, Vingt-cinq ans de bonheur, Les Évadés de l'an 4000* and *L'Affaire des poisons*), films that would have earned me three to four million. I refused Otto Abetz's proposal to leave Paris for Baden-Baden [for a propaganda journey]. I replied I preferred Paris-Paris to Baden-Baden, my affair being purely sentimental and in no way linked to political events."[9]

If Arletty's affair with Hans Jürgen Soehring has been well documented, what happened to Mireille Balin is still mysterious to a degree. She was rumored to have been arrested near the Italian border on September 28, 1944, with her lover, a German officer. Then, it was stated she was raped and her lover murdered. A French police report from November 9, 1945, tells a completely different story. Balin met Alois Diessbock, nicknamed Birl, in Kitzbühel, Austria, in February 1938.[10] At that time, he worked as a chemist for a pharmaceutical company. In 1939, he was mobilized in the artillery before becoming interpreter for the army. In 1942, the German Embassy in Paris discharged him, and he then became a diplomatic courier between Berlin, Madrid, and Lisbon. It was during that time that he met Balin a second time in Monte Carlo, her native city, and they subsequently decided to live together. Shortly before the liberation of France, Birl made contact with the British Intelligence Service, which asked him to make some propaganda in German in favor of the Allies. He also prevented the arrest of the state minister of the Monaco principality,

Émile Roblot, by the Italians by contacting his former head of department in Paris. Following Roblot's advice, Birl and Mireille Balin stayed in Monte Carlo in order to make themselves available to the American authorities. They were both arrested on September 13, 1944, by the French Forces of the Interior at the Palais Miramar. Birl was kept in custody at the Suisse Hotel in Nice, and during interrogations, he noted he never joined the Nazi party. He provided a lot of information about people in contact with the Gestapo and later became an informer for the French counterintelligence agency. As for Balin, she was sent to Nice Prison before being liberated, free of charges, on December 22. The two lovers then settled in Villa Catari at Le Canet, a property owned by Mireille, and went on living as if they were husband and wife. One possible reason this version of events differs considerably from the one that was current is that if Birl indeed became an informer for French intelligence, the official version offered the perfect cover.

Among the famous personalities arrested, there was of course playwright and filmmaker Sacha Guitry. His arrest was worthy of a French farce: "Arrested at my home on August 23, at around eleven in the morning, by six men armed to the teeth but who did not have a warrant, I was taken away on foot, dressed in my pajamas, to the seventh arrondissement town hall. A murderer caught in the act would not have been treated more rigorously."[11] Guitry told his apprehenders that he had indeed received an offer from Continental: "They offered me three million for one film. And I refused. I refused in front of witnesses, in front of Mr. [Guy] de Carmoy, Mr. [Raoul] Ploquin, and Mr. [Édouard] Harispuru. I told them categorically that I only wanted to work with French people. And the next day, we agreed, Harispuru and I, to make *Désirée Clary*."[12]

Various actors who participated in *Le Corbeau* have often been described as having been victims of zealous purging operations. Yet the sanctions taken against them, their files reveal, were not so much related to their film activity as to their participation at Radio-Paris programs or gala evenings tainted by their association with collaborationists. For example, Noël Roquevert and Jean Brochard both received a suspension because of their work on propaganda programs at Radio-Paris. Similarly, Micheline Francey was barred from working for a year because of her participation in ninety programs on the same radio station.

The actors from Comédie-Française, Antoine Balpêtré, Pierre Bertin, and Louis Seigner, were also sanctioned by the purge committee of their own theater. Balpêtré was excluded from the Comédie-Française without pension for having been a member of the Groupe Collaboration and, in addition, for having read poetry written by notorious collaborator Philippe Henriot in his youth during the ceremony in his memory that was held in August 1944.[13] Bertin got compulsory retirement for having been a frequent visitor at the German Institute. As for Seigner, owing to his heavy family responsibilities, he received only a three-month suspension for having directed programs at Radio-Paris. In the end, their participation in *Le Corbeau* was not even mentioned.

As he had become a resident member of the Comédie-Française in January 1944 to perform in Molière's *Le Bourgeois gentilhomme*, the theater's purge committee also investigated Raimu. He replied to that accusation that *Les Inconnus dans la maison* had been screened in Germany under the title *Jeunesse française* by stating he could not have known that would happen.[14] He added that he simulated an illness, with the help of French doctors, and suspended his performances at the Comédie-Française rather than execute his contract with Continental. He received no sanction.

Among other lead actors at Continental was Fernandel. The French people's favorite comedian was violently attacked in the satirical newspaper *Le Canard Enchaîné* for having joined the firm as early as 1941. "One of the first, he set the example. You'll tell me that Mr. Fernandel, millionaire and actor, could have gone to reign elsewhere or even could have retired to the country to plant his cabbages and sleep on his bank account. Everybody will tell you he was playing a good trick on the Germans in making films for them and in selling the smoke of his exaggerated expressions and the wind of his fantasy. That day, nevertheless, Mr. Fernandel didn't make us laugh quite as much."[15] In front of the committee, the actor put up a very unconvincing defense: "I worked at Continental for a fee. . . . I was offered an exclusive contract, but I refused it. I swear on my honor that I was not under a yearly contract with Continental. I didn't know in 1941, actually, what Continental was. I made three pictures in total. The second one was in 1942. For the third one, I tried to avoid it by postponing it to 1943. But the war was not finished; I had to do it."[16] The actor was hardly credible when he said he was not aware Continental was German, especially given that he made *L'Héritier des Mondésir* for UFA in Berlin shortly before the start of the war, a production that had been approved of personally by Greven. And his agent Robert Beunke didn't hesitate to tell screenwriter Carlo Rim and his wife shortly before the shooting of *Simplet* that the actor preferred Continental, as he was paid more by Continental. However, Fernandel's case was simply closed. He received no sanction.

A famous singer had a quick stint at Continental, between May and June 1943, where he made a single picture. Tino Rossi played the lead for *Mon amour est près de toi* (1943), under the direction of Richard Pottier. That musical did not elicit any protest or comments from the purge committee. If the handsome Rossi was arrested, it was because of his friend Étienne Léandri, a Corsican gangster linked to the Gestapo. The singer said he didn't know his childhood friend kept such bad company. He got suspended for four months.

Character actor Robert Le Vigan's case was, of course, of a completely different order. He had played only a small part in *L'Assassinat du Père du Noël*, but he had thanked Greven effusively for this opportunity to collaborate. He had hoped to be hired again by the firm in 1942 for *La Fausse maîtresse*. He had written to Bauermeister to get an appointment with him: "Continental Films summoned me fifteen days ago to describe a character in Mr. Cayatte and Michel Duran's picture. I took the opportunity to tell these people, as well as your stage manager Olive, that I agreed to play this character. Since then, when I have stated my name and in spite of the favorable frame of mind of the authors and director, things are at a standstill. . . . Over the past forty-eight hours, I have come twice and phoned your secretaries six times to get an appointment with you. I could not get one."[17] Probably hurt to see his eagerness to collaborate ignored, he later effectively refused a small part in *La Symphonie fantastique* by asking for an excessive fee, knowing it would be refused. In addition to this short collaboration with Continental, Le Vigan's file shows that he faced serious charges for his regular participation in propaganda programs at Radio-Paris and that he was even accused of being a member of the French Popular Party in 1943. His flight to Sigmaringen in Germany in 1944 in the company of antisemitic writer Louis-Ferdinand Céline made matters even worse. When he appeared in front the Paris Court of Justice, in spite of the support of an impressive number of artists and directors, he was condemned to ten years' hard labor.

The purge among directors, producers, and technicians was, as noted, more professional than it was for the actors. The Committee for the Liberation of French Cinema took possession of the former Organizing Committee of the Cinema Industry building at 92 avenue des Champs-Élysées. A three-member committee was formed for each group. For directors, the committee was composed of two directors, Léon Mathot and André Berthomieu, and one production manager, Paul Guien. The Continental directors were among the first to be interviewed in October 1944. There wasn't any hostility toward them. Each one was invited to explain his activity. This first committee didn't sanction those called before it; its job was to gather testimonies and possibly to bring witnesses to the stand. Later, members suggested possible sanctions that might or might not be approved by the cabinet committee supervised by the ministry.

In his memoirs, Marcel Carné was not that truthful when he complained that he had to explain himself in front of a jury that included one of his former dressers. In reality, he only had to face Mathot, Berthomieu, and Guien. In addition, Carné received a simple official warning, the least severe sanction for directors who signed a contract at Continental. It didn't stop him from painting himself as a martyr of an unfair purge. "While some of my colleagues who had made several films for the same company were never troubled; I was sanctioned for not having made a film! Make of that what you will."[18] Unfortunately, his statement doesn't stand up to facts. Maurice Tourneur, André Cayatte, Christian-Jaque, Richard Pottier, Georges Lacombe, René Jayet, and Maurice Gleize all received an official warning, just like the filmmaker of *Les Enfants du paradis*.

Among the Continental directors, there was a very special case, that of Pierre Caron. The inept picture he directed, *Ne bougez plus* (1941), was of little importance compared with the trafficking he engaged in for the Germans. He nevertheless was able to direct a picture without a trade card while receiving a comfortable salary of 500,000 francs, much higher than the one received by other directors. He later moved to metal trafficking on a grand scale, selling wagonloads of barbed wire to a German buying office. This trade looked perfectly legal to him, as he even dared to mention it to his actors. Paul Meurisse was flabbergasted when he told him he had sold a train full of railroad tracks to the Germans. He justified this activity on the grounds that he was unable to get his Organizing Committee of the Cinema Industry card. At the liberation, he had the nerve to present himself as a late-hour resistance fighter. His lie did not hold out. He was sent to the Paris Court of Justice. Taking advantage of an early release, he fled to Spain. He was sentenced in absentia in 1946 to five years' imprisonment and charged with national disgracefulness.[19]

Unlike most of his colleagues at Continental, Jean Dréville was in a difficult position with respect to the purge committee not only because of his haughty attitude during his interview but also because of the letters he sent to Greven, Bauermeister, and Henking offering to direct another film for Continental after finishing *Annette et la dame blonde*. The process proved particularly slow due to the thousands of cases to deal with, and he only received his sanction in November 1946, which was suspension without pay. He immediately contested this punishment, as he had already made *La Cage aux rossignols* (1945) and *La Ferme du pendu* (1945) and was on the verge of starting another picture. Dréville believed the committee should have gone through the directors' cases first before those of the thousands of technicians so as to allow the film industry to get back on track. In addition, his sanction, according to him, was "a measure that seems more fitting for a civil servant and looks unenforceable for a filmmaker."[20] The sanction was lifted on January 23, 1947.

Henri Decoin, Albert Valentin, and Henri-Georges Clouzot faced more serious trouble, as their pictures had been considered antinational. Because of *Les Inconnus dans la maison*, Decoin got a particularly rigorous sanction in July 1945: a ban from working in a managing job in the profession, which meant he couldn't work at all. But the director asked for a review of his case, producing various petitions signed by numerous technicians and actors who had been in the Resistance, as well as Billancourt grips who certified that Decoin had always been openly anti-German inside Continental. His sanction was lifted on June 24, 1946.

Albert Valentin was treated more severely than his colleagues, probably because he was Belgian. The director of *La Vie de plaisir* was hit with a double sanction: an official warning as well as a ban from occupying a managing job. His case was even sent to a justice court, but the case was closed and no action was taken. However, he only narrowly escaped deportation thanks to the intercession of filmmaker Jean Grémillon when he went to renew his identity papers in 1946. Valentin was struggling to make a living until February 1948 when his sanction was finally lifted. He was certainly the director who suffered the most during the purge process.

Yet Clouzot has always been presented as the expiatory victim of blinkered committee members. But this picture doesn't hold up. He received a sanction similar that of Valentin and Decoin, a ban from occupying a managing job in August 1945. But as early as September 1, 1946, he was allowed to go back to work.[21] His later brilliant career demonstrates he didn't suffer that much harm. During a meeting of a preparatory committee on November 9, 1944, one of the committee members, director Jacques Becker, a Resistance fighter, came to Clouzot's defense: "There has been some kind of Clouzot hysteria; there is no doubt. We mustn't be influenced by that and we mustn't refuse to take it into account either. . . . We must judge clearly and know that most people judge Mr. Clouzot behaved badly." "But if we examine his case closely and objectively," continued Becker, and "if we do not discover any new fact, we cannot, then, treat this man as a scapegoat, just because, everyone in this corporation feels he is guilty."[22]

If Clouzot was able to resume his livelihood rather quickly compared to some of his colleagues, the fate of *Le Corbeau* remained a burning issue after the liberation. That film was banned, along with *Les Inconnus dans la maison* and *La Vie de plaisir*. When *Les Caves du Majestic* was finally released in October 1945, the ban of Clouzot's masterpiece received renewed attention from critics. Georges Charensol in *Les Nouvelles littéraires* wondered why the government department managing state property, which sequestrated defunct Continental productions, authorized the release of certain films but not others: "Because, really, if *Les Caves du Majestic* can have an exclusive run in the biggest cinema on the Champs-Élysées, we cannot understand why *Le Corbeau* which is no less 'commercial,' but infinitely more 'artistic,' should remain banned. Did it owe its ban to its quality?"[23]

Film critic and historian Georges Sadoul, who had been a member of the editorial staff of the supplement for the underground paper *Lettres françaises*, launched an offensive and replied to Charensol. While recognizing the picture's qualities, he didn't appreciate its content.

> This secondhand work would be successful enough that we could forget it was financed by Goebbels if quality was the only reason. But *Le Corbeau*, like *Les Inconnus dans la maison*, was a picture which assented to portraying France as a rotten, degenerate, petty bourgeois, vicious, and decadent nation in accordance with the assertions from *Mein Kampf*. It's possible that the authors of the picture never had this intention in their hearts. It's probably not true that *Le Corbeau* had been screened in Germany under the title *Une petite ville française*. But it is certain that this picture, finished during the occupation for an enemy firm, paints a picture of a small French town whose inhabitants are all equally sick, liars or criminals. One can say that other works, and bigger ones, are just as dark. But Stroheim didn't make *The Wedding March* for the Viennese Gauleiter, and in *La Bête humaine*, neither Zola nor Renoir carried out a command under the authority of general Stülpnagel.[24]

Sadoul's obvious hypocrisy didn't in the end prevent the rerelease of Clouzot's picture on Parisian screens on September 4, 1947.

The release of *Les Caves du Majestic* coincided with Georges Simenon's departure to the United States. He thus avoided a hearing in front of the purge committee for writers, authors, and composers and the sanction he was handed, which was a two-year ban on publication in France.[25] The picture and its director were torn to pieces by the reviewers, who had a field day demolishing a Continental picture that was described as "a bad main course (gentlemen from Continental across the Rhine, please forgive me for this ungraceful allusion)."[26]

The Continental assets seized by the state were considerable, as they included the circuit of film theaters formerly owned by Greven. With these assets, the French state created the Union Générale Cinématographique on September 25, 1946. The producer André Halley des Fontaines was appointed CEO of the firm.[27] The company is still one of the major distribution and movie theater companies in France, even if it doesn't own most of the Continental pictures anymore.

CHAPTER 26

Greven's Last Years

Alfred Greven's life after his hasty departure in the summer of 1944 was certainly less flamboyant than during his prosperous years in occupied France. However, it showed that Continental's former boss had an extraordinary ability to adapt.

Back in Germany, Greven didn't remain idle. He had not been officially dismissed from his post as head of Continental, even if he wasn't managing the firm anymore. He went on producing reports about the end of production to his superior until December 1944. He was finally officially dismissed on December 21, 1944, by the Cautio firm. He was offered a new contract for a different job inside the firm. However, Greven already had other projects in mind. By mid-January 1945, SS-Gruppenführer Hans Hinkel was surprised to come across him in Prague. "I personally met Greven in Prague; I don't know what was behind his journey and his stay, and none of our people there ([Josef] Hein, [E. W.] Emo, etc.) knew anything about it. I also heard that Greven had visited our studios in Berlin, Vienna, and Ischl and had met with Mr. Jannings."[1]

When Germany surrendered on May 8, 1945, Greven was in Thuringia, where he ended up being jailed by the Soviets for a few months. During his imprisonment, he was the one who kept order, even establishing a morning physical exercise regime for his fellow prisoners.[2] When he was freed, he left for West Germany, then occupied by the Allies.

In 1949, he was living near Hamburg and wanted to produce pictures in collaboration with film actor Willy Birgel.[3] He asked for an authorization from the British authorities, who were then the occupying power in this region. The British authorities asked for information from the French authorities regarding his activities during the war. General Kœnig, then commander in chief in Germany, immediately sent a request for information to the head of the Centre national de la Cinématographie in Paris.[4] The reply was crystal clear:

I have the honor of letting you know that, in my opinion, the request from this character must be received with utmost express reservation. . . . Mr. Greven was the head of French cinema during the occupation, and, as such, was responsible for the subordination of the French film industry to the interest of German firms. Mr. Greven managed besides to derive substantial personal benefits from his privileged position. . . . The activity thus engaged in during the occupation by Mr. Greven looks to me to be a reason to ban him now from any managing job in a private firm and a fortiori in an organization authorized by the French authorities.[5]

The year 1949 proved to be a very bad one for the former Continental manager. The UFA liquidators filed claims against Greven for about 100,000 Reichsmarks (equivalent to 10,000 Deutschemarks) he had illegally taken. He was offered a settlement to reduce the amount, but Greven refused it.

I have only accepted my dismissal under duress. Winkler expressly assured me that it was only a formality and that I would assist him in the rebuilding of the film industry after the war. . . . I have lost my Paris apartment and all my savings with the Reichskreditkasse. . . . I would like UFA to make me a decent offer. As a former board member of UFA, I was not able to hold an executive position in the German film industry. Therefore, UFA ought to compensate me, as my only work in the film business has been with them.[6]

In 1963, the liquidators finally relinquished their claims.

In 1953, Greven was on the verge of being appointed head of a new production company, Norddeutsches Filmkontor in Hamburg. While he was considered the most qualified candidate, his past caught up with him. "If German film is to get back on a firm financial footing it will depend on foreign markets. Its natural markets are to be found mostly in countries recently occupied by Germany and ravaged by Nazism. Does the trade union council genuinely believe it would be possible in France, Belgium, and Holland to market films made under the auspices of a man who used to be the Nazi film commissioner for France? Surely, it does not want to provoke a boycott."[7] In the end, the project was abandoned.

In October 1953, Greven created the firm Alfred Greven Film GmbH in Düsseldorf. During the next decade, he produced three pictures, among them *Bonjour Kathrin* (1956), directed by Karl Anton with Caterina Valente, a musical with a garish color scheme similar to the B musicals produced by MGM.

The sets re-creating Montmartre and its artists were made by an old Continental acquaintance, Russian art director André Andrejew.

It was likely that Greven had wanted to become a director for a long time. He managed to make his dream come true in 1959 when he directed the documentary *Alarm im Mittelmeer*, which recorded the everyday work of several NATO units with a small element of fiction added. He concluded his career as producer-director with the documentary *NATO-Manöver* (1963), about the NATO maneuvers. A former Nazi sympathizer promoting NATO is one of the numerous paradoxes of the Cold War. His long career as producer ended in 1972 with the children's TV series *Peter is der Boss*, made for ZDF, West Germany's second TV channel.

Alfred Greven died of cancer on February 9, 1973, in Cologne. His nephew Klaus-Jörg Hoppe, who had come to see him shortly before his death, recounted his last words: "I destroyed all my archives. Open a bottle of Sekt when I'm dead."[8] This last stunt perfectly accorded with the personality of the extravagant Continental boss; he had no regrets and no remorse. He didn't want to leave any trace behind him. His name was never credited on the titles of any Continental film. It certainly wasn't modesty on his part but just a step he took to avoid hindering the commercial prospects of his pictures.

Greven remains an anomaly in the history of French film. This German producer made some masterpieces, a number of very good pictures, and some turkeys at Continental. Nevertheless, he is not entirely responsible for the quality of these films. The film directors fought to have their vision honored and to maintain the quality of French cinema during a period when the country was under German rule. If Greven is still now a name in film history, he owes it to the Continental filmmakers. And thanks to Bertrand Tavernier's picture *Laissez-passer* (2002), based on the memoirs of assistant director Jean Devaivre, Greven became a movie figure. No doubt, he would have never dreamed of being so recognized on the big screen. The producer left the shadows for the limelight.

Acknowledgments

I am indebted to the following people who helped me in various degrees in my research for this book. First, I wish to thank Arndt Pawelczik, who translated into English all the articles and books in German, and Marc Alizon, Kevin Brownlow, Jean-Pierre Ferrière, and Stéphanie Salmon from the Fondation Jerôme Seydoux-Pathé.

I would also like to thank the staff of the Bibliothèque nationale de France, the Bibliothèque du film, the German Historical Institute library in Paris, the Archives nationales in Pierrefitte-sur-Seine, the Archives de Paris, the Archives de la préfecture de police, and the Dépôt central d'archives de la justice militaire.

At the University of Wisconsin Press, I would like to thank my editor, Sheila McMahon, and my copyeditor, MJ Devaney.

And finally, I wish to thank Patrick McGilligan for his unflagging support.

Filmography

Films are listed in chronological order. The names of uncredited cast or crew members are italicized.

Feature Fiction Films

L'Assassinat du Père Noël
RELEASE DATE: October 16, 1941
DIRECTOR: Christian-Jaque
ADAPTATION AND DIALOGUE: Charles Spaak after a novel by Pierre Véry
CINEMATOGRAPHY: Armand Thirard
ART DIRECTOR: Guy de Gastyne
EDITOR: *René Le Hénaff*
MUSIC: Henri Verdun
CAST: Harry Baur, Renée Faure, Marie-Hélène Dasté, Raymond Rouleau, Robert Le Vigan, Fernand Ledoux, Jean Brochard, Héléna Manson, Jean Parédès
SHOOTING: February 17–April 25, 1941; Neuilly studios; Chamonix

Le Dernier des six
RELEASE DATE: September 16, 1941
DIRECTOR: Georges Lacombe, *Jean Dréville*
ADAPTATION AND DIALOGUE: Henri-Georges Clouzot after a novel by Stanislas-André Steeman
CINEMATOGRAPHY: Robert Le Febvre
ART DIRECTOR: André Andrejew
EDITOR: *Marguerite Beaugé*
MUSIC: Jean Alfaro
CAST: Pierre Fresnay, Michèle Alfa, Suzy Delair, Jean Tissier, Jean Chevrier, Lucien Nat, André Luguet, Georges Rollin, Raymond Segard
SHOOTING: February 28–April 15, 1941; Billancourt studios

Premier Rendez-vous
RELEASE DATE: August 14, 1941
DIRECTOR: Henri Decoin

ADAPTATION AND DIALOGUE: Michel Duran after a story by *Max Colpet* (title
   credits list Henri Decoin)
CINEMATOGRAPHY: Robert Le Febvre
ART DIRECTOR: Jean Perrier
MUSIC: René Sylviano
CAST: Danielle Darrieux, Jacqueline Desmarets, Suzanne Dehelly, Gabrielle Dorziat,
   Rosine Luguet, Elisa Ruis, Fernand Ledoux, Louis Jourdan, Jean Tissier, Jean
   Parédès, *Georges Marchal, Daniel Gélin*
SHOOTING: April 22, 1941–unknown; Billancourt studios

Le Club des soupirants
RELEASE DATE: September 26, 1941
DIRECTOR: Maurice Gleize
ADAPTATION AND DIALOGUE: *André Cayatte*, Maurice Gleize, and Jean Manse after
   a story by Marcel Aymé
CINEMATOGRAPHY: Léonce-Henri Burel
ART DIRECTOR: Georges Wakhevitch
EDITOR: *Christian Gaudin*
MUSIC: Philippe Parès and Georges Van Parys
CAST: Fernandel, Louise Carletti, Annie France, Colette Darfeuil, Saturnin Fabre,
   Andrex, Max Dearly, Marcel Vallée
SHOOTING: April 26, 1941–unknown; Marcel Pagnol studios (Marseille); around
   Nice

Péchés de jeunesse
RELEASE DATE: November 16, 1941
DIRECTOR: Maurice Tourneur
ADAPTATION AND DIALOGUE: Michel Duran and Charles Spaak after a story by
   Albert Valentin
CINEMATOGRAPHY: Armand Thirard
ART DIRECTOR: Guy de Gastyne
EDITOR: *René Le Hénaff, Jacques Desagneaux*
MUSIC: Henri Sauguet
CAST: Harry Baur, Lise Delamare, Monique Joyce, Suzanne Dantès, Marguerite
   Ducouret, Jeanne Fusier-Gir, Yvette Chauviré, Guillaume de Sax, Pierre Bertin,
   Fred Pasquali, *Jean Bobillot, Jacques Varennes*
SHOOTING: May 12, 1941–unknown; Neuilly studios

Caprices
RELEASE DATE: February 16, 1942
DIRECTOR: Léo Joannon
ADAPTATION AND DIALOGUE: *Jacques Companeez, Jean-Jacques Bernard*, and
   Raymond Bernard after a script by *Jacques Companeez* (title credits list André
   Cayatte after a script by Léo Joannon)

CINEMATOGRAPHY: Jules Kruger
ART DIRECTOR: André Andrejew
EDITOR: *Charlotte Guilbert*
MUSIC: Georges van Parys
CAST: Danielle Darrieux, Albert Préjean, Jean Parédès, *Jean Gobet, Maupi, Pierre Labry, Louis Florencie, Gildès, Sinoël, Ginette Catriens, Fred Pasquali, René Stern, Bernard Blier, Gabriello, Jean Brochard, Marcel Pérès, Germaine Reuvère, Arthur Devère*
SHOOTING: June 30, 1941–unknown; Billancourt studios

Ne bougez plus
RELEASE DATE: October 31, 1941
DIRECTOR: Pierre Caron
SCREENPLAY: Roméo Carlès and Pierre Caron
CINEMATOGRAPHY: Armand Thirard
ART DIRECTOR: Guy de Gastyne
EDITOR: *Jacques Desagneaux*
MUSIC: Jehan Charpentier
CAST: Saturnin Fabre, Annie France, Colette Fleuriot, Germaine Charley, Paul Meurisse, Guillaume de Sax, Jean Mayer, Pierre Etchepare, Roger Legris, Marcel Carpentier
SHOOTING: July 21, 1941–unknown; Neuilly studios

Mam'zelle Bonaparte
RELEASE DATE: January 16, 1942
DIRECTOR: Maurice Tourneur
ADAPTATION AND DIALOGUE: H. André Legrand after a novel by Gérard Bourgeois and Pierre Chanlaine
CINEMATOGRAPHY: Jules Kruger
ART DIRECTOR: Guy de Gastyne
EDITOR: *Christian Gaudin*
MUSIC: Henri Verdun
CAST: Edwige Feuillère, Monique Joyce, Simone Renant, Marguerite Pierry, Nina Sinclair, Raymond Rouleau, Guillaume de Sax, Aimé Clariond, Armontel, Noël Roquevert, Jacques Maury, *Simone Valère, André Varennes, Louis Florencie, Elmire Vautier, Louis Salou*
SHOOTING: September 1, 1941–unknown; Neuilly and Billancourt studios

Annette et la dame blonde
RELEASE DATE: March 16, 1942
DIRECTOR: Jean Dréville
ADAPTATION AND DIALOGUE: *Henri Decoin* and Michel Duran after a short story by Georges Simenon
CINEMATOGRAPHY: Robert Le Febvre

ART DIRECTORS: Waldimir Meingard and Robert Hubert
EDITOR: *Charlotte Guilbert*
MUSIC: René Sylviano
CAST: Louise Carletti, Mona Goya, Rosine Luguet, Simone Valère, Rexiane, Henry Garat, Georges Rollin, Georges Chamarat
SHOOTING: September 20, 1941–unknown; Billancourt and Neuilly studios; Cannes

La Symphonie fantastique
RELEASE DATE: April 1, 1942
DIRECTOR: Christian-Jaque
ORIGINAL SCRIPT AND DIALOGUE: Jean-Pierre Feydeau and H. André Legrand
CINEMATOGRAPHY: Armand Thirard
ART DIRECTOR: André Andrejew
EDITOR: *Jacques Desagneaux*
MUSIC: Hector Berlioz (Musical director: Maurice-Paul Guillot)
CAST: Jean-Louis Barrault, Renée Saint-Cyr, Lise Delamare, Jules Berry, Bernard Blier, Gilbert Gil, *Catherine Fonteney*
SHOOTING: October 17, 1941–unknown; Billancourt studios; Cirque d'Hiver

Les Inconnus dans la maison
RELEASE DATE: May 16, 1942
DIRECTOR: Henri Decoin
ADAPTATION AND DIALOGUE: Henri-Georges Clouzot after a novel by Georges Simenon
CINEMATOGRAPHY: Jules Kruger
ART DIRECTOR: Guy de Gastyne
EDITOR: *Marguerite Beaugé*
MUSIC: Roland-Manuel and *Manuel Rosenthal*
CAST: Raimu, Juliette Faber, Gabrielle Fontan, Héléna Manson, Tania Fédor, Marguerite Ducouret, Jean Tissier, Jacques Baumer, Noël Roquevert, André Reybaz, Jacques Grétillat, Lucien Coëdel, Marc Dolnitz, Jacques Denoël, Pierre Ringel, Marcel Mouloudji, Raymond Cordy
NARRATOR: *Pierre Fresnay*
SHOOTING: December 9, 1941–unknown; Neuilly studios

Simplet
RELEASE DATE: September 11, 1942
DIRECTOR: Fernandel (technical assistant: Christian Gaudin)
ORIGINAL SCRIPT AND DIALOGUE: Carlo Rim
CINEMATOGRAPHY: Armand Thirard
ART DIRECTOR: André Andrejew
EDITOR: *Charlotte Guilbert, Christian Gaudin*
MUSIC: Roger Dumas

CAST: Fernandel, Colette Fleuriot, Milly Mathis, Maximilienne, Mathilde Alberti, Édouard Delmont, Andrex, Henri Poupon, Georges Alban, Charles Blavette, Geo Georgey, Charles Lavialle, Max Dalcourt, Edmond Castel
SHOOTING: February 7, 1942–unknown; Billancourt studios; Marseille; Nice

Mariage d'amour (working title: Divorce sans mariage)
RELEASE DATE: December 22, 1942
DIRECTOR: *Henri Decoin, Richard Pottier*
SCENARIO AND DIALOGUE: Henri Decoin after a script by *Max Colpet* (title credits list Jean-Lec)
CINEMATOGRAPHY: Jules Kruger, Charles Bauer
ART DIRECTOR: Guy de Gastyne
EDITOR: *Charlotte Guilbert, Marguerite Beaugé*
MUSIC: René Sylviano
CAST: Juliette Faber, François Périer, Georges Rollin, Paul Meurisse, Michel Vitold, Henri Vilbert, Gabriello, Louis Florencie, Georges Bever, Georges Péclet, Charlotte Lysès, Jeannine Viénot
SHOOTING: April 27, 1942–unknown; Neuilly studios

La Fausse maîtresse (working title: Une Paire d'amis)
RELEASE DATE: August 14, 1942
DIRECTOR: André Cayatte
SCENARIO AND ADAPTATION: André Cayatte and Michel Duran after a novel by Honoré de Balzac
CINEMATOGRAPHY: Robert Le Febvre
ART DIRECTOR: André Andrejew
MUSIC: Maurice Yvain
CAST: Danielle Darrieux, Lise Delamare, Monique Joyce, Huguette Vivier, Gabrielle Fontan, Bernard Lancret, Alerme, Jacques Dumesnil, Guillaume de Sax, Michel Duran, Gabriello, Charles Blavette, Guy Sloux, Maurice Baquet, Maupi
SHOOTING: May 1, 1942–unknown; Billancourt studios; Perpignan

L'Assassin habite au 21
RELEASE DATE: August 7, 1942
DIRECTOR: Henri-Georges Clouzot
ADAPTATION AND DIALOGUE: Henri-Georges Clouzot after a novel by Stanislas-André Steeman
CINEMATOGRAPHY: Armand Thirard
ART DIRECTOR: André Andrejew
EDITOR: *Christian Gaudin*
MUSIC: Maurice Yvain
CAST: Pierre Fresnay, Suzy Delair, Jean Tissier, Pierre Larquey, Noël Roquevert, René Génin, Jean Despeaux, Marc Natol, Huguette Vivier, Odette Talazac, Maximilienne, Sylvette Saugé, Louis Florencie, Gabriello, Raymond Bussières
SHOOTING: May 4, 1942–unknown; Billancourt studios

Défense d'aimer (working titles: Totte et sa chance and Le Cœur sur la main)
RELEASE DATE: October 30, 1942
DIRECTOR: Richard Pottier
ADAPTATION AND DIALOGUE: *Jean Aurenche* and Michel Duran after the
operetta *Yes* by Albert Willemetz, René Pujol, Jacques Bousquet, and Pierre
Soulaine
CINEMATOGRAPHY: *Walter Wottitz*, Charles Bauer
ART DIRECTOR: Guy de Gastyne
EDITOR: *Gérard Bernsdorp*
MUSIC: Maurice Yvain
CAST: Suzy Delair, Paul Meurisse, Gabriello, Mona Goya, Guillaume de Sax, Josée
Bisbal, Louis Salou, Jean Rigaux
SHOOTING: July 28, 1942–unknown; Neuilly studios

La Main du diable (working title: La Main enchantée)
RELEASE DATE: April 21, 1943
DIRECTOR: Maurice Tourneur
ADAPTATION AND DIALOGUE: Jean-Paul Le Chanois after a novel by *Gérard de Nerval*
CINEMATOGRAPHY: Armand Thirard
ART DIRECTOR: André Andrejew
EDITOR: *Christian Gaudin*
MUSIC: Roger Dumas
CAST: Pierre Fresnay, Josseline Gaël, Noël Roquevert, Guillaume de Sax, Pierre
Palau, Pierre Larquey, Gabriello, Antoine Balpêtré, Rexiane, André Varennes,
Georges Chamarat, Jean Davy, Jean Despeaux, *Robert Vattier, Jean Coquelin,
André Bacqué, Georges Douking, Garzoni, Paul Marcel*
SHOOTING: August 21, 1942–unknown; Billancourt studios

Picpus
RELEASE DATE: February 12, 1943
DIRECTOR: Richard Pottier
ADAPTATION AND DIALOGUE: Jean-Paul Le Chanois after a novel by Georges
Simenon
CINEMATOGRAPHY: Charles Bauer
ART DIRECTOR: André Andrejew
EDITOR: *Gérard Bernsdorp*
MUSIC: Jacques Metehen
CAST: Albert Préjean, Juliette Faber, Jean Tissier, Gabriello, Noël Roquevert,
Guillaume de Sax, Édouard Delmont, Antoine Balpêtré, Henri Vilbert, Pierre
Palau, Gabrielle Fontan, Colette Régis, *Maximilienne, Héléna Manson, Marguerite
Ducouret, Sinoël, Huguette Vivier*
SHOOTING: October 28, 1942–unknown; Billancourt studios

Vingt-cinq ans de bonheur
RELEASE DATE: May 25, 1943
DIRECTOR: René Jayet, *Richard Pottier*
ADAPTATION AND DIALOGUE: Germaine Lefrancq and Jean-Paul Le Chanois after a play by Germaine Lefrancq
CINEMATOGRAPHY: Charles Bauer
ART DIRECTOR: Guy de Gastyne
EDITOR: *Marguerite Beaugé*
MUSIC: Louis Sédrat
CAST: Jean Tissier, Denise Grey, Annie France, André Reybaz, Noël Roquevert, Tania Fédor, Rexiane, Rosine Luguet, Gabriello, Guillaume de Sax, Jeanne Fusier-Gir, Marcelle Monthil
SHOOTING: January 13–March 6, 1943; Neuilly studios

Au Bonheur des dames
RELEASE DATE: July 20, 1943
DIRECTOR: André Cayatte
ADAPTATION AND DIALOGUE: André Cayatte, H. André Legrand, and Michel Duran after a novel by Émile Zola
CINEMATOGRAPHY: Armand Thirard
ART DIRECTOR: André Andrejew
EDITOR: *Gérard Bernsdorp*
MUSIC: Louis Sédrat
CAST: Michel Simon, Albert Préjean, Blanchette Brunoy, Suzy Prim, Juliette Faber, Huguette Vivier, Santa Relli, Catherine Fonteney, Jacqueline Gautier, Maximilienne, Rexiane, Suzet Maïs, André Reybaz, Jean Tissier, Jean Rigaux, Georges Chamarat, Pierre Bertin, René Blancard, *Pierre Labry*
SHOOTING: February 1–March 3, 1943; Billancourt studios

Adrien
RELEASE DATE: December 27, 1943
DIRECTOR: Fernandel (technical assistant Christian Gaudin)
ADAPTATION AND DIALOGUE: Jean de Letraz, Jean Manse, *Jean Aurenche*, and *René Wheeler* after a play by Jean de Letraz
CINEMATOGRAPHY: Armand Thirard
ART DIRECTOR: Guy de Gastyne
EDITOR: *Christian Gaudin*
MUSIC: Roger Dumas
CAST: Fernandel, Paulette Dubost, Huguette Vivier, Dorette Ardenne, Jane Marken, Gabriello, Jean Tissier, Roger Duchesne, Paul Azaïs, Georges Chamarat, Albert Duvaleix, Georges Douking, *Rivers Cadet, René Alié, Charles Lavialle, Georges Péclet, Joe Alex, Paul Mirvil, Gesky, Gustave Gallet*
SHOOTING: April 1–May 12, 1943, Neuilly studios; Paris region

Le Corbeau (working titles: Laura and Maladie contagieuse)
RELEASE DATE: September 28, 1943
DIRECTOR: Henri-Georges Clouzot
ORIGINAL SCRIPT AND DIALOGUE: Louis Chavance and Henri-Georges Clouzot
CINEMATOGRAPHY: Nicolas Hayer
ART DIRECTOR: André Andrejew
EDITOR: *Marguerite Beaugé*
MUSIC: Tony Aubin
CAST: Pierre Fresnay, Ginette Leclerc, Micheline Francey, Héléna Manson, Jeanne
    Fusier-Gir, Sylvie, Liliane Maigné, Pierre Larquey, Noël Roquevert, Bernard
    Lancret, Antoine Balpêtré, Jean Brochard, Pierre Bertin, Louis Seigner, Roger
    Blin, Robert Clermont, Pierre Palau, Marcel Delaitre, *Gustave Gallet, Étienne
    Decroux, Albert Malbert, Yvernes*
SHOOTING: May 10–July 3, 1943; Billancourt studios; Monfort L'Amaury

Mon amour est près de toi
RELEASE DATE: September 29, 1943
DIRECTOR: Richard Pottier
ORIGINAL SCRIPT AND DIALOGUE: Camille François
CINEMATOGRAPHY: Charles Bauer
ART DIRECTOR: André Andrejew
EDITOR: *Gérard Bernsdorp*
MUSIC: Vincent Scotto, Roger Lucchesi, Francis Lopez
CAST: Tino Rossi, Annie France, Paul Azaïs, Jean Tissier, Édouard Delmont, René
    Génin, Mona Goya, Jean Rigaux, Jean Davy
SHOOTING: May 11–June 19, 1943; Billancourt studios

Le Val d'enfer
RELEASE DATE: September 22, 1943
DIRECTOR: Maurice Tourneur
ORIGINAL SCRIPT AND DIALOGUE: Carlo Rim
CINEMATOGRAPHY: Armand Thirard
ART DIRECTOR: Guy de Gastyne
EDITOR: *Christian Gaudin*
MUSIC: Roger Dumas
CAST: Ginette Leclerc, Gabrielle Fontan, Nicole Chollet, Colette Régis, Gabriel
    Gabrio, Édouard Delmont, Lucien Gallas, Charles Blavette, Raymond Cordy,
    André Reybaz, Paul Fournier
SHOOTING: June 10–July 31, 1943; Billancourt and Neuilly studios; Moret-sur-Loing

La Ferme aux loups
RELEASE DATE: December 14, 1943
DIRECTOR: Richard Pottier
ORIGINAL SCRIPT AND DIALOGUE: Carlo Rim

CINEMATOGRAPHY: Armand Thirard
ART DIRECTOR: André Andrejew
EDITOR: *Gérard Bernsdorp*
MUSIC: Roger Dumas
CAST: François Périer, Paul Meurisse, Gabriello, Guillaume de Sax, Martine Carole, Suzanne Dantès, Pierre Palau, Georges Chamarat, Georges Vasty, Eugène Frouhins, Jean Reynols, Victor Tcherniavsky, Georges Zagrebelsky, *Fernand Blot, Paul Barge, Jean Paley, Daniel Royer, Léon Mazeau, Jacques Courtin, Jules Vibert, André Chanu, Pierre Maindaiot, Jean Vallois, Cécile Marcyl, Fred Herbault, Jean Halle, Henri Charett, Albert Brouett*
SHOOTING: August 19–September 29, 1943; Billancourt and Neuilly studios

Pierre et Jean
RELEASE DATE: December 29, 1943
DIRECTOR: André Cayatte
ADAPTATION AND DIALOGUE: André Cayatte and André-Paul Antoine after a novel by Guy de Maupassant
CINEMATOGRAPHY: Charles Bauer
ART DIRECTOR: André Andrejew
EDITOR: *Marguerite Beaugé*
MUSIC: Roger Dumas
CAST: Renée Saint-Cyr, Noël Roquevert, Jacques Dumesnil, Gilbert Gil, Bernard Lancret, René Génin, Georges Chamarat, Solange Delporte, Huguette Vivier, Dany Bill, Raymond Raynal
SHOOTING: August 30–October 15, 1943; Billancourt and Neuilly studios; Gournay-sur-Marne

La Vie de plaisir
RELEASE DATE: May 16, 1944
DIRECTOR: Albert Valentin
ADAPTATION AND DIALOGUE: Charles Spaak after a story by Albert Valentin
CINEMATOGRAPHY: Charles Bauer, Paul Coteret
ART DIRECTOR: Guy de Gastyne
EDITOR: *Christian Gaudin*
MUSIC: Paul Durand
CAST: Albert Préjean, Claude Génia, Yolande Laffon, Hélène Constant, Claude Nollier, Aimé Clariond, Jean Servais, Maurice Escande, Noël Roquevert, Jean Paqui, Yves Deniaud, Roger Karl, Pierre Magnier, Marcel Carpentier, *Paul Delauzac, Louis Vonelly, Léon Walther*
SHOOTING: September 27–October 25, 1943; Neuilly studios

Le Dernier sou
RELEASE DATE: January 23, 1946
DIRECTOR: André Cayatte

ORIGINAL SCRIPT AND DIALOGUE: André Cayatte and Louis Chavance
CINEMATOGRAPHY: Charles Bauer
ART DIRECTOR: André Andrejew
EDITOR: Marguerite Beaugé
MUSIC: Georges Dupont
CAST: Gilbert Gil, Ginette Leclerc, Noël Roquevert, Annie France, Charpin, Gabrielle Fontan, René Génin, Zélie Yzelle, Eugène Frouhins, Paul Faivre, Pierre Labry, Raymond Raynal, René Blancard, Michel Salina, Guy Decomble, Georges Collin, Fabienne Vérani, Vitzoris, Jacques Berlioz, Maurice Salabert, André Marion
SHOOTING: December 15, 1943, restarted on February 17, 1944–unknown; Billancourt studios

Cécile est morte!
RELEASE DATE: March 8, 1944
DIRECTOR: Maurice Tourneur
ADAPTATION AND DIALOGUE: Jean-Paul Le Chanois and Michel Duran after a novel by Georges Simenon
CINEMATOGRAPHY: Pierre Montazel
ART DIRECTOR: Guy de Gastyne
EDITOR: *Gérard Bernsdorp*
MUSIC: Roger Dumas
CAST: Albert Préjean, Santa Relli, Germaine Kerjean, Luce Fabiole, Liliane Maigné, Gabriello, Jean Brochard, André Reybaz, Yves Deniaud, Marcel Carpentier, Marcel André, Henri Bonvalet, Charles Blavette
SHOOTING: December 20, 1943–January 1944; Neuilly studios

Les Caves du Majestic
RELEASE DATE: October 31, 1945
DIRECTOR: Richard Pottier
ADAPTATION AND DIALOGUE: Charles Spaak after a novel by Georges Simenon
CINEMATOGRAPHY: Pierre Montazel
ART DIRECTOR: Guy de Gastyne
EDITOR: Christian Gaudin
MUSIC: René Sylviano
CAST: Albert Préjean, Suzy Prim, Jacques Baumer, Denise Grey, Jean Marchat, Gabriello, Gina Manès, René Génin, Florelle, Charpin, Denise Bosc, Gabrielle Fontan, Jeanne Manet, Marcel Lévesque, Georges Chamarat, Jean-Jacques Delbo, Raymond Rognoni, Robert Demorget, *Julienne Paroli, Marie-José, Henri Vilbert*
SHOOTING: February 16–April 1944; Neuilly studios

Documentaries (in alphabetical order)
À l'ombre du Canigou (1943), directed by Robert Le Febvre
Abricots en boîte (1943), directed by Robert Le Febvre

Les Bouchons (1943), directed by Robert Le Febvre
Carambolage (1943), directed by Robert Le Febvre
Le Champagne (1945), directed by Armand Thirard
Collioure (1943), directed by Robert Le Febvre
Coup d'œil sur le Roussillon (1943), directed by Robert Le Febvre
De l'Étoile à la Place Pigalle (1941), directed by Rudolf Hornecker
Les Enfants s'amusent (1942), directed by Robert Le Febvre
Les Espadrilles (1943), directed by Robert Le Febvre
Fouette cocher (1944), directed by Robert Le Febvre
Paris sur Seine (1941), directed by Robert Le Febvre
La Pêche aux anchois (1942), directed by Robert Le Febvre
La Petite reine (1942), directed by Robert Le Febvre
Le Piano (1942), directed by Robert Le Febvre
Porcelaines de Sèvres (1941), directed by Robert Le Febvre
Les Sapeurs-pompiers de Paris (1944), directed by Lucien Ganier-Raymond
Le Sucre (1944), directed by Armand Thirard

Notes

Prologue

1. Universum Film AG, established in 1917, was the largest German film production company.

2. Rim, *Le Grenier d'Arlequin*, 288.

3. Rim, *Le Grenier d'Arlequin*, 316.

4. Rim, *Le Grenier d'Arlequin*, 289.

Chapter 1. Paris, Fall 1940

1. Articles from this periodical are reprinted in *Où sortir à Paris?*

2. Transcript, April 17, 1945, Pierre Blanchard (aka Pierre Blanchar) file, Archives de Paris.

3. Transcript, April 17, 1945.

Chapter 2. Alfred Greven

1. Feuillère, *Les Feux de la mémoire*, 131; Le Chanois, *Le Temps des cerises*, 136.

2. The following biography is derived from Bock, *CineGraph*, installment 34, D1–D15.

3. Elberfeld is today a suburb of Wuppertal.

4. In France, it is often said that Greven met Hermann Göring when he was in the air force. However, they were in different squadrons, and Göring finished the war as head of Jagdgeschwader 1 (Fighter Wing 1). Moreover, there are no references to Göring in any of the German biographies of Greven I consulted.

5. *Filmwelt*, no. 41 (October 11, 1941).

6. It is possible he underwent trephination following this accident rather than during the war.

7. Klaus-Jörg Hoppe, interview, in *Tarnname Continental*.

8. Goebbels, *Die Tagebücher von Joseph Goebbels*, 4:329.

9. Goebbels, *Die Tagebücher von Joseph Goebbels*, 4: 329.

10. Guy de Carmoy, interview, in *Tarnname Continental*.

Chapter 3. The Beginnings of a Company

1. Cautio Treuhand to Greven, December 17, 1940, cited in Bock, *CineGraph*, installment 34, D2.

2. Transcript, November 13, 1946, Aimé Chemel file, Archives de Paris.

3. Transcript, April 17, 1945, Pierre Blanchard (aka Pierre Blanchar) file, Archives de Paris.

4. Transcript, October 13, 1944, Marcel Carné file, Archives de Paris. Mary was deputy of the head of film services for the French government.

5. Transcript, October 19, 1944, Christian Maudet (aka Christian-Jaque) file, Archives de Paris.

6. For more details, see my biography of Maurice Tourneur.

7. Statement, April 17, 1945, Maurice Thomas (aka Maurice Tourneur) file, Archives de Paris.

8. Transcript, October 26, 1944, Roger Forster file, Archives de Paris.

Chapter 4. First Productions

1. Christian-Jaque to Continental Films, October 17, 1940, Christian Maudet (aka Christian-Jaque) file, Archives de Paris.

2. *Le Film*, no. 10 (March 1, 1941): 11.

3. Transcript, Robert Coquillaud (aka Robert Le Vigan) interrogation, September 29, 1945, Cour de justice de la Seine file, Archives Nationales.

4. Robert Le Vigan to Alfred Greven, January 31, 1941, Robert Coquillaud (aka Robert Le Vigan) file, Archives Nationales.

5. Note (in German), October 31, 1940, Harry Baur file, German Archives of the Occupation, Archives Nationales.

6. Note, July 22, 1941, Harry Baur file, Archives allemandes de l'occupation, Archives nationales.

7. Pierre Véry to purge committee, August 20, 1946, Pierre Véry file, Archives de Paris.

8. Transcript, October 14, 1944, Guy Benoist (aka Guy de Gastyne) file, Archives de Paris.

9. Undated note in Christian Maudet (aka Christian-Jaque) file, Archives de Paris.

10. René Le Hénaff to the president of the purge committee, November 20, 1946, René Le Hénaff file, Archives de Paris.

11. M. Haller to Maurice Bessy, October 23, 1941, Maurice Bessy file, Archives de Paris.

Chapter 5. Decoin and Greven

1. Undated statement, Henri Decoin file, Archives Nationales. Georges Loureau was a producer at Tobis. He produced *La Kermesse Héroïque* (1935), directed by Jacques Feyder, among other films. Lucachevitch produced *La Citadelle du silence* (1937), directed by Marcel L'Herbier, and *Hôtel du nord* (1938), directed by Marcel Carné. He left France for the United States at the start of the German invasion in spring 1940.

2. *Le Film*, no. 17 (June 7, 1941): 59.

3. Undated statement. Henri Decoin married Danielle Darrieux on August 19, 1935.

4. Undated statement.

5. Undated statement.

6. Desmarets, *Les Mémoires de Sophie*, 94–95.

7. Decision, Troisième chambre du Tribunal civil de la Seine, March 28, 1944, Archives de Paris.

8. Pierre Mallot, review, *Le Matin*, August 8, 1941.

9. Jacques Audiberti, review, *Comœdia*, August 23, 1941.

Chapter 6. Henri-Georges Clouzot, Screenwriter

1. Transcript, October 17, 1944, Henri-Georges Clouzot file, Archives de Paris.

2. Transcript, October 17, 1944.

3. Fresnay and Possot, *Pierre Fresnay*, 65.

4. Transcript, November 16, 1945, Léonie Bathiat file (aka Arletty), Archives de la Préfecture de Police de Paris.

5. Paul Olive to Rudolph Hans Bauermeister, June 6, 1941, Paul Olive file, Archives de Paris.

6. Transcript, November 3, 1944, Jean Dréville file, Archives de Paris.

7. Undated statement, Henri Decoin file, Archives Nationales.

8. François Vinneuil (aka Lucien Rebatet), review, in *Je suis partout*, September 20, 1941.

9. Gilles, *Ginette Leclerc*, 101.

10. Undated statement.

11. Undated statement.

12. Undated statement. The character was named Ephraïm in the film. He was renamed Amédée after the liberation.

13. Georges Simenon to Pierre Léaud, August 9, 1941, Georges Simenon file, Archives Nationales.

14. Georges Simenon to A. Keller, August 23, 1941, Georges Simenon file, Archives Nationales. Journalist Jean Luchaire (1901–46), was the founder of collaborationist newspaper *Les Nouveaux Temps* and president of the Parisian Press Association.

15. Cortanze, *Pierre Benoit*, 322.

16. Raimu to Henri Decoin, July 4, 1941, Henri Decoin file, Archives Nationales.

17. Undated statement.

18. Although in his statement, Decoin noted that shooting started November 15, 1941, the professional magazine *Le Film* stated the date was December 9, 1941. Dates mentioned by the press are probably not reliable.

19. Undated statement.

20. Transcript, October 19, 1944, Maurice Thomas (aka Maurice Tourneur) file, Archives de Paris.

Chapter 7. *Les Inconnus dans la maison*

1. Mouloudji, *La Fleur de l'âge*, 92.

2. de Beauvoir, *La Force de l'âge*, 696.

3. Jean Rossi had been denounced to the German Propaganda Office by actor René Bergeron (Gennaro Rossi [aka Jean Rossi] file, Archives de Paris).

4. Transcript, October 18, 1944, Henri Decoin File, Archives de Paris.

5. *L'Écran français*, no. 1 (December 1943): 3.

6. *Comœdia*, May 23, 1942.

7. *Le Film*, May 23, 1942, 13.

8. *Je suis partout*, May 23, 1942.

9. *Paris Soir*, June 1, 1942.

10. Transcript, October 18, 1944, Henri Decoin file, Archives de Paris. The cinematographer selected by Greven was Jules Kruger. On Georges Metchikian, see chapter 10.

11. Georges Simenon to Alfred Greven, received June 12, 1942, Georges Simenon file, Archives Nationales.

12. Transcript, October 18, 1944.

Chapter 8. Greven's Empire

1. Transcript, December 7, 1946, Correspondance de l'épuration du cinéma, Archives de Paris.

2. Note, April 20, 1942, Épuration des sociétés cinématographiques, Archives Nationales.

3. Statement, November 14, 1941, Épuration des sociétés cinématographiques, Archives Nationales.

4. Alfred Greven to Cinéma Tirage L. Maurice, received August 8, 1941, Léopold Gratioulet file, Archives de Paris.

5. Continental Films to Léopold Maurice, October 20, 1941, Léopold Gratioulet file, Archives de Paris.

6. Marcel Chavet to Tobis, October 4, 1940, Marcel Chavet file, Archives de Paris.

7. Marcel Chavet to Tobis, October 8, 1940, Marcel Chavet file, Archives de Paris.

8. Undated transcript, Marcel Chavet file, Archives de Paris.

9. German sound equipment supplied by Tobis-Klangfilm was only used at the Neuilly studios.

10. Transcript, November 4, 1944, Jean-Armand Anderlé File, Archives de Paris.

11. Statement, November 14, 1941.

12. Marcel Bertrou file, Archives de Paris.

13. Undated statement, Henri Decoin file, Archives Nationales.

Chapter 9. Leaving Continental

1. Transcript, October 13, 1944, Marcel Carné file, Archives de Paris. The Marcel Aymé story was *Les Bottes de sept lieues*. Henri Jeanson said he had been asked by Continental to join the company. Because he refused, he was banned from working with all French producers by the Germans (transcript, December 20, 1945, Comité de libération du cinéma français—Commission d'épuration, Archives de Paris).

2. *Le Film*, no. 17 (June 7, 1941).

3. Carné, *La Vie à belles dents*, 150.

4. Transcript, October 13, 1944.

5. Transcript, October 13, 1944.

6. Christian-Jaque to Continental Films, October 17, 1940, Christian Maudet (aka Christian-Jaque) file, Archives de Paris.

7. Transcript, October 19, 1944, Christian Maudet (aka Christian-Jaque) file, Archives de Paris.

8. Undated statement, Henri Decoin file, Archives Nationales.

9. Undated statement.

10. Undated statement.

11. Henri Decoin to Alfred Greven, June 2, 1942, Henri Decoin file, Archives Nationales.

Chapter 10. The Russians at Billancourt

1. Grégoire Metchikian to Fritz Klotsch, September 30, 1940, Grégoire Metchikian naturalization file, Archives Nationales.

2. Grégoire Metchikian to Alfred Greven, December 18, 1940, Grégoire Metchikian naturalization file, Archives Nationales.

3. Grégoire Metchikian to the president of the purge committee, August 19, 1946, Grégoire Metchikian file, Archives de Paris.

4. Grégoire Metchikian to Rudolph Hans Bauermeister, February 28, 1941, Grégoire Metchikian naturalization file, Archives Nationales.

5. Grégoire Metchikian to Rudolph Hans Bauermeister, March 6, 1941, Grégoire Metchikian naturalization file, Archives Nationales.

6. Grégoire Metchikian to Rudolph Hans Bauermeister, March 6, 1941.

7. Continental Films to Grégoire Metchikian, July 25, 1941, Grégoire Metchikian naturalization file, Archives Nationales.

8. Grégoire Metchikian to Alfred Greven, July 27, 1941, Grégoire Metchikian naturalization file, Archives Nationales.

9. Transcript, October 17, 1944, Grégoire Metchikian file, Archives de Paris.

10. He was assistant director on *Eine kleine Sommermelodie* (1944), directed by Volker von Collande. IMDb mistakenly mentions his father's name instead of his own.

11. Transcript, October 17, 1944. Metchikian here was playing on the expression of being a fifth wheel.

12. Henri Decoin to Grégoire Metchikian, June 12, 1945, Grégoire Metchikian file, Archives de Paris.

13. November 16, 1944, Archan Chakhatouny file, Archives de Paris.

14. Transcript, November 16, 1944. The headquarters of the Organizing Committee of the Cinema Industry were at 92 avenue des Champs-Élysées. After the liberation, the building was used by the Committee for the Liberation of French Cinema.

15. Transcript, February 16, 1945, Archan Chakhatouny file, Archives de Paris.

16. Transcript, February 16, 1945.

17. Transcript, February 16, 1945.

18. Transcript, February 16, 1945.

19. Transcript, November 16, 1944.

20. Resistance fighter Missak Manouchian was shot by the Germans on February 21, 1944.

21. Devaivre, *Action!*, 109.

22. Statement, July 10, 1945, André Andrejew file, Archives de Paris.

23. Transcript, November 7, 1944, André Andrejew file, Archives de Paris.

24. Osmin Lafon, testimony, September 1, 1945, André Andrejew file, Archives de Paris.

25. Staff is a material made of plaster and fibers used to make ornaments and statues for film sets.

26. Transcript, March 2, 1945, André Kuczura file, Archives de Paris

27. *Le Petit Parisien*, January 16, 1941,3.

28. Note by Wladimir Meingard, April 24, 1945, Wladimir Meingard file, Archives de Paris.

29. Statement, March 27, 1946, Nicolas Wilcké file, Archives de Paris.

30. Statement, March 27, 1946.

31. Transcript, November 16, 1944, Boris Fastovitch (aka Boris de Fast) file, Archives de Paris.

32. Rudolph Hans Bauermeister to Victor de Fast, April 12, 1941, Boris Fastovitch (aka Boris de Fast) file, Archives de Paris.

33. Georgette Wichnevetsky to the Préfet de la Seine, October 26, 1945, Boris Wichné file, Archives de Paris.

Chapter 11. A Trip to Berlin

1. Bertin-Maghit, *Le Cinéma sous l'Occupation*, 51.

2. Transcript, November 30, 1944, Henri André Legrand file, Archives de Paris.

3. Transcript, October 17, 1944, Christian Maudet (aka Christian-Jaque) file, Archives de Paris.

4. Transcript, November 30, 1944.

5. Transcript, November 30, 1944.

6. Transcript, November 30, 1944.

7. Her brother Olivier Darrieux, born in 1921, was later called up by the compulsory work service to go to work in Germany.

8. Undated statement, Henri Decoin file, Archives de Paris.

9. Transcript, January 25, 1945, Henri Decoin File, Archives de Paris.

10. Transcript, November 30, 1944.

11. Report, January 8, 1945, Suzanne Delaire (aka Suzy Delair) file, Archives Nationales.

12. Transcript, November 29, 1944, Michel Durand (aka Michel Duran) file, Archives Nationales. Hans Jurgen von Eike und Polwitz was one of Continental's authorized representatives (see chapter 3).

13. Statement, November 8, 1945, André Préjean file, Archives Nationales.

14. See Anatole Clément Mary (aka René Dary) file, Archives Nationales.

15. Pierre Heuzé, *Ciné-Mondial*, April 10, 1942.

16. Transcript, November 30, 1944. It is possible Legrand mistook foreign journalists for attachés.

17. Pierre Heuzé, *Ciné-Mondial*, April 24, 1942.

18. Pierre Heuzé, *Ciné-Mondial*, May 1, 1942.

19. Günther Sawatzki, review, in *Filmwelt*.

20. Pierre Heuzé, *Ciné-Mondial*, May 8, 1942.

21. Transcript, November 30, 1944.

22. Goebbels, *Die Tagebücher von Joseph Goebbels*, 3:526.

23. Transcript, November 30, 1944.

24. Transcript, November 30, 1944.

25. Heyworth, *Otto Klemperer*, 389.

26. Transcript, November 30, 1944.

27. Pierre Heuzé, *Ciné-Mondial*, May 29, 1942.

28. Pierre Heuzé, *Ciné-Mondial*, June 5, 1942.

29. Pierre Heuzé, *Ciné-Mondial*, June 12, 1942.

30. Transcript, April 17, 1945, Pierre Blanchard (aka Pierre Blanchar) file, Archives de Paris. The shooting of *Pontcarral, colonel d'empire*, directed by Jean Delannoy, started on June 10, 1942.

31. Transcript, April 17, 1945.

32. Goebbels, *Die Tagebücher von Joseph Goebbels*, 4:295–96.

Chapter 12. The Harry Baur Affair

1. Statement, April 28, 1947, Harry Baur file, Archives Nationales.

2. Statement, April 28, 1947.

3. Turkish Consulate to German Propaganda Office, October 25, 1940, Archives allemandes de l'occupation, Archives Nationales.

4. Turkish Consulate to German Propaganda Office, October 25, 1940.

5. *Comœdia*, August 16, 1941, 5.

6. Note, August 23, 1941, Archives allemandes de l'occupation, Archives Nationales.

7. Statement, April 16, 1947, Harry Baur file, Archives Nationales.

8. Statement, April 28, 1947.

9. In October 1941, Henri Jeanson was no longer editor in chief of the daily newspaper *Aujourd'hui*. He had left the paper in November 1940.

10. Statement, March 27, 1947, Harry Baur file, Archives Nationales.

11. Statement, May 17, 1947, Harry Baur file, Archives Nationales.

12. Statement April 16, 1947.

13. Statement, April 28, 1947.

14. É. Bouchez's comments cited in Capitaine Sézille's report from December 23, 1941, Harry Baur file, Archives Nationales.

15. Loëna Meyer's statement from April 29, 1947, Harry Baur file, Archives Nationales.

16. Statement, August 28, 1948.

17. Statement, March 27, 1947.

18. Statement, March 27, 1947. The Cagoule was an extreme-right terrorist group active during the 1930s.

19. Report, December 23, 1941, Harry Baur file, Archives Nationales.

20. Statement, May 17, 1947.

21. Statement, May 17, 1947.

22. Statement, April 1, 1947, Harry Baur file, Archives Nationales.

23. Statement, March 27, 1947, Harry Baur file, Archives Nationales.

24. Statement, April 1, 1947.

25. Statement, March 27, 1947.

26. Statement, April 1, 1947.

27. Note by Dr. P. Soulié, June 5, 1947, Harry Baur file, Archives Nationales.

28. Statement, April 1, 1947.

29. Goebbels, *Die Tagebücher von Joseph Goebbels*, 5:481.

30. The sentence of national disgracefulness was passed by a special court (Cour de justice de la Seine) on French collaborators and resulted in the loss of civil liberties.

Chapter 13. Shooting on the French Riviera

1. Statement, November 26, 1946, Marcel Pagnol file, Archives de Paris.

2. Note, November 6, 1940, Renseignements généraux, Archives Nationales.

3. Transcript, November 14, 1944, Marcel Pagnol file, Archives de Paris.

4. Transcript, November 14, 1944.

5. Undated statement, Henri Decoin File, Archives Nationales.

6. Undated statement.

7. Transcript, November 7, 1944, Georges Wakhevitch file, Archives de Paris.

8. Fernand Contandin (aka Fernandel) file, Archives Nationales.

9. Statement, November 26, 1946.

10. In a 1965 interview, Marcel Pagnol stated he destroyed only part of the film, as it was unusable owing to defects on the Lumière celluloid film, which had shrunk. The part of the film that he had preserved for a possible resumption of the production decomposed (bonus included on the *Melusse* DVD.)

11. Report (in German), November 14, 1941, Épuration des sociétés cinémato-graphiques, Archives Nationales.

12. Transcript, November 3, 1944, Jean Dréville file, Archives de Paris.

13. Transcript, November 3, 1944.

14. Transcript, November 3, 1944.

15. Transcript, November 3, 1944.

16. Transcript, November 3, 1944.

17. Transcript, November 3, 1944.

18. Transcript, November 3, 1944.

19. Transcript, November 22, 1944, Jean-Marius Richard (aka Carlo Rim) file, Archives de Paris.

20. Statement, December 16, 1945, Jean-Marius Richard (aka Carlo Rim) file, Archives de Paris.

21. Transcript, November 22, 1944.

22. Transcript, November 22, 1944.

23. Transcript, of phone call between Carlo Rim and Robert Beunke, November 15, 1941, Renseignements généraux, Archives Nationales.

24. Transcript of phone call between Alice Richard and Robert Beunke, November 15, 1941, Renseignements généraux, Archives Nationales.

25. Alice Richard to the purge committee, December 7, 1944, Jean-Marius Richard (aka Carlo Rim) file, Archives de Paris.

26. Alice Richard to the purge committee, December 7, 1944.

27. Fernandel to Alfred Greven, April 7, 1942, Fernand Contandin (aka Fernandel) file, Archives Nationales.

28. André Andrejew file, Archives de Paris.

29. Transcript, November 22, 1944.

30. Transcript, November 22, 1944.

31. I do not know the correct spelling of Goertik's name. Therefore, I used the one given in the transcripts.

32. Transcript, November 22, 1944.

33. Transcript, November 22, 1944.

Chapter 14. New Directors

1. Transcript, October 17, 1944, Henri-Georges Clouzot File, Archives de Paris.

2. Transcript, October 17, 1944.

3. Transcript, November 22, 1944, Claude Vermorel file, Archives de Paris.

4. Transcript, November 22, 1944.

5. Henri-Georges Clouzot to Georges Simenon, March 12, 1942, Georges Simenon file, Archives Nationales.

6. Possot and Fresnay, *Pierre Fresnay*, 70.

7. Undated statement, André Galopet (aka Gabriello) file, Archives Nationales.

8. Undated statement.

9. *La France Socialiste*, August 12, 1942.

10. The Vel' d'Hiv' roundup was a mass arrest of Jewish people that took place between July 16 and July 17, 1942, in Paris.

11. Transcript, October 17, 1944, André Cayatte file, Archives de Paris.

12. Transcript, October 17, 1944.

13. Transcript, October 17, 1944.

14. Transcript, October 17, 1944.

15. Transcript, October 17, 1944.

16. Transcript, October 17, 1944.

Chapter 15. The *Caprices* Affair

1. The managers were the Belgian Roger Janssen de Van Loo, French naturalized citizen Alexandre Mnouchkine, and Raymond Eger. Eger was Jewish.

2. Judgment, Paris Industrial Tribunal, May 15, 1944, Raymond Bernard vs. Majestic Film, Léo Joannon file, Archives de Paris. Jean Grémillon only left Paris on June 10, four days before the arrival of the Germans.

3. Jacques Companeez to Raymond Bernard, March 12, 1941, Léo Joannon file, Archives de Paris.

4. Transcript, December 12, 1944, Léo Joannon file, Archives de Paris.

5. Transcript, December 12, 1944.

6. Transcript, December 12, 1944.

7. Jacques Companeez to Raymond Bernard, March 12, 1941.

8. Transcript, December 12, 1944.

9. Raymond Bernard to the president of the purge committee, July 23, 1945, Léo Joannon file, Archives de Paris.

10. Undated statement, Léo Joannon file, Archives de Paris.

11. Statement, Edwige Feuillère collection, Bibliothèque nationale de France.

12. The pseudonym Huguette Ex-Micro is a reference to silent actress Huguette Duflos, who adopted the name Ex-Duflos after her divorce. Jeanson is making a joke using the colloquial expression "mouche du coche" (coach's fly, meaning a goad, a nuisance) and "mouche du Boche" (hun's fly, meaning Joannon's behavior).

13. Transcript, December 12, 1944.

14. Goebbels, *Die Tagebücher von Joseph Goebbels*, 4:279.

Chapter 16. Richard Pottier

1. Transcript, October 18, 1944, Richard Deutsch (aka Richard Pottier) file, Archives de Paris.

2. Transcript, October 18, 1944.

3. The film Pottier had made with Borderie was *Le Monde tremblera* (1939), starring Claude Dauphin, Madeleine Sologne, and Erich von Stroheim, with a script by Henri-Georges Clouzot.

4. Transcript, October 18, 1944.

5. Kögl was one of Dr. Diedrich's henchmen inside the Propaganda Office.

6. Transcript, October 18, 1944.

7. Oberleutnant Kögl to Alfred Greven, February 13, 1941, Archives de Paris.

8. Transcript, October 18, 1944.

9. Transcript, October 18, 1944.

10. Transcript, October 18, 1944.

11. The film had several working titles: *Le Cœur sur la main* and *Totte et sa chance*.

12. Meurisse, *Les Éperons de la liberté*, 156.

13. Transcript, October 17, 1944, Gennaro Rossi (aka Jean Rossi) file, Archives de Paris.

14. Transcript, October 18, 1944.

Chapter 17. Maurice Tourneur

1. For further information, see my biography of Tourneur.

2. Transcript, October 19, 1944, Maurice Thomas (aka Maurice Tourneur) file, Archives de Paris.

3. Transcript, October 18, 1944, René Le Hénaff file, Archives de Paris.

4. Transcript, October 18, 1944.

5. Louise Lagrange, interview with Kevin Brownlow, 1966, K. Brownlow Collection.

6. The occupying authorities considered them both to be American citizens, even though they had been stripped of their nationality according to the laws of the time owing to the fact that they had not lived in the United States for a long time.

7. Edwige Feuillère to Continental Films, July 30, 1941. Edwige Feuillère collection, Bibliothèque nationale de France.

8. Transcript, October 19, 1944.

9. Transcript, October 19, 1944.

10. Transcript, October 19, 1944.

11. Police report, June 8, 1944, Maurice Thomas (aka Maurice Tourneur) file, Archives de la Préfecture de police.

Chapter 18. *La Main du diable*

1. *Le Film*, February 15, 1941.

2. Transcript, November 23, 1944, Jean Aurenche file, Archives de Paris.

3. Transcript, November 20, 1944, Jean-Paul Dreyfus (aka Jean-Paul Le Chanois) file, Archives de Paris.

4. Transcript, November 20, 1944.

5. Transcript, November 20, 1944.

6. Transcript, November 20, 1944.

7. Transcript, November 20, 1944. Lieutenant Hirsch was one of Dr. Diedrich's henchmen.

8. Transcript, November 20, 1944.

9. Transcript, November 20, 1944.

10. Transcript, November 20, 1944.

11. Devaivre joined Continental in October 1942 at Le Chanois's instigation (Jean Devaivre file, Archives de Paris).

12. Alfred Greven to Armand Thirard, November 19, 1941, Armand Thirard file, Archives de Paris.

13. Possot and Fresnay, *Pierre Fresnay*, 69–70.

14. *Comœdia*, May 1, 1943.

15. Purge questionnaire filled out by Roland-Manuel, November 9, 1945, Archives nationales.

Chapter 19. Maneuvers in the Unoccupied Zone

1. Robert Beunke to Continental Films, August 17, 1942, Renseignements généraux, Archives nationales.

2. Robert Beunke to Continental Films, August 17, 1942. Actress Renée Dennsy had appeared in Maurice Tourneur's *Justin de Marseille* (1935).

3. Police report, September 17, 1942, Archives nationales.

4. Following her interview with the purge committee, Danielle Darrieux received no sanction.

5. Maurice Bessy, *Aujourd'hui*, September 10, 1940. *À nous la liberté* is a 1931 René Clair picture. The title translates as "freedom for us!"

6. Julien Duvivier to Pierre Duvivier, March 1, 1942, Archives nationales.

7. Julien Duvivier to the French consul in Los Angeles, January 7, 1942, Archives nationales. The picture was not released in France until October 9, 1945

8. Julien Duvivier to Pierre Duvivier, May 2, 1941, Archives nationales.

9. Maurice Bessy, *Aujourd'hui*, September 11, 1940.

10. *Le Pilori*, June 19, 1941. The journalist made a mistake; Viviane Romance's real last name was Ortmans. Jean-Jacques Meccati was an extremely rich man from Nice who knew nothing about filmmaking.

11. Transcript of phone call between Abel Gance and the German vice consul, March 24, 1942, Renseignements généraux, Archives nationales.

12. Transcript of phone call between Abel Gance and the German vice consul, March 24, 1942.

Chapter 20. Documentaries

1. Robert Muzard file, Archives de Paris.

2. *Forces occultes* was only forty-three minutes long.

3. Cinéma Épernay-Palace to Films Albert Lauzin, August 16, 1943, Albert Lauzin file, Archives de Paris. *Ces Dames aux chapeaux verts* is a 1937 picture directed by Maurice Cloche.

4. Police report, October 16, 1940, Archives nationales.

5. Police report, October 16, 1940.

6. Report by Jean Ramigeau about Robert Muzard, March 6, 1947, Robert Muzard file, Archives de Paris.

7. Transcript, January 9, 1945, Joseph-Louis Mundviller file, Archives de Paris.

8. Transcript, January 9, 1945.

9. Transcript, January 9, 1945.

10. Joseph-Louis Mundviller to Rudolph Hans Bauermeister, March 1, 1943, Joseph-Louis Mundviller file, Archives de Paris.

11. Ramelot had died in September 1942 (Serge Griboff file, Archives de Paris).

12. Transcript, October 23, 1946, Serge Griboff file, Archives de Paris.

13. A forty-two-minute version of *Travailleurs de France* can be viewed at the Archives Françaises du Film. The original prints released lasted only thirty-five and fifteen minutes each, according to *Le Film*.

14. *Le Film*, July 1, 1944, 6.

15. Transcript, October 18, 1944, Richard Deutsch (aka Richard Pottier) file, Archives de Paris.

16. Georges Zevaco, review, *Mondes*, November 21, 1945.

Chapter 21. *Le Corbeau*

1. Transcript, October 17, 1944, Henri-Georges Clouzot file, Archives nationales.

2. Goebbels, *Die Tagebücher von Joseph Goebbels*, 4:317.

3. He only mentioned *La Symphonie fantastique* (May 15, 1942), *Caprices* (May 12, 1942), *Annette et la dame blonde* (May 19, 1942), and a picture whose title he did not give, which he rated as bad (May 17, 1942).

4. Goebbels, *Die Tagebücher von Joseph Goebbels*, 4:427.

5. Goebbels, *Die Tagebücher von Joseph Goebbels*, 9:93.

6. Fresnay and Possot, *Pierre Fresnay*, 67.

7. Fresnay and Possot, *Pierre Fresnay*, 67.

8. Fresnay and Possot, *Pierre Fresnay*, 66.

9. Transcript, November 8, 1944, Sacha Voyen (aka Jean Sacha) file, Archives de Paris.

10. Transcript, November 8, 1944.

11. Report, October 6, 1944, Nicolas Hayer file, Archives de Paris.

12. Cameraman Jacques Lemare and assistant cameraman Étienne Laroche had been requisitioned to work in Germany.

13. Report, October 6, 1944.

14. Transcript, October 23, 1944, Marguerite Beaugé file, Archives de Paris.

15. Marguerite Beaugé to Rudolph Hans Bauermeister, August 30, 1943, Marguerite Beaugé file, Archives de Paris.

16. Transcript, October 23, 1944.

17. Marguerite Beaugé to the president of the purge committee, December 14, 1945, Marguerite Beaugé file, Archives de Paris.

18. Marguerite Beaugé to the president of the purge committee, December 14, 1945.

19. Marcel Colin-Reval to the president of the purge committee, October 20, 1944, Henri-Georges Clouzot file, Archives nationales.

20. François Holbane, review, *Paris-Midi*, October 7, 1943.

21. Jacques Audiberti, review, *Comœdia*, October 4, 1943.

22. *Panorama*, October 14, 1943.

23. Roger Charmoy, review, *L'Appel*, October 14, 1943.

24. *L'Écran français*, no. 1 (December 1943): 3.

25. Marcel Colin-Reval to the president of the purge committee, October 20, 1944.

26. Transcript, November 17, 1944, Nicolas Katkoff file, Archives de Paris.

27. *Le Film*, no. 71 (August 21, 1943): 5.

28. Suzanne Delaire (aka Suzy Delair) file, Archives nationales.

29. Transcript, October 17, 1944.

30. Henri Jeanson to Henri-Georges Clouzot, undated, Henri-Georges Clouzot file, Archives nationales. *Pension Mimosas* is a 1935 film directed by Jacques Feyder, *Pépé le Moko* a 1937 film directed by Julien Duvivier, *La Bête humaine* a 1938 film directed by Jean Renoir, *Quai des brumes* a 1938 film directed by Marcel Carné, and *Goupi mains rouges* a 1943 film directed by Jacques Becker. Capitaine Hurluret is the main character in the play *Les Gaîtés de l'escadron* by Georges Courteline that was adapted to the screen in 1932 by Maurice Tourneur.

31. Jacques Prévert to Louis Chavance, October 18, 1944, Henri-Georges Clouzot file, Archives nationales.

32. Jean-Paul Sartre to H.-G. Clouzot, undated, Henri-Georges Clouzot file, Archives nationales. Two of the signees worked for Continental: screenwriter Claude Vermorel and actor Michel Vitold.

33. de Beauvoir, *La Force de l'âge*, 731.

34. Transcript, January 22, 1947, Nicolas Hayer file, Archives de Paris.

Chapter 22. The Difficult Years

1. Fernandel had been considered as Tissier's costar for the picture (*Le Film*, no. 55 [December 19, 1942]).

2. Transcript, October 18, 1944, René Jayet file, Archives de Paris.

3. Transcript, October 18, 1944.

4. Transcript, November 22, 1944, Jean-Paul Dreyfus (aka Jean-Paul Le Chanois) file, Archives de Paris.

5. Jean-Paul Le Chanois to Jean Tissier, November 7, 1945, Jean Tissier file, Archives nationales.

6. *Paris-Midi*, July 23, 1943.

7. Saint-Cyr, En toute mauvaise foi, 139.

8. This contract is located in the Renée Saint-Cyr Collection, Bibliothèque nationale de France.

9. Saint-Cyr, *En toute mauvaise foi*, 144.

10. Géo Sandry was also the author with Marcel Carrère of the excellent *Dictionnaire de l'argot moderne* (Aux Quais de Paris, 1953).

11. Transcript, October 24, 1944, Gabriel Bleinat (aka Géo Sandry) file, Archives de Paris.

12. Transcript, November 22, 1944.

13. Transcript, November 22, 1944.

14. Transcript, January 10, 1945, Jean Devaivre file, Archives de Paris.

15. Saint-Cyr, *En toute mauvaise foi*, 141.

16. See chapter 10.

17. *Actu*, February 27, 1944.

18. Denise Delamare (aka Rosine Delamare) file, Archives de Paris. Vaillant was the pseudonym of Jean de Vogüé.

19. Robert Brasillach, review, *L'Écho de la France*, January 8–9, 1944.

20. *Les Nouveaux Temps*, January 8, 1944.

21. Paul Strecker, review, *Pariser Zeitung*, January 24, 1944.

22. Clouzot had offered her the lead in *La Chatte*, a project that never materialized.

23. Ginette Leclerc recalled that Greven had propositioned her. It was therefore not unusual behavior for him. Gilles, *Leclerc*, 102.

24. Paul Olive to Rudolph Hans Bauermeister, December 28, 1943, Paul Olive file, Archives de Paris.

25. *Le Club des soupirants* (1941), *Ne bougez plus* (1941), *Vingt-cinq ans de bonheur* (1943), *Mon amour est près de toi* (1943), and *Le Dernier sou* (1946).

26. Transcript, November 22, 1944, Jean-Marius Richard (aka Carlo Rim) file, Archives de Paris.

27. The company wanted him to make *Garou-Garou*, a Marcel Aymé adaptation, as well as *L'Indésirable*, written and directed by André Cayatte. Neither of these pictures was ever made (*Le Film*, January 3, 1942).

28. Meurisse, *Les Éperons de la liberté*, 166.

29. This organization was in charge of building the Atlantic Wall (a system of fortifications along the Atlantic coast).

30. Meurisse, *Les Éperons de la liberté*, 168.

31. François Vinneuil (aka Lucien Rebatet), review, *Le Petit Parisien*, December 18, 1943.

32. Max Bihan, review, *Comœdia*, December 25, 1943.

Chapter 23. *La Vie de plaisir*

1. Transcript, October 19, 1944, Albert Valentin file, Archives de Paris.

2. Transcript, October 19, 1944.

3. *Marché noir* was a film project intended for Maurice Tourneur that was never shot (transcript, November 22, 1944, Charles Spaak file, Archives de Paris).

4. Transcript, November 22, 1944.

5. Transcript, November 22, 1944.

6. Transcript, October 19, 1944.

7. Transcript, October 19, 1944.

8. Transcript, November 22, 1944.

9. Transcript, October 19, 1944.

10. *Le Dernier sou* and *Les Caves du Majestic*, produced after *La Vie de plaisir*, were not released until January 1946 and October 1945, respectively.

11. Roger Charmoy, review, *L'Appel*, May 25, 1944.

12. François Vinneuil, review, *Le Petit Parisien*, May 20, 1944.

13. Jacques Bar, review, *El Rachid*, May 31, 1944

14. Pierre Maudru, review, unidentified newspaper, May 31, 1944.

15. Arlette Jazarin, review, *Révolution Nationale*, June 3, 1944.

16. *Les Lettres françaises*, no. 17 (June 1944).

17. Cited in Barrot, *L'Écran français*, 14.

Chapter 24. Game Over

1. Noël Bénévent (aka Noël Roquevert) file, Archives nationales.

2. Noël Bénévent (aka Noël Roquevert) file.

3. Ginette Leclerc managed to get Continental colleagues André Legrand and Albert Préjean to participate in the board meetings of the club.

4. Transcript, October 31, 1944, Geneviève Menut (aka Ginette Leclerc) file, Archives de la Préfecture de Police de Paris.

5. Charles Spaak to Alfred Greven, April 7, 1943, Charles Spaak file, Archives de Paris.

6. *Les Nouveaux temps*, April 18, 1944.

7. *Au Pilori*, April 6, 1944. Dr. Marcel Petiot (1897–1946) was one of the worst serial killers in French history. He was sentenced to the death penalty in 1946 for murdering twenty-seven people.

8. Actually, Spaak was not married to his new partner, Claudie Perrier, as he had not yet divorced his first wife.

9. Soutzo ran the Ile-de-France Films firm and produced *Volpone* (1941), directed by Maurice Tourneur.

10. Transcript, November 22, 1944, Charles Spaak file, Archives de Paris.

11. Transcript, November 22, 1944.

12. *Le Collier de la reine* was directed by Marcel L'Herbier and stars Viviane Romance.

13. Préjean, *The Sky and the Stars*, 211.

14. *L'Affaire des poisons* was made in 1955, directed by Henri Decoin and starring Danielle Darrieux, Viviane Romance, and Paul Meurisse. The notorious black mass scene was included. The director of photography was Pierre Montazel.

15. *Le Film*, July 22, 1944.

16. Transcript, October 11, 1944, Pierre. Montazel file, Archives de Paris.

17. Alfred Greven to Max Winkler, March 10, 1944, cited in Bock, *CineGraph*, installment 34, D5.

18. Bauer to Max Winkler, March 10, 1944, cited in Bock, *CineGraph*, installment 34, D5.

19. Wolf Albach-Retty (1906–67) was actress Romy Schneider's father.

20. Transcript, October 17, 1944, Paul Olive File, Archives de Paris.

21. Aurenche worked with screenwriter René Wheeler on the script of that picture in order to help Wheeler, who was destitute. Aurenche, *La Suite à l'écran*, 114.

22. Transcript, November 23, 1944, Jean Aurenche file, Archives de Paris.

23. Goebbels, *Die Tagebücher von Joseph Goebbels*, 12:307.

Chapter 25. A Professional Purge

1. Albert Préjean to the president of the purge committee, undated, Albert Préjean file, Archives nationales.

2. Pierre Laudenbach (aka Pierre Fresnay) file, Archives de la préfecture de police.

3. Bourdet was officially appointed delegate for theater and cinema for the education and art ministry after the liberation.

4. Note by Édouard Bourdet, September 1944, Pierre Laudenbach (aka Pierre Fresnay) file, Archives nationales.

5. Report, May 18, 1945, Pierre Laudenbach (aka Pierre Fresnay) file, Archives de la préfecture de police.

6. Report, May 21, 1945, Pierre Laudenbach (aka Pierre Fresnay) file, Archives de la préfecture de police.

7. Tourneur was living with Louise Lagrange, whose sister Marthe was married to Blanchar.

8. Geneviève Menut (aka Ginette Leclerc) file, Archives nationales.

9. Transcript, October 21, 1944, Léonie Bathiat (aka Arletty) file, Archives de la préfecture de police. Otto Abetz was the German ambassador to Vichy France.

10. Diessbock was born in Wasserburg am Inn in Bavaria on May 7, 1910. The police report about him can be found in the Renseignements généraux du cinema, Archives nationales.

11. Statement, October 7, 1944, Renseignements généraux, Archives nationales.

12. Statement, October 7, 1944. De Carmoy was the government commissioner in charge of cinema, Ploquin was the head of the Organizing Committee of the Cinema Industry, and Harispuru was a producer.

13. Philippe Henriot was one of the most fervent collaborationists on Radio-Paris. He was killed by Resistance fighters on June 28, 1944.

14. Raimu was not aware that the picture had been released under the title *Das unheimliche Haus*.

15. Undated article, Fernand Contandin (aka Fernandel) file, Archives nationales.

16. Statement, December 12, 1944, Fernand Contandin (aka Fernandel) file, Archives nationales.

17. Robert Le Vigan to Rudolph Hans Bauermeister, March 25, 1942, Robert Coquillaud (aka Robert Le Vigan) file, Archives nationales.

18. Carné, *Ma Vie à belles dents*, 202.

19. Pierre Caron file, Archives de Paris.

20. Jean Dréville to the president of the purge committee, February 28, 1946, Jean Dréville File, Archives de Paris.

21. Sanction index cards of filmmakers, Archives nationales.

22. Becker intervention, Henri-Georges Clouzot File, Archives de Paris.

23. *Les Nouvelles littéraires*, November 22, 1945.

24. *Les Lettres françaises*, December 1, 1945.

25. Georges Simenon file, Archives nationales.

26. Georges Zevaco, review, *Mondes*, November 21, 1945. The critic is making a pun with "un mauvais plat de resistance," meaning a "bad main course" or literally "a bad Resistance dish."

27. He produced *Monsieur Vincent* (1948), directed by Maurice Cloche and starring Pierre Fresnay.

Chapter 26. Greven's Last Years

1. Hans Hinkel to Max Winkler, January 13, 1945, cited in Bock, *CineGraph*, installment 34, D6.

2. Klaus-Jörg Hoppe, interview, in *Tarnname Continental*.

3. Actor and director Wilhelm Birgel (1891–1973) performed in Nazi propaganda pictures.

4. General Kœnig to Michel Fourré-Cormeray, July 25, 1949, Épuration des sociétés cinématographiques, Archives nationales.

5. Michel Fourré-Cormeray to André François-Poncet, August 22, 1949, Épuration des sociétés cinématographiques, Archives nationales.

6. Friedrich Merten to Max Winkler, April 25, 1955, cited in Bock, *CineGraph*, installment 34, D6–7.

7. *Deutschland-Union-Dienst*, no. 51 (March 13, 1953), cited in Bock, *CineGraph*, installment 34, D7.

8. Sekt is a sparkling German sweet wine often wrongly compared to Champagne.

Selected Bibliography

Aurenche, Jean. *La Suite à l'écran*. Actes Sud/Institut Lumière, 1993.

Barrot, Olivier. *L'Écran français (1943–1953): Histoire d'un journal et d'une époque*. Les Éditeurs français réunis, 1979.

Beauvoir, Simone de. *La Force de l'âge*. Gallimard, 1960.

Bertin-Maghit, Jean-Pierre. *Le Cinéma français sous l'Occupation*. Perrin, 2002.

Bock, Hans-Michael, ed. *CineGraph: Lexikon zum deutschsprachigen Film*. 9 vols. Text + Kritik, 1984–.

Brownlow, Kevin. *Napoléon: Abel Gance's Classic Film*. Jonathan Cape, 1983.

Carné, Marcel. *La Vie à belles dents*. L'Archipel, 1996.

Cavanna, François. *Les Russkoffs*. Pierre Belfond, 1979.

Cortanze, Gérard de. *Pierre Benoit: Le Romancier paradoxal*. Albin Michel, 2012.

Desmarets, Sophie. *Les Mémoires de Sophie*. Fallois, 2002.

Devaivre, Jean. *Action!* Nicolas Philippe, 2002.

Feuillère, Edwige. *Les Feux de la mémoire*. Albin Michel, 1977.

Gilles, Christian. *Ginette Leclerc: Le Désir des hommes*. L'Harmattan, 2000.

Goebbels, Joseph. *Die Tagebücher von Joseph Goebbels*. Part 2, *Dikate, 1941–1945*. 15 vols. Edited by Elke Fröhlich. K. G. Saur, 1996–.

Heyworth, Peter. *Otto Klemperer: His Life and Times*. Vol. 1, *1885–1933*. Cambridge University Press, 1996.

Le Chanois, Jean-Paul. *Le Temps des cerises: Entretiens avec Philippe Esnault*. Actes Sud/Institut Lumière, 1996.

Leteux, Christine. *Maurice Tourneur réalisateur sans frontières*. La Tour Verte, 2015.

Meurisse, Paul. *Les Éperons de la liberté*. Robert Laffont, 1979.

Mouloudji, Marcel. *La Fleur de l'âge*. Bernard Grasset, 1991.

Où sortir à Paris? Le Guide du soldat allemand, 1940–1944. Alma, 2013.

Possot, François, and Pierre Fresnay. *Pierre Fresnay*. La Table Ronde, 1975.

Préjean, Albert. *The Sky and yhe Stars*. Harvill Press, 1956.

Rim, Carlo. *Le Grenier d'Arlequin*. Denoël, 1981.

Saint-Cyr, Renée. *En toute mauvaise foi*. Rocher, 1990.

Documentary

Tarnname Continental: Alfred Greven—ein deutscher Filmproduzent in Paris. Written and directed by Peter H. Schröder and Hans Peter Kochenrath. Arte/ZDF, 1997.

Index

WISCONSIN FILM STUDIES